TOM INGL

MORAL MONOPOLY

The Catholic Church in Modern Irish Society

GILL AND MACMILLAN

Published in Ireland by
Gill and Macmillan Ltd
Goldenbridge
Dublin 8
with associated companies in
Auckland, Dallas, Delhi, Hong Kong,
Johannesburg, Lagos, London, Manzini,
Melbourne, Nairobi, New York, Singapore,
Tokyo, Washington

© Tom Inglis 1987

0 7171 1565 8

British Library Cataloguing in Publication Data
Inglis, Tom
Moral monopoly: the Catholic church in Irish society.
1. Catholic Church – Ireland – History
2. Ireland – Religious life and customs
I. Title
306'.6'09417 BX 1503
ISBN 0-7171-1499-6
0-7171-1565-8 pbk

Print origination in Ireland by
Design and Art Facilities, Dublin
Printed in Great Britain by
The Camelot Press, Southampton

For Aileen

Contents

Acknowledgments

Much of the research of this book was completed while I was a doctoral student at Southern Illinois University. I owe a great deal intellectually to many of the ideas and insights provided by faculty and colleagues while I was there, especially Tom Burger, but also Charles Lemert, Charles Snyder and Garth Gillan. My interest in the role of the Catholic Church in Irish society was cultivated during the time I worked with the Episcopal Commission for Research and Development. Don Bennett, Tony Fahey, Eugene Hynes, Bridget Lunn, Carol MacKeogh and two anonymous reviewers read and commented on earlier drafts of the text and were most generous and helpful in their criticisms. Ann Coogan typed a good deal of the manuscript, and Conor Ward provided facilities when they were most urgently needed. I owe a tremendous amount to friends and members of my family who I am lucky to say are too numerous to mention. They have provided continual support and have participated in numerous discussions which have helped clarify many of the issues raised in this book. My wife, Aileen MacKeogh, and son Arron have borne the greatest burdens. They have been a tower of strength and affection during the production of the text. It is dedicated with love to Aileen, with the hope that one day Arron will also be able to read and appreciate it.

1
Introduction

IRELAND is an island to the extreme north-west of Europe. One of the first impressions of the country that marks it out as different from other Western societies is that the Catholic Church is a strong and active force in everyday life. Visitors are impressed by the pious devotion of the people. They see the crowded churches on Sundays, with sometimes six or more masses being said to accommodate the numbers who attend. They see people stopping whatever they are doing to pray when they hear the Angelus. They see thousands of people making annual pilgrimages to various shrines, mountains, and wells. They see people blessing themselves as they pass a church. They see people salute with reverence the large numbers of priests, nuns, and brothers. It is as if the Irish have always been a holy and religious people who are devoted to the Catholic Church. Should anyone ask why this is so, they may well be told the old story of how we were all pagans until St Patrick arrived, but that once he converted us we became fervent Christians—an island of saints and scholars that exported the faith all over the world. In later years, we were to remain loyal to Rome despite centuries of oppression from Protestant England. This is the same old story which has been told and accepted by many Irish Catholics. The aim of this study is to provide some alternative explanation as to why the Irish adhere so strongly to the Catholic Church, and to examine critically how the Church came to have such power and influence in Irish society.

The notion that the Irish are almost naturally Catholic has become part of what is sometimes accurately referrred to as 'the simple faith'. The criterion of a good Irish Catholic has traditionally been perceived as one who received the sacraments regularly and who followed as well as possible the rules and regulations of the Church. Innocence was regarded as a virtue. People were not encouraged to question their religion or their priests. The appropriate responses to any questions one might have about religion were learnt off by heart in the catechism. One could be forgiven for breaking the rules of the Church, but questioning them was a different matter. The dominance of 'the simple faith' has meant that many Irish Catholics have not developed an intellectual interest in, or critical attitude towards, their religion. While there have been frequent public debates and critical assessments made of the State, political parties, trade unions and other national organisations, the Catholic Church has, until recently, remained aloof from rigorous criticism and public accountability. In the past, many Irish Catholics secretly bickered and complained about the Church, often in anger and frustration, without being coherent or consistent in their criticisms.

Much of this can be related to the fact that the Church has dominated Irish education, and has been slow to accept or encourage criticism. Indeed the Church has tended to demand reverence and obedience and has been inclined to see any public debate about its position as part of what one bishop termed, 'a cancer of criticism and dissent' which 'is the result of ignorance' or 'downright antagonism'.[1] But 'the simple faith' and the walls of censorship and silence which protected the Church in the past from criticism are beginning to crumble. The Catholic Church in Ireland has to learn to accept criticism and to defend its position reasonably rather than by appealing to dogma and tradition. The absence of a systematic, rigorous critique of its power has been a handicap both to the Church itself, and to a new generation of Irish people who seek a coherent explanation of its influence in their personal lives and in Irish society generally.

There has already been quite an amount written about the Catholic Church in Ireland, but much of this comes from a liturgical, pastoral or theological perspective and has been written by committed members. There has also been some important social research done on Catholicism and the Church in Ireland. Again much of this has been done by the Church itself as part of a policy of research and development. The main problem with this research is that it has concentrated on gathering facts and data, usually through social surveys, and has avoided dealing with the larger, more general, questions about the position and influence of the Church. This is not to say that there have been no previous studies which have provided a critical assessment of the power of the Catholic Church in Ireland. One can think of observers from outside such as Blanshard and Messenger whose works have all too readily been dismissed as being unobjective, unscholarly, and out of touch with the ethos of Irish society.[2] One can also think of many Irish authors whose literary genius would appear to have been born on the back of a critical reaction to the Church and its influence in their lives. Their literary descriptions have provided some good insights into how the Church has operated within Irish society. Yet, in the past, these writers have often been dismissed as disloyal misfits.

On a more academic level, sociological analyses have generally proved inadequate. Peillon, for example, provides a good overall analysis of contemporary Irish society, but he argues that the main social forces in ireland are social classes and that the Catholic Church, while once a social force, has now only a marginal influence. But Peillon fails to explain why Ireland continues to have one of the highest levels of religious practice in Western Europe; why so many Catholics still adhere to the rules and regulations of the Church; why divorce and abortion are unconstitutional; why the Irish continue to have one of the highest levels of postponed marriage and permanent celibacy in Western Europe; why Ireland did not industrialise until the beginning of the 1960s; and, generally, why (in his own words) 'numerous facets of traditional Irish society, far from being on the point of disappearance, are being given a new lease of life and are being mobilised to stem the tide of encroaching modernisation'.[3]

While Irish sociology has failed generally to produce a systematic description and analysis of the power of the Catholic Church in contemporary Irish society, Irish historiography has had more success in identifying when and why Irish people became so strongly attached to the Church. Four main reasons have been put forward for the development of this institutional adherence, or for what Larkin has termed the 'Irish Devotional Revolution'. Larkin's own explanation is that it was a response to a loss of language and cultural identity in the nineteenth century, i.e. the Irish, in search of stability in a time of rapid social change, attached themselves to the Church because they feared they were being effectively Anglicised.[4] Cullen has argued that the adherence to romantic notions of an island of saints and scholars, which arose in the last century, was part of a crisis of identity caused by rapid social change.[5] Miller has put forward a different type of reason for the devotional revolution. He has argued that before the Famine, labourers and cottiers, who formed the majority of the population, were oriented towards magical practices. With the virtual elimination of these classes during the Famine, magical practices declined rapidly and were replaced by institutional church practices favoured by the higher social order of Catholics.[6] This reasoning has been developed by Connolly. He suggests that there was an inherent appeal to the rationalisation of Catholicism 'as a religion, a system of beliefs, values and rules of behaviour supported by an appeal to supernatural realities'. He links this rationalisation to a change in the class structure of the population which brought in a 'new and respectable society in which the Church's discipline was from the start more readily accepted.'[7] This leads to a third type of reasoning put forward by Hynes, i.e. that the new and respectable society was created in and through the Church. In other words, the growth in institutional adherence was part of an overall growth in discipline involving the sacrifice of short-term goals for long-term planning. This moral discipline was exercised through a newly adopted stem-family system and was a prerequisite for the modernisation of Irish society.[8] The final type of explanation for the 'devotional revolution' is a Marxist type one, and can be stated as follows: the growth of the institutional Catholic Church and an adherence to its practices were part of an ideological apparatus of the English State, fostered in order to contain the growing class antagonisms which had resulted from divisions that arose with the new mode of agricultural production, i.e. the transformation from tillage to pasture farming. Such an explanation argues that popular, essentially class, grievances were sublimated in mass devotionalism, and that repressed sexuality, necessary in the new mode of production and stem-family system, found a socially acceptable form of emotional relief in Catholic revival.[9]

Much of the reasoning behind these different types of explanations is, with certain exceptions, incorporated into the present study. First, although any simplistic notion that the devotional revolution was an ideological apparatus of the English State is rejected, emphasis is given to the role State-financed education played in instilling a new system of discipline, and how the State gradually handed the implementation of this discipline over to the Catholic Church. Secondly, the growth in institutional adherence was not so much a reaction to becoming Anglicised, but rather part of a modern civilising process that had been spreading throughout Europe since the sixteenth century. This process was imported into Ireland and made acceptable to most Catholics by the Church. Thirdly, besides being a means to becoming as civil and moral as other Europeans, especially English Protestants, a rigid adherence to the rules and regulations of the Church became the means to adopting stem-family practices, avoiding the subdivision of already small farms, and improving the standard of living which farming could provide. But because the Catholic Church was the means behind this new system of moral discipline and social control, Irish Catholics became socialised into an ideology of spirituality, frugality and celibacy. This ideology was maintained through practices which centred on individuals surrendering to the interests of Church, family and community, and through an uncritical commitment to traditional rules and regulations. It was partially for these reasons that Ireland did not develop a mature system of capitalist agricultural production and modernise fully until the second half of the twentieth century. Fourthly, this study seeks to explain how it was, in comparison with other European societies, that a high level of institutional adherence was sustained up to the present day. In this regard, emphasis is given to the Church's influence in Irish family life and, in particular, the dependence of mothers on the Church for moral power within the home. It was primarily through this dependence that the Church maintained control of women and sex and was able to develop a rigid adherence to its rules and regulations. Finally, in order to gain an overall understanding of what may be termed, 'the long nineteenth century of Irish Catholicism', this study develops a sociological perspective which helps explain how being religious, or ethical, fits into certain aspects of Irish social, political and economic life.

The Catholic Church has become an integral part of Irish social life. In attempting to provide an alternative and systematic explanation of its power and influence, this study develops a radically different outlook not just on the Church, but on social life in general. Instead of seeing the Church as a voluntary body to which people subscribe on the basis of shared beliefs, values and practices, I examine it in terms of a large bureaucratic organisation which, like other organisations, is primarily interested in maintaining its power and influence in society. I look at the Church as a compulsory and coercive organisation that, regardless of the intentions of individual members, has limited Irish discourse and practice, i.e. the general range of possibilities of what Irish people could do or say. In this regard, the Catholic Church in Ireland is a power bloc that operates mainly in the social and moral spheres of Irish life, but which has a major influence on political and economic life. Membership of the Church can be understood as having been maintained through a rigid system of physical and moral discipline centred on the elimination of individual freedom.

Why, then, do Catholics ally themselves with this power bloc? I explain adherence to the Church not so much in terms of commitment to its teachings and practices in order to live a good life and gain salvation in the next world, but rather in terms of how it helps people attain and maintain power, particularly economic possessions, occupational positions and social prestige. In other words, I examine the reasons why Irish Catholics adhere to the Church in terms of a rational, instrumental calculation of means towards more immediate, specific, material ends.[10] This perspective on Catholic behaviour being a means to attain worldly ends, and on the Church as a coercive organisation that curtails individual freedom, is maintained throughout the text. It may seem to some, especially the more traditional kind of Irish Catholic, that this perspective is negative and prejudiced, and takes a poor view not just of the Church and being Catholic in Ireland, but of social life in general. But such a perspective can be liberating, especially for those who feel oppressed and dominated. Many Irish Catholics have clung to a one-dimensional understanding of the Church, and while they have been willing to admit and accept its weaknesses and failures, they have been unable to admit and accept that it is a power bloc.

This is a sociological study which presents an overall understanding of the Catholic Church in modern Ireland. The attempt is to provide a reasonable and coherent explanation of its power. The methodology is based on devising general concepts in order to develop some new insights. Reference is made to a wide range of primary and, mainly, secondary sources. There is no attempt or claim to give a complete picture of the Catholic Church in Irish society. The objective is to challenge the orthodox view. This is essential if the power and domination of the Church is to be recognised and if there is to be liberation from this domination.

The book begins by stating how many Roman Catholics there are in Ireland, and to what extent the Church exercises control over their ethical behaviour. It is suggested that there are three main types of ethical religious behaviour in Irish society—magical practices, adherence to Church rules and regulations, and individual moral responsibility. It is argued that the power of the Church has derived from a maintenance of magical practices, both formally and informally within the Church, together with an ability to confine the definition of what is right and wrong to its own teachings, rules, and regulations (Chapter 2). This moral power is maintained through the hierarchical organisation of the Church, its physical and human resources, and the dominant position it has held in Irish education, health and social welfare (Chapter 3). But the organisational strength of the Church is not sufficient to explain its power and influence in Irish society and, in the fourth chapter, I examine the more instrumental, material reasons why Irish Catholics have remained committed members. I analyse the Church's moral power in its effect upon political and economic life in Ireland—particularly the relations between Church and State—and relate how in recent times the Church's power has been gradually undermined by the media.

In the second part of the book I examine when and how the Church became so powerful and the mechanisms by which this power was maintained. It is argued that the Church first emerged as a power block during the last century when the English State, recognising the failure of political and economic repression, gradually changed its policy and sought to pacify and control the Irish population. After a series of conflicts and compromises with Rome and the Irish hierarchy, it gradually handed this task over to the Church whose organisational strength had increased rapidly during the first half of the nineteenth century (Chapter 5). But the growth of the institutional Church was also based on an interest among Irish Catholics in becoming as civil and morally respectable as other modern Europeans. In importing the civilising process into Ireland, the Church gained control of many of the buildings and mechanisms through which modern manners and civility were incorporated and developed among Irish Catholics (Chapter 6). But the development of the Church's power was also related to the widespread adoption of a new sexual morality which helped develop and maintain a system of stem-family practices, which were linked to an economic interest in improving the standard of living of one's family (Chapter 7). The link between past and present, and the institutional Church and the individual, is then identified as having been Irish mothers. Having become dependent on the Church for power in the home, it was the mother who instilled the moral discipline necessary to sustain a new form of family life, who transformed houses into neat, ordered and respectable homes, and who nurtured the vocations on which the Church depended (Chapter 8). Finally, it is argued that it was the power alliance between Church and mother that played a major part in the initial modernisation of Irish society. But once the alliance became established, it helped maintain Ireland as a conservative, rural society and delayed its full modernisation until the second half of the twentieth century.

PART ONE

The Catholic Church in Contemporary Ireland

2
The Religious Behaviour of
Irish Catholics

WHAT MAKES the Republic of Ireland different from other Western European societies is the high level of adherence to the Roman Catholic Church. More than nine in ten of the population identify themselves as Church members, and of these more than eight in ten attend Mass at least once a week. The vast majority of Irish people are born, marry, and die within the Church. They regard their Church membership as important. Religion is not merely a question of accepting certain beliefs and teachings, it is something which is actively practised. Irish Catholics regularly receive the sacraments. They obey Church teachings and accept its definition of what constitutes good moral conduct. It is for these reasons that being Irish and being Catholic have become synonymous. The Irish have often been characterised as a deeply spiritual people, but this does not explain how and why this spirituality is manifested in a strong adherence to institutional Catholicism. The answer to this question, as will be argued in the first part of this book, lies in the organisational manpower and resources of the Church, and the role being a good Catholic plays in the struggle for, and distribution of, power in Irish society. The task of the present chapter is to describe the religious behaviour of Irish Catholics in terms of how they decide what is good or bad, right or wrong. However, before doing this, it is necessary to draw attention to the way in which the island is divided politically and ecclesiastically, and to the high proportion of Roman Catholics that live in the Republic of Ireland.

Irish Catholics

Ireland has been divided politically into the North and South since 1922. The six north-eastern counties of Antrim, Derry,

Tyrone, Fermanagh, Armagh and Down comprise Northern
Ireland, which is part of the United Kindom. The remaining
twenty-six counties comprise the Republic of Ireland. The Irish
Catholic Church extends throughout the whole island, and the
ecclesiastical divisions have little or no correspondence with the
political divisions. For example, the northern ecclesiastical
province of Armagh has two dioceses, Meath and Ardagh which
are completely in the Republic, and four dioceses, Armagh,
Clogher, Derry and Kilmore which are divided by the political
boundary. One of the main reasons for the introduction of the
boundary in 1922 was to create a political state in which the
Protestant minority of the island would be in the majority. The
boundary also meant that the southern part of the island became
almost completely Catholic. Its imposition continued to affect the
proportion of Catholics in both areas for some time afterwards. In
the twenty-five years between 1911 and 1936, the proportion of
Catholics in Northern Ireland fell by six per cent, whereas in the
Republic it rose by four per cent (see table 1).

Table 1.   Roman Catholic population as percentage of Northern
Ireland, The Republic of Ireland, and all Ireland, 1861–1981

	1861 %	1911 %	1936 %	1961 %	1981 %
Northern Ireland	41.0	39.5	33.5	34.9	38.0*
Republic of Ireland	89.4	89.6	93.5	94.9	93.0
All Ireland	78.1	75.3	75.4	74.7	76.8
Number in thousands	5,768	4,391	4,248	4,243	4,925

Adapted from Brendan Walsh, *Religion and Demographic Behaviour in Ireland* (Dublin:
Economic and Social Research Institute paper 55, 1970), p.7; and Census of Population
1981 (Ireland and Northern Ireland).

* Estimated figure.

The proportion of Catholics in the Republic of Ireland increased
steadily throughout the twentieth century until it reached a peak

of 95 per cent in 1961. There are four main reasons for this increase:

(1) Soon after its foundation in 1922, thousands of Protestants began to leave the Irish Free State. The main factors were economic uncertainty, loyalty to the English crown, and the incorporation of Catholic teachings in the State's constitution and laws. Indeed the population of the Free State would have increased slightly between 1926 and 1946 had it not been for the 24 per cent decline in the number of Protestants.[1]

(2) There was a low rate of disaffiliation from the Catholic Church. Although the actual numbers of Catholics and Protestants who have changed their religion may not differ much, the impact on the Protestant minority has been far greater. Even as late as 1974, a national survey of religious practices, attitudes and beliefs showed that 7.5 per cent of Protestants had changed their affiliation, compared to only 0.3 per cent of Catholics.[2]

(3) The Catholic Church teaching of *Ne Temere* requires that in a mixed marriage involving a Catholic, the children must be brought up as Catholics. A mixed marriage in one generation meant, if the regulation was obeyed, an all-Catholic family in the next. An indication of the long-term effect of mixed marriages is that in one year alone (1961), it was estimated that 30 per cent of Other Denomination (mostly Protestant) grooms, and 20 per cent of Other Denomination brides, married Catholics in Catholic ceremonies.[3] As one southern Protestant commentator put it: 'the process of intermarriage continues, and with it the leaching of the Protestant community'.[4]

(4) Another major reason for the increase in the proportion of Catholics in the Republic, and indeed in Northern Ireland, is their higher level of fertility. In the Republic of Ireland between 1960 and 1962, the Catholic birth rate (for married women aged 15–44) was 254.6 per thousand; for Protestants it was 151.3 per thousand. This means that, on average, Catholic families were 50 per cent larger than Protestant families.[5] The differential, as Kennedy shows, was maintained across occupational and social groups. It would seem that regardless of knowledge or access to artificial means of birth control, Catholics wanted and had larger families than non-Catholics.[6]

Since 1961, there has been a small decline in the proportion of Catholics in the Republic. This has been due to an increase in the number who have been leaving the Church. They have either not supplied information in their Census returns about their religious denomination, or have declared that they have 'no religion'. An interesting aspect of this process of disaffiliation is that most of those who leave the Church do not join another Christian denomination. Many no longer even regard themselves as Christians. A survey of Irish university students in 1976 showed that one in seven of the students who had been brought up within the Catholic Church no longer identified themselves as members. The majority of these students regarded themselves as agnostics, even though the most frequently mentioned reason for leaving the Church was disagreement with particular teachings.[7]

A Typology of Irish Religiosity

Christianity is a salvationary religion based on ethics. To be saved in and from this world, and to gain entry to the next, depends upon what one does in this world. There are three main types of ethical behaviour in Christianity: (1) magical—fulfilling traditional prescriptions and formulas in order to achieve material transformations in this world, (2) legalistic—adhering to the institutional rules and regulations of a Church, and (3) principled—methodically following an individually reasoned set of ethical guidelines. These types of ethical behaviour are often seen in terms of developmental stages with individually principled ethics as the most rational. In other words, societies as well as individuals go through stages in which their ethical behaviour develops from being predominantly magical, to being legalistic, to finally becoming individually principled. Until the first half of the nineteenth century, unorthodox religious practices, many of which were magical, appear to have been the dominant type of religious behaviour in Ireland.[8] Throughout the next one hundred years a legalistic adherence to the rules and regulations of the Catholic Church became the dominant type. Since the end of the 1960s, religious legalism has begun to be replaced by individually principled ethics in which Catholics develop their own principles about what is morally right and wrong.[9]

The least rationally developed type of religious behaviour is magic. It is based on the correct use of traditional formulas and objects which, if properly enacted, will bring success or reward. In its most basic form, magic is non-institutionalised. The status of the magician has often depended on his ability to compel a god or spirit to do his will. In other words, magical behaviour is good if it works. The practices of prayer and sacrifice have their origins in magic in so far as their ritual fulfilment is associated with attaining material advantage in this world, e.g. novenas, or donations to a saint in order to obtain favours. In this way magic can be part of institutional Catholic behaviour. Indeed, as Weber points out, 'magical coercion is universally diffused, and even the Catholic priest continues to practise something of this magical power . . .'[10]

In contrast to magic, religious legalistic behaviour is based on supplication and entreaty of God through adherence to the stable, systematic, consistent doctrine enunciated by a Church. This doctrine may be presented as formal abstract principles, but it is generally translated into specific rules and regulations. Obedience to the law is seen as the distinctive way to win God's favour, and any infraction of the Church's doctrine constitutes a sin. In legalistic religious ethics, behaviour is assessed in terms of the intentions and consequences of numerous individual actions. This is what traditionally occurs in Confession. It is associated with an absolute conviction that the rules and regulations of the Church or sect are divinely ordained and, consequently, are universally binding. In principled ethics, it is the total conduct of the individual and his personality that is evaluated. The assessment is not simply in terms of whether a particular action conforms to the rules and regulations of the Church. The individual makes moral judgments independently of the authority of the priest and the Church. He or she has come to recognise and accept the existence of other ethical principles and the necessity to defend his or her principles through reasoned debate rather than relying solely on the conviction of their sacredness.[11]

Now there are many aspects of modern Irish Catholicism that would link it to an ethic of principles, but ethical principles are rarely incorporated systematically by individual Catholics. This is due to the dominance of priests and the miracle of sacraments, both of which prevent Catholics from developing a consistent ethical systematisation of conduct and good works and, consequently, becoming autonomous, subjectively responsible individuals. Weber gives a good description of the difference between Catholicism, which still contains many elements of magic, and a highly rationalised religious ethic such as Calvinism:

> The priest was a magician who performed the miracle of transubstantiation, and who held the key to eternal life in his hand. One could turn to him in grief and penitence. He dispensed atonement, hope of grace, certainty of forgiveness, and thereby granted release from that tremendous tension to which the Calvinist was doomed by an inexorable fate, admitting of no mitigation. For him such friendly and human comforts did not exist. He could not hope to atone for hours of weakness or of thoughtlessness by increased good will at other times, as the Catholic or even the Lutheran could. The God of Calvinism demanded of his believers not single good works, but a life of good works combined into a unified system. There was no place for the very human Catholic cycle of sin, repentance, atonement, release, followed by renewed sin.[12]

This is not to say that the Catholic Church is devoid of general ethical principles, but that the Church acts as interpreter and defines explicitly, in terms of laws and regulations, how these principles are to be transformed into practice. It is the Church, rather than the individual, that decides what specific regulations of behaviour follow from general ethical principles. Salvation can be attained through a legalistic, external compliance with the Church's regulations. Consequently, there can often be a compliance with the Church's regulations without an explicit awareness of the ethical principles from which they are derived.

The Catholic Church, then, through its priesthood establishes a comprehensive ruling and direction of all spheres of behaviour. Everyone who is a member can be saved through adhering to its rules and regulations. Salvation does not depend upon being ethically perfect. Through good works and the miracle of institutional grace, a person who has been perfectly irreligious can become perfectly religious. Members who do more good works than necessary for their own salvation, accumulate grace for the credit of the institution, which distributes it to those in need.[13] Grace, the miracle of the sacraments, and the regulation of ethical behaviour by priests, spare Catholics the necessity of developing an individual pattern of life based on general ethical principles. It is the extent to which Irish Catholics are dispensing with the need for grace and are making up their own minds about what is good or bad moral behaviour, which indicates that they are moving towards a more Protestant type faith. However even though there has been a definite shift away from the dominance of religious legalistic behaviour towards individually principled ethics, there are still many Irish Catholics who are orientated towards magical practices. Indeed rarely does any modern Irish Catholic adhere specifically to one type of ethical behaviour. Rather is Irish religiosity an amalgam of all three types, with one type, an adherence to the rules and regulations of the Church, dominant over the other two.

Magical Practices

The analytical distinction between magical practices and legal religious behaviour is often difficult to distinguish in everyday Catholic life in Ireland. There are many aspects of the Church's rituals which could be seen as magical. Even the most solemn ritual of the transformation of bread and wine into the body and blood of Christ could in some respects be interpreted as magical. The more transubstantiation is taken to be an actual, physical rather than symbolic transformation, and the more the trans-formation is taken to be dependent on the precise repetition of actions and words, the more the sacrament becomes magical. There is one further crucial distinction. The miracles operated by priests are quite different from the magic of a magician in that they are part of an institution of grace founded on the principles of a stable doctrine. In other words, any magical power that the priest has, comes from the institution rather than from his own personal, charismatic power.

Magical practices are based on the enactment of a formula or ritual which, if followed correctly, will coerce the god into bringing about the desired results. Legalistic religious behaviour is based on winning God's favour by supplication, entreaty and being holy through following the Church's teachings and rituals. It is the priests who interpret God's will and actions, and tell the laity how to be holy and obtain God's favour. Ritual prayer becomes magical when the main interest is in obtaining a temporal favour or the material transformation of existing conditions. Indeed the religious behaviour of Irish Catholics has often been directed as much towards influencing and controlling the irrational forces of nature as it has been to gaining salvation in the next world. It is for this reason that the Catholic Church has institutionalised magical objects and practices, e.g. relics, medals, holy water, novenas, pilgrimages, etc. These are what the Church has traditionally called 'sacramentals' and they are used 'in imitation of the sacraments, to obtain from God spiritual favours'.[14] The Catholic Church has allowed these practices to continue even though they may go against the systematic rational control of behaviour. This has been necessary because, until recently, Ireland was a rural society in which the majority of the people came from peasant backgrounds and were bound to traditions based on magic. Indeed, the acceptance and incorporation of magical practices within the institutional Church would seem to have fostered a non-intellectual approach to doctrine and ethical conduct and helped maintain a simple, unquestioning devotion to its rules and regulations.

There are two main types of magical practice that exist within Irish Catholicism: (1) traditional practices, rituals, and superstitions which are pagan, i.e. non-Christian, in origin, and (2) sacred objects and practices approved by the Church and used to obtain temporal favours. Again the formal distinction between these two types of magical practice is often blurred in reality. There are, as we shall see, many traditional pagan practices which have been successfully incorporated in formal Church rituals.

Irish social life contains myriads of little rituals that are used to avoid bad luck and bring good fortune. Many of these rituals and objects, e.g., not killing a house-spider, not walking under a ladder, putting up horseshoes, keeping lucky pennies, etc., may have nothing to do with the Catholic Church, but they are practised by Catholics and they are an aspect of magical religious behaviour. Even if they are done tongue-in-cheek, and 'not really' believed in, they are significant simply because they continue to be practised. There are many Irish Catholics who would not consider themselves to be influenced by magic but who would go to enormous extremes not to walk under a ladder, or to catch sight of a lone magpie. Irish people may scorn the primitive tribesman who chants ditties to make the seeds grow, yet in their everyday life many of them engage in similar practices. The National survey in 1974 found, for example, that one in ten respondents believed that it was bad luck to walk under a ladder (table 2).

Table 2.   Magical Beliefs and Superstitions of the Irish*

Percentage who believed	%
(a) *That it is bad luck to:*	
Walk under a ladder	10.4
Break a chain letter	3.5
Put up an umbrella in the house	8.3
Oppose or contradict a priest	24.9
(b) In lucky numbers/charms/colours	9.4
In fortune telling	6.4

Source: Nic Ghiolla Phadraig, personal communication.

* Based on sample of 2,623 of which 2,499 were Catholic.

It is not that the Irish are more superstitious and magical than people from other Western societies. A survey of Londoners in 1968 found that three-quarters of the respondents touched wood in certain circumstances, while almost half threw salt over their shoulders when some was spilt.[15] These findings give credence in Martin's claim that Western society, although supposedly secular, remains deeply imbued with every type of superstition.[16] The findings also reveal that even though an individual or society may in most cases adhere to principled ethics, this does not mean that there are not magical aspects to their religious behaviour.

Irish folklore is full of pagan practices and superstitions. The proportion who engage in these practices is generally higher than the proportion who say they really believe in them. In other words, in contrast to other aspects of Irish religiosity, the level of practice is higher than the level of actual belief. People may search desperately for a piece of wood to touch, even though they claim they do not believe in magic or superstition. It has been, and in many respects still is, the ability of the Catholic Church to combine magical practices and superstitions with a predominantly legalistic type of religious ethic that has aided the growth of the institutional Church both in Ireland and elsewhere. This combination has also helped maintain a rich heritage of folklore. It cannot be denied that fairies, leprechauns, banshees and the like have almost disappeared from the Irish landscape. However, they would seem to have endured for a long time in the face of the onslaught of modern civilisation, science, and technology. This is because they have been compatible with institutional Catholicism. Pagan practices were suppressed only when they posed a direct threat. This is what happened to the wake which the Church gradually began to change from a festive celebration of death into a ritual occasion of mourning. Instead of a party involving games, some of which were sexually explicit, the wake has become a subdued and decorous occasion where prayers are said for the dead person, and visitors sit talking quietly among themselves.[17]

Another popular magical practice which is still prevalent in Ireland is faith-healing. There are numerous people throughout Ireland who have 'the cure' for specific ailments. The cure is generally performed by rubbing the afflicted spot in a ritualised manner with a sacred object such as a stone. Often the ritual has been Christianised through the recital of a few prayers and the use of a crucifix or medal instead of a stone. Again it is the mixture of object and ritual that creates the cure. There are also those who have the power of healing through touch alone. These faith-healers operate outside the institutional Church. They generally do not claim to get their powers from Christ and often charge for their services. Some of these faith-healers are the 'seventh son of a seventh son'. Logan goes so far as to suggest that 'one quarter of the medical practice in Ireland today is done by people who are not on the Medical Register'.[18]

There are many pagan practices which the Catholic Church in Ireland has adopted into its own rituals, for example pilgrimages to holy wells. Wells are essential for survival, and over time some became renowned as having greater properties than others. Consequently many became identified as holy. Over 3,000 holy wells have been catalogued in Ireland, of which over two hundred are still in use. Logan estimates 'that there are few parishes in which there is not at least one, but in many parishes there are more'.[19] Most of the wells have become associated with particular saints and, although they are undoubtedly pre-Christian in origin, the Church openly encourages pilgrimages to them. But there was a time in the nineteenth century when these pilgrimages were officially discouraged, not so much because they were pagan practices as because, like wakes, they were occasions of passionate, drunken, and often sexually immoral festivities.

Whereas Ireland may not differ from other Western societies in terms of the persistence of practices such as touching wood and believing in lucky numbers, it is different in terms of the variety and frequency with which pagan practices are enacted as part of Catholic religious behaviour. Even the rosary, the most traditional form of common ritual prayer, has many similarities with pagan practices—e.g. the ritual counting of beads (stones) as one proceeds in a circle. Instead of being imposed by coercion, such practices have become penitential acts of supplication and entreaty. However, very often the ritual is enacted for the purpose of a magical transformation of existing conditions. This is especially the case when a rigid adherence to the details of the ritual are held to be central to achieving the desired result. There is often a thin line between the legalistic enactment of a magical practice and a ritual adherence to the Church's regulations concerning what constitutes good moral conduct.[20] Forming a circle around the fire at home to say the rosary may be done to adore God—that is, with a more spiritual motivation. It may be done to keep the family together. It may also be done for more practical, material ends such as to bring rain or sunshine to help the crops grow.

Pilgrimages to Lough Derg, Croagh Patrick and Knock (where the Blessed Virgin is said to have appeared in 1879 and which, like Lourdes, is associated with miracle cures) are part of a wide range of popular devotional practices that have been enacted for centuries. In the national survey in 1973/74, half of the respondents had made a pilgrimage.[21] Some of the practices involve penitential exercises, e.g. climbing the rocky slopes of Croagh Patrick in one's bare feet, or going round the 'beds' (of rocks) in Lough Derg in the middle of the night having fasted for two days. Throughout the summer of 1985, there was an upsurge in popular devotion to Our Lady. This manifested itself mainly in outdoor vigils before a small number of the many hundreds of statues to her throughout the country. People gathered, sometimes in their thousands, in front of these statues and sang hymns and said the rosary. The devotional upsurge, while undoubtedly linked to changes in social and economic conditions, was sparked off by claims of material transformations in the statues, which were said to have moved, cried, bled, etc. . . .[22]

The nine-day novena has been making something of a comeback as a devotional practice. It was very popular during the 1950s and 1960s, but like many other devotional practices it became de-emphasised in the aftermath of Vatican II. However in 1979 it was estimated that up to 40,000 attended a nine-day novena to Our Lady of Perpetual Succour in Limerick.[23] Similar levels of attendance have been recorded for other centres in which the novena has been held. A traditional feature of the novena is the petitions for material benefits which, as Kelly points out, 'seem to reflect every need of human existence; petitions for positions, for homes, for a good wife or husband, for success in examinations, for advancement in work, for a chance to return to Ireland. . . .'[24]

As well as novenas, there are also a number of other private, devotional practices associated with the attempt to obtain temporal favours. Nearly every church in Ireland has statues, or a shrine, in front of which are candles. The 'penny candle' is paid for and lit, and a prayer is said, often for a special intention. What makes the practice magical in nature is the highly ritual format used to obtain the favour. There are special saints to whom one prays and specific acts are done in order to obtain favours. One prays to Saint Jude for a husband, to Saint Anthony if something is lost, and to Saint Christopher for a safe journey.

The most common sacramental object used in Ireland is holy water. It is generally found outside every church, and inside the door of many homes. It is associated with spiritual protection. Some holy water, e.g. from Lourdes or from a holy well, is often used for a cure. Medals are also common. They are used for spiritual as well as physical protection. For example, a St Christopher medal is often hung in a car to protect the travellers against accidents. Relics of saints or holy people are another type of sacred object used to obtain favours, especially cures from illnesses. In the national survey of 1974, half of the respondents had worn medals, and three-quarters put up holy pictures or statues.

The devotional piety of Irish Catholics is evidenced by the finding from the 1974 survey that 97 per cent of the respondents prayed at least once a day. Almost seven in ten (69 per cent) prayed when things went wrong or when they wanted something.

When asked why they prayed, '45 per cent stated that they prayed for material reasons and mentioned such "temporal" favours as protection from illness, comfort, or prosperity'.[25] Examples of thanksgiving for favours obtained from saints through this type of petitionary prayer are found in many newspapers and popular Catholic publications.

There is a similarity between magical practices and religious legalistic behaviour. The person who engages in magic believes that unless the formula is followed exactly, the gods will not be coerced and the desired result will not be achieved. The religious legalist holds that unless there is strict adherence to the letter of the law there will be no salvation. Consequently, there is often a compatability in Irish Catholicism, both within the formal structures of the institution and at the level of individual religious behaviour, between a strict adherence to the rules and regulations of the Church and engagement in magically oriented practices. Some of the magical practices described in this section are officially sanctioned by the Church, others are condoned, and some, especially those conducted by individual magicians, are discouraged. In general, as long as the practice is engaged in under the auspices of the Church it is tolerated. Material transformations directly attributed to God and his saints are a major aspect of Irish Catholic behaviour. Indeed some aspects of the sacraments, which are the keystone of the Catholic faith, are quite magical. But the sacraments are not simply received for their magical grace. They are received as part of an adherence to the Church's definition of what it is to be holy. Salvation in the next world is attained by keeping the commandments. But the catechism states that keeping the commandments cannot be done without the grace of God which is obtained through prayer and the sacraments. Receiving the sacraments has become part of adhering to the Church's definition of how to attain salvation. The more one prays, receives the sacraments and follows the teachings of the Church as to how to be holy, the more likely it is that one will be saved. Sacramental practice has less to do with magic than it has to do with the legalistic fulfilment of Catholic teaching which is central to attaining salvation. It is the fear of being denied moral respectability and salvation which is central to the power that bishops and priests have of limiting what the laity do and say.

Legalistic Religious Behaviour

The dominant form of religious behaviour in contemporary Ireland is an adherence to the rules and regulations of the Catholic Church. The way to be a good moral person and to save one's soul is to follow its teachings and practices. Moral respectability and salvation are attained through the unquestioning use of rituals, regulations and good works. This is how one becomes holy. Salvation becomes the 'sole' preserve of the Church. It is through a regular and habitual performance of rituals and good works that a state of grace is maintained. Questions of morality and salvation are left in the hands of the experts—bishops and priests. Moral problems for the laity are solved by confessing them to a priest and then, as a penance, actively engaging in some traditional, devotional practice.

Throughout the last hundred years or more in which institutional Catholicism has been dominant in Ireland, the principal form of entry into the rules and regulations of the Church was the Catechism of Catholic Doctrine; the 'penny' catechism or 'little green book'. Although the catechism was used in hedge-schools throughout the eighteenth century, its large-scale use did not begin until the development of confraternities in the first half of the nineteenth century. Its use among the mass of the Catholic population was delayed until the Church gained full control of the national school system during the latter half of the century. The catechism that was used in all Catholic schools in Ireland until the end of the 1960s was little different from Dr James· Butler's catechism, which was used throughout the nineteenth century, and itself was based on many of the teachings first promulgated at the Council of Trent. It is within the catechism that the general principles of Christian behaviour are given specific interpretations. The importance attached to religious practice as a means of maintaining adherence to its teachings is evident in the Church's commandments:

1. First: To hear Mass on Sundays and holydays of obligation.
2. Second: To fast and abstain on the days appointed.
3. Third: To confess our sins at least once a year.
4. Fourth: To receive worthily the Blessed Eucharist at Easter time.
5. Fifth: To contribute to the support of our pastors.

6. Sixth: To observe the marriage laws of the Church.[26]

In the national survey in 1974, respondents were asked questions about some of these Church commandments (table 3).

Table 3. Attitudes of Irish Catholics to Church Commandments
(Based on Sample of 2,499 Catholics)

Church Commandment	Always Wrong %	Generally Wrong %	Ambivalent/ Right/Other %
Missing Mass on Sundays*	24.4	61.5	14.1
Failing to do your Easter duty	59.4	19.4	21.2
Not paying dues	47.6	41.6	10.8
Not marrying in church	73.0	11.7	15.3

Source: Research and Development Commission "Report No. 3, Moral Values" pp. 2–47.
* Respondents were also asked to agree or disagree, or state if they were undecided about whether 'You can be a good Catholic without going to Mass:' 41% agreed, 2.3% were undecided and 56.6% disagreed with the statement.

The vast majority of the respondents considered it wrong to contravene the commandments of the Church. A high percentage took a rigid line regarding failure to do one's Easter Duty and not marrying in church. A less rigid approach was taken regarding missing Mass on Sundays and not paying dues. However the only exception generally mentioned for not obeying these two commandments were 'if ill' and 'if were not able to afford it'.

An adherence to rules and regulations is closely associated with, if not maintained by, regular ritual practice. For example 97 per cent of the respondents who thought missing Mass on Sundays was always wrong, and did not mention any exception, attended at least once a week. More remarkable is that six in ten of those who thought it was all right to miss Sunday Mass, or that it was up to the individual, attended regularly every Sunday. In general, the higher the level of religious practice, the higher the level of adherence to Church teachings and regulations. It is for this reason, perhaps, that the Church has concentrated on a pastoral strategy which, as Kirby points out, aims 'to maintain the moral standards on sexual matters and a strong family life through opposing the liberalisation of laws on contraception, divorce and abortion'.[27]

Results from the national survey in 1974 would suggest that nine in ten Irish Catholics adhere to the minimum criterion of a practising Catholic and attend Mass once a week, and Confession and Communion at least once a year (table 4).

Table 4.   Overall attendance at Mass, Holy Communion and Confession

Frequency	Mass		Communion		Confession	
	Act. %	Cum. %	Act. %	Cum. %	Act. %	Cum. %
Daily	5.6	5.6	3.6	3.6	—	—
More than once a week	17.8	23.4	6.1	9.7	—	—
Once a week	67.5	90.9	18.3	29.0	0.8	0.8
2 or 3 times a month	2.5	93.4	16.2	44.2	5.3	6.1
Once a month	0.9	94.3	21.4	65.6	40.4	46.5
About 6 times a year	0.8	95.1	13.5	79.2	23.3	69.8
Up to 3 times a year	0.8	95.9	12.7	91.9	20.0	98.8
Less than once a year	(1.4)	—	(5.1)	—	(6.4)	—
Never	(2.6)	—	(3.0)	—	(3.7)	—
no. =	2,499		2,495		2,495	

Act. = Actual   Cum. = Cumulative
Source: Nic Ghiolla Phadraig, "Religion in Ireland", p. 129.

A significant proportion of Irish Catholics would appear to do more than the Church's required minimum of religious practice. Nearly a quarter (23 per cent) of the 1973 survey respondents went to Mass more than once a week; nearly half (47 per cent) attended Confession at least once a month; and two thirds received Holy Communion at least once a month. Regular reception of the sacraments by the majority of Irish Catholics is an indication of their acceptance of the Church's definition of the path to salvation. A prominent conviction among many Irish Catholics would seem to be that as long as one attends Mass every Sunday, confesses any infractions of the Commandments and Church regulations to a priest, and worthily receives Holy Communion, one can be described as a moral person who has a good chance of being saved. However, the more frequently one receives the sacraments the higher one's state of grace becomes and, consequently, the better the possibility of keeping the commandments and being saved. The way to salvation is a complete trust in the Church's definition of moral conduct, and this is maintained by adhering to its minimum standards regarding a practising Catholic.

The level of attendance at Mass, Confession and Communion is lower among certain subgroups of the Irish population, e.g. the young, males, and those living in cities. A rigid adherence to the Church's definition of sin is generally less likely among the young and better educated. Whereas eight in ten respondents in the university survey in 1976 went to Mass once a week and received Holy Communion once a year, only 65 per cent attended Confession the required once a year. When it is considered that six in ten disagreed with the Church's teaching on contraception, then the indication is that many Catholic university students are following their own definition of sin and are receiving Holy Communion even though the Church may formally consider them unworthy.[28] It is the movement away from Confession and the Church's definition of what constitutes sin and good moral conduct, to an individual interpretation of morality, which is a sign of the development of individually principled ethics within this subgroup of the population. A further indication of this trend comes from the 1984 update, after ten years, of the national survey. The results indicated that while the proportion attending weekly Mass had not changed dramatically (from 91 per cent in 1974, to 87 per cent in 1984), the proportion who did not go to Confession at least once a year had risen from 10 per cent in 1974, to 24 per cent in 1984.[29]

Evidence that sacramental attendance among Irish Catholics is primarily a legal fulfilment of a Church prescription is that not only did the vast majority of respondents in the national survey regard missing Mass on Sundays and failing to do your Easter Duty as wrong, but when asked why it was wrong, over two-thirds gave the general reason that it was against the law of God or Church, or that it was failing in their duty. Analysing the responses from the 1974 survey in more depth, Nic Ghiolla Phadraig found that one in two gave legalistic-type reasons for regarding the following as wrong: missing Mass on Sundays, failing to do your Easter Duty, not paying dues, not marrying in Church, and not bringing up your children as Catholics. She also found a positive and linear relationship between levels of religious practice and the likelihood of using legalistic reasoning, e.g. 'against the law of God', 'against Church law', in the assessment of moral conduct. Indeed she found that those who relied on extrinsic legalistic reasoning were, in terms of the indices used, more religious than those who used spiritual reasoning such as 'would lose contact with God', or 'would miss the graces'. She concluded: 'The legalist group, as predicted, were significantly over-represented in traditional categories and had significantly the highest levels of religiosity on most indices. It had been predicted that the spiritual group would be mainly distinguished by high levels of religiosity, but their performance was below average.' However even the spiritual group were best distinguished by their 'attitudinal and behavioural endorsement of the institutional Church' rather than by their 'beliefs, values, experiences or perceived social support for such endorsement'.[30]

Further evidence that religious legalistic behaviour is a characteristic of Irish Catholic religiosity comes from the survey of university students in 1976; a young, educated subgroup of the population among whom such behaviour might not be expected to be prominent. In fact less than a quarter of the Catholic respondents agreed with any of the three statements that were used to measure religious legalism: 'You cannot be a good Christian without going to church on Sundays,' 'It is wrong to work on Sundays if it is not necessary,' and 'In order to be saved it is necessary to have been baptised.' In subsequent statistical analysis, these three attitudinal items, along with three other measures ('belief that the Catholic Church is the one true Church,' 'belief that the Pope can teach infallibly,' and 'frequency of attendance at Confession'), formed a separate dimension to being religious. Again it was only a minority (less than three in ten) of the Catholic students who fully accepted these beliefs and who attended Confession at least once a month. What is important about these findings is that religious legalism was found to be a separate dimension of Irish religiosity, even among university students. Students who were classified as religious legalists were more likely to consider premarital sex, abortion, killing and the use of contraceptives as being wrong primarily because they are contrary to the teachings of the Church.[31]

Attendance at Confession is a major aspect of religious legalistic behaviour since the individual submits his conduct to the priest for an assessment of its morality in terms of the institution's laws. If Confirmation is the assessment of the individual's knowledge of the rules and regulations by which salvation can be attained, Confession is the continuous assessment of whether or not it is being attained. The rigid legalist does not follow his own conscience. He does not derive his own code of moral behaviour from the principles given to him in the Bible. He follows the norms and regulations which the Church has derived from these principles. It is the legalist who, in the absence of a specific regulation, is often forced to consult with a priest so as to find out what is morally right or wrong.

The Church necessarily advocates a legalistic adherence to its rules and regulations. It discourages following one's own conscience because, as the Irish hierarchy put it, 'it can err, and in fact often does'.[32] Faithful Catholics are expected to accept all of the Church's teachings. As Bishop Newman of Limerick put it, there are 'some Catholics [who] manage to persuade themselves that they are faithful to their Church even though they reject some points of its teaching'.[33] To make a moral decision, according to the Irish hierarchy, the individual conscience must not only be informed, it 'must be guided by Church authority'. In other words, it is permissible for a Catholic to follow his or her conscience as long as it is guided by Church principles and does not contravene any specific regulation. As the Bishops' pastoral put it: 'It is for conscience to consider each new situation in the light of the overall command of love and the relevant moral values, and make the appropriate response. This response must always be in accordance with the specific commandments of God, as authoritatively interpreted by the Church, and must never violate the prohibitions contained in them.'[34]

Principled Ethics

The Catholic Church is founded on a systematic doctrine of ethical principles. It is a complete system within which the morality of any act can be determined. The principles are rationally and logically related to one another. But in the hierarchical organisation of the Church it is not the task of the laity to understand how these principles are logically interrelated. This is the task of the pope, bishops, and theologians who devise specific rules and regulations for the laity to follow. The 'simple faith' is the embodiment of these rules and regulations without any questioning or individual interpretation. Indeed, as O'Doherty found, there can be a strict adherence to the disciplinary obligations of the Church and an absence of any awareness of general Catholic principles.[35]

There are Catholics who strictly adhere to the regulations of the Church and who are aware of the general principles of their faith. But unless these principles are recognised, internalised, and adopted for their own sake rather than simply because of Church demands, they remain closer to religious legalism than to individually principled behaviour. There are other Catholics who do not have an explicit awareness of general Catholic principles and who appear to follow their own consciences in that they disobey certain teachings and regulations. They adhere to some regulations, but not to others. But many of these Catholics are closer to religious legalism rather than individually principled ethics in that they continue to interpret their own behaviour, and that of others, as right or wrong in terms of the categories and definitions of the Church. Fully developed principled ethics are based on the ability of an individual to interpret the morality of behaviour in terms of abstract principles, to internalise these principles as his or her own, to adapt them to particular situations, and to explain and justify them to others.

Individually principled ethics do not appear to be very common among Irish Catholics. The majority seem to follow the Church's interpretation of Christ's teachings. Even though they may be disobedient, most Irish Catholics rarely seem to disagree with the Church's teachings. In the 1974 survey, two-thirds of the respondents said they had no difficulty with any of the Church's teachings.[36] A similar percentage fully accepted the belief in papal infallibility. Such is the acceptance of the Church's interpretation of Christ's teachings and what constitutes good Christian behaviour that most Irish Catholics do not bother to read the Bible or gospels.[37]

There are approximately one-third of Irish Catholics who still identify themselves as Church members but who no longer adhere strongly to its teachings. Some of these still assess what is good moral behaviour in terms of the Church's teachings, even though they may contravene these themselves. Others adopt their own criteria for deciding whether behaviour is good or bad, and assume an individual moral responsibility for their own conduct and lifestyle. These Catholics are generally better educated and live in urban areas. In the 1974 survey, six in ten of the respondents who had third-level education said they had difficulty with some aspect of the Church's teaching, whereas only two in ten of those with no more than primary-level education said they had any difficulty.[38] In his survey of Dubliners in 1972, MacGreil found that the level of monthly confession attendance was significantly lower among those with third-level education. Yet they had a significantly higher frequency of receiving Holy Communion.[39] Among Catholic university students, the author found that a majority (57 per cent) disagreed with the Church's teaching on contraceptives and thought that their use was right. Yet this did not make many of them feel immoral or unworthy since more than two-thirds (69 per cent) received Holy Communion up to twice a month.[40]

Conclusion

Three types of ethical religious behaviour which are found in Irish Catholicism have been described in this chapter: magical practices, legalism (adherence to the rules and regulations of the Church), and principled ethics (individually reasoned principles about moral conduct). This analytical framework helps us to understand the religious behaviour of Irish Catholics. It is not to suggest that Catholics are oriented solely towards one type of behaviour. There are Catholics in Ireland who assess the morality of behaviour in terms of specific Church regulations, but who are also oriented to magical-type practices such as using relics to produce cures. Equally there are many Catholics who follow a set of individually principled ethics, but who in illness might surrender themselves to a faith-healer. Irish Catholic religious behaviour vacillates between all three different types in much the same way that the Church itself does. There are many institutional Church rituals that are quite magical in their orientation. On the one hand, the Church can advocate that moral behaviour is dependent on a reasonable, informed conscience. On the other, it can foster practices such as the use of relics and holy water which are typically magical. Indeed one of the reasons for the persistence of the Catholic Church in modern Ireland is its ability to reconcile the three types of religious behaviour, and to avoid the rational systematisation of ethics that occurs in certain forms of Protestanism, especially Puritanism. Nevertheless it has been shown that adherence to the rules and regulations of the Church is the dominant form of religious behaviour among Irish Catholics. When, how, and why it came to be and remain the dominant form of religiosity will occupy much of the remainder of this study.

What makes Irish Catholics different from Catholics in other Western European societies is the high level of institutional adherence to the Church (especially in terms of sacramental attendance), the persistence of many magical and devotional practices, and the general acceptance of the Church as the legislator and arbiter of morality. In a recent comparative study of values and practices in different European societies, the weekly attendance at church by the Irish (82 per cent) was found to be three times higher than the general European average (25 per cent), and twice as high as traditionally Catholic countries such as Spain (41 per cent) and Italy (36 per cent) where the proportion of Catholics in the population is also nine in ten. The Irish respondents also had a higher level of confidence in their Church and thought that its answers on individual moral problems were adequate.[41] The power, then, of the Catholic Church in Ireland is essentially a moral one. Instead of a shift towards principled ethics and a more secular ethic of individual responsibility which has taken place in other European societies, there is still in Ireland not only a persistence of magical practices, but also an adherence to the rules and regulations of the Church and a general acceptance of its definition of what is morally right or wrong.

3
Church Organisation and Control

THE HIGH level of adherence to the rules and regulations of the Church among Irish Catholics has been maintained through a vast physical organisation that was developed in the nineteenth century. It was within this institutional network of churches, schools, hospitals, and homes that Irish Catholics became disciplined within the rules and regulations of the Church. It was through the dedicated work of priests, nuns, and brothers that the ability to control the moral discourse and practice of the Irish people was first established. It was they who looked after the health, education, and social welfare of Irish Catholics. It was this care and supervision which laid the basis for, and maintained, institutional adherence. The physical reorganisation of the Irish Church during the last century was part of the extension of bureaucratic control from Rome. A rigorous system of hierarchical discipline was implemented. Bishops and priests were brought into Roman line. To understand the moral power of the Church in Ireland, it is, then, necessary to describe how it is physically organised and hierarchically structured; the position and role of bishops, priests, nuns, and brothers; the contribution of part-time voluntary workers; and the various strategies and tactics by which this hierocratic power has regulated the laity. It is partly because of its organisational strength that the Church is able to limit what Irish people do and say. It is through its highly developed bureaucratic apparatus that the Church, like the State in political matters, has been able to maintain control over Irish moral discourse and practice, regardless of whether people are fully committed to it. Indeed, other than the State, there is no institution in Irish society that has the same level of organisation and depth of resources as the Catholic Church. It has a strict bureaucratic organisation with a hierarchical structure of command from the pope down to bishops and priests. Its legal system, Canon Law, is as detailed and complex as that of the State. It has enormous economic resources. It owns large quantities of valuable land, much of which is located near the centre of towns and cities. Many of the largest buildings that dominate the Irish countryside are owned by the Church. It has over twenty-five thousand full-time workers. It has thousands more who work on a part-time basis. Through its dominance of education, health, and social welfare the Church has been largely responsible for the civilisation, moralisation, discipline, and supervision of Irish people. It is partly because the overwhelming mass of the Irish people spend a considerable proportion of their lives in buildings owned and run by the Catholic Church, and under the direct or indirect supervision of priests, nuns, and brothers, that the Church has been able to maintain its moral power. Unless one has an understanding of the size of the organisation and the way in which it operates, one cannot appreciate how the Catholic Church continues to dominate Irish society.

Physical Organisation

The physical organisation of the Catholic Church in Ireland is based on the twenty-six dioceses within the whole island. The dioceses are subdivided into parishes, of which there were 1,322 in 1982. Each of these parishes contains, on average, two churches (table 5).

Table 5.   Physical Organisation of the Catholic Church in Ireland, 1982

Diocese	Parishes	Churches	Religious Houses Priests	Brothers	Convents	Charitable Institutions	Schools Primary	Post-Primary	Catholic Population	% of Total Pop.
Armagh	60	140	10	7	24	11	170	33	183,691	66.8
Ardagh & Clonmacnoise	41	78	2	1	23	8	96	25	67,843	98.1
Clogher	39	87	3	4	11	5	103	23	81,900	75.4
Derry	52	105	1	2	13	11	149	27	173,766	68.2
Down and Connor	81	149	6	9	34	42	188	39	295,000	29.9
Dromore	20	47	2	2	14	7	52	14	63,334	48.7
Kilmore	36	97	1	—	11	3	93	17	57,030	91.1
Meath	68	145	10	6	43	32	185	36	160,000	98.2
Raphoe	29	70	2	1	11	9	116	18	78,542	88.0
Dublin	185	234	106	73	272	186	550	203	990,000	91.2
Ferns	48	101	3	4	23	9	98	23	99,000	96.1
Kildare & Leighlin	55	116	8	15	38	8	175	52	151,100	96.4
Ossory	42	105	5	6	31	36	89	30	71,275	97.2
Cashel	46	89	4	7	21	8	132	28	82,879	99.2
Cloyne	46	105	1	10	23	15	132	33	118,000	98.5
Cork and Ross	64	121	17	15	51	49	265	53	205,750	95.0
Kerry	53	110	2	7	31	54	184	40	125,000	98.4
Killaloe	58	133	2	5	26	10	160	28	112,114	97.5
Limerick	59	93*	11	6	34	12	114	32	129,200	98.3
Waterford & Lismore	44	84	11	12	30	14	100	30	115,702	99.4
Tuam	57	131	2	10	29	10	240	42	116,969	99.0
Achonry	23	47	1	1	12	6	72	19	34,000	99.1
Clonfert	24	48	2	1	10	13	68	9	33,812	96.7
Elphin	33	90	2	3	19	16	146	22	70,240	99.0
Galway	37	66	6	6	24	11	89	22	74,407	99.0
Killala	22	48	—	1	6	6	78	12	37,657	98.0
Total	1,322	2,639	219	213	859	591	3,844	900	3,732,211	77.1%

* 1980

Source: Irish Catholic Directory, 1983 (Dublin: Universe, 1983), p. 349
Annurio Pontificio, 1983 (Vatican: Libreria Editrice Vaticana, 1983), pp. 9–667.

There is approximately one church for every one thousand four hundred Catholics in Ireland. This average varies throughout the island, from one church to every 587 Catholics in the diocese of Kilmore, to one church to every 4,230 Catholics in Dublin.

Besides actual churches, there are numerous other buildings which belong to the Church. Religious Order priests have 219 houses, just under half of which are centred in Dublin. Orders of Brothers have 213 houses. This is quite a large number given that there were only 1,490 brothers in the country in 1981, i.e. one house for every seven brothers. The number of houses reflects a time when vocations were more plentiful There are 859 convents throughout the island with over a quarter of these located in Dublin. It is mainly nuns and brothers who run the 591 Catholic charitable institutions in Ireland which include hospitals, homes for the deaf, blind, etc., as well as reformatories.

One of the main assets of the Church, especially in terms of instilling a commitment to the institution, is the 3,844 primary schools and the 900 secondary schools which it owns. It is within these schools that each new generation of Irish Catholics is imbued with the beliefs and practices of the Church. Although adherence to institutional rules and regulations has begun to decline in recent years, it is certainly not as dramatic as what would happen if there were an end to denominational education. Ownership and control of buildings and land, especially schools, hospitals and charitable institutions, are an important aspect of the Church's power in Ireland. This power has been maintained over generations because property is held collectively as part of the organisation rather than privately. Indeed Weber argues that the original reason for the emphasis on celibacy was to prevent inheritance rights being claimed by the heirs of priests.[1]

Bureaucratic Organisation

The Catholic Church is a compulsory organisation. It is not something which people often join voluntarily. It has an established order of rules and regulations into which one is usually born and which are enforced by the threatened denial of salvation. The highly complex legal structure of the Church, which is central to its domination, is administered through the bureaucratic staff of priests, nuns, and brothers. This administrative staff is quite different from that of the State. Its members are generally life-long and often dedicated through vows of obedience, celibacy, and poverty. It is these vows, together with their clerical dress, which make priests and religious highly distinctive. It is this cultural distinctiveness, combined with high occupational status, which is central to their power.

The Catholic Church is a centralised, multinational organisation which claims a universal, legal competence that is exercised by bishops and priests throughout the world. The most important outcome of the Vatican Council of 1870 was not so much the dogma of Papal Infallibility as the universal episcopate of the people which, in Weber's words, 'created the ecclesiastical bureaucracy, and turned the bishop and parish priest, in contrast to the Middle Ages, into mere officials of the central power, the Roman Curia'.[2] The dogma of Papal Infallibility and the rational-isation of eccesiastical bureaucracy were the culmination of a process which had begun in earnest in the eighteenth century, and were in many ways a response to the domination being exercised by the new centralised power of nation-states. As we shall see in the second part of this study, the growth of the Catholic Church in Ireland was part of this process. From the end of the eighteenth century, but particularly from the granting of Catholic Emancipation in 1829, there was a tightening of administrative control which was associated with increased communication between bishops, their priests, Rome and London. But it was not until Paul Cullen, who had spent twenty years in Rome as head of the Irish College, was appointed Archbishop of Armagh in 1850, that the entire Irish Church was reshaped in discipline and devotion along Roman lines.

One of the best ways to give an idea of the bureaucratic structure of the Catholic Church in Ireland is to describe how it is hierarchically organised in terms of bishops, priests, brothers, and nuns, and what role each of these plays in the day-to-day running of the Church:

Bishops: Since the thirteenth century the Catholic Church in Ireland has been divided into dioceses. Each of these dioceses has at least one bishop. For example, Dublin which is the largest diocese with just over a quarter of the island's Catholic population, has five auxiliary bishops. There are four ecclesiastical provinces administered by archbishops. There is generally one Cardinal appointed who is the formal head of the Irish Church and who presides over the Conference of bishops. The four archbishops have very limited power over the bishops in their archdiocese. It is still the individual bishop in charge of his own diocese who is the crucial link between Rome and the Irish Church.

Each bishop is the authority for matters concerning his own diocese. Matters concerning Ireland as a whole are dealt with in full meetings of the Irish hierarchy which meets three times a year for two days. There are also some extraordinary meetings—for example, to draft joint pastoral statements. A Standing Committee of the hierarchy, consisting of the four archbishops and eight other bishops, meets about six times a year to deal with current affairs and to draw up the agenda for the full meetings.

Public squabbling between bishops and disregard of directives from Rome, which were quite common in the first half of the nineteenth century, have virtually disappeared. As one bishop described the present-day scene: 'Each bishop has a responsibility before the Lord for his own diocese. . . . But you won't find bishops contradicting one another'.[3] During the 1970s the hierarchy began to issue pastorals and joint statements more frequently. While these are undertaken independently, they rely heavily on papal encyclicals and statements. Individual bishops with special competencies will often issue public statements on contemporary issues; sometimes as individuals, sometimes as spokesmen for the rest of the hierarchy. It is also common for a bishop to issue his own pastoral statement which differs from any joint statement of the Episcopal Conference. This is what happened in 1971 when the hierarchy issued a statement with reference to the proposal to change the legislation on contraception. The statement declared that: 'There are many things which the Catholic Church holds to be morally wrong and no one has ever suggested, least of all the Church herself, that they should be prohibited by the State.' However, in his Lenten pastoral the Archbishop of Dublin, Dr McQuaid went beyond the joint statement, and declared that the proposed legislation offended 'the objective moral law', was a 'curse upon our country', and 'an insult to our Faith'.[4]

Like any other modern bureaucratic organisation, the Conference of Irish Bishops has a number of commissions and advisory bodies each of which is under the supervision of two or three bishops. These commissions gather and disseminate information and statements concerning various aspects of the Church in Ireland. There are twenty-one altogether dealing with: catechetics, clergy, communications, doctrine, ecumenism, education, emigrants, finance, foreign aid, justice and peace, the laity, liturgy, missions, pastoral matters, press and information, the religious, research and development, seminaries, social welfare, unwanted pregnancies and vocations.

Under the hierarchical organisation of the Church, bishops are accountable to Rome, priests are accountable to their bishops, and the laity is accountable to their priests. Canon law obliges bishops to visit the whole or part of their diocese in order to safeguard good customs and rectify evil ones, and to promote peace, innocence, piety, and discipline amongst the people and clergy. It is only in exceptional circumstances that a member of the laity makes direct contact with a bishop. Indeed there is something of a tradition of bishops remaining aloof from the ordinary people. This was often due to the fact that many bishops were appointed from the National Seminary in Maynooth, or some other third level institution, and had little or no experience of regular contact with the laity. It would also seem part of a deliberate policy to maintain doctrinal orthodoxy among the bishops, i.e. the less contact with the theologically illiterate, the less possibility of contamination. This helped maintain the status of bishops. Members of the laity, including the democratically elected leaders of the people, had to come to see them in their palaces if there was reason to meet. For example, during the Mother and Child controversy in 1951, it was the Archbishop of Dublin who summoned the Minister for Health to his residence. In 1963, Blanchard could claim that the bishops of Ireland 'have more power in practice than those of any country in the world,' and that 'a member of the congregation listens much more readily to his Bishop than he does, for instance, to his deputy [elected member of political constituency]'.[5] There was a tendency immediately after Vatican II to appoint bishops with pastoral rather than theological experience, but this trend has been reversed in recent years. This is in spite of the fact that in the national survey in 1973/74, two-thirds of the respondents agreed that the leaders of the Catholic Church were out of touch with the real needs of its members, and that half of the respondents felt that lay people should have a say in electing bishops.[6] In effect, as in any other multinational organisation, bishops are appointed directly by the headquarters in Rome. Other bishops within the archdiocese are consulted, as are priests and some lay leaders within the actual diocese itself. However their choice is never made known and may be overlooked. Far from being an open democratic process, the appointment of bishops is an autocratic Roman preserve which is clouded in secrecy. The internal organisational struggles are probably as great as those concerning the appointment of any politician, but they are clouded in the belief that all the machinations are really an expression of the Holy Spirit.

The methods by which bishops supervise and control their priests are numerous. Most of the formal procedures are set out in the Decrees of the Maynooth Council in 1956. As part of the hierarchical power of the Church in which the business of bishops and priests is deliberately hidden from the laity, these decrees are written in Latin and are not available to members of the general public. Similarly, members of the laity are denied access to the meetings of the Conference of Irish Bishops, and after the meetings only brief statements are issued about what took place. Blanchard notes that under the Maynooth decrees each parish is formally visited by the bishop every two to three years. The parish priest is required to complete a questionnaire concerning the spiritual welfare of his parish before the visit. Like the Maynooth decrees, the details of the questionnaire and an account of the visit are never made public. Besides this more formal procedure, bishops can supervise and obtain information about their priests, their problems, and their conduct through diocesan chapter meetings, various committee meetings and, most important of all perhaps, during the annual diocesan retreat.[7]

Bishops are also responsible for overseeing the operations of clerical religious orders of priests, brothers, and nuns. Here the level of control and supervision is greatly reduced unless, as has been happening in recent years, a religious order of priests is running a parish. A bishop cannot censure a member of a clerical religious order as easily as he can a curate, and he certainly does not have the same power to say where he or she should go, and what he or she should do.

Diocesan Priests: Although the Catholic Church exercises global control from Rome, and there are regulations under canon law which must be followed, there is nonetheless a certain autonomy afforded to bishops and priests in their day-to-day running of the Church. This independence means that bishops in one country can behave quite differently from bishops in another, and yet still be part of the same Church. Similarly, priests can be quite different from their bishops, and from each other, in the way that they interpret, teach, and enforce the teachings of the Church. Throughout Irish history there have been numerous rebel priests who have disregarded the directives of their bishops, especially with regard to political matters, and who have never been censured, let alone excommunicated. In fact it has been one of the organisational strengths of the Catholic Church for the pope and bishops to state one thing, and for the priests, often reflecting pressure from the laity, to state and do the opposite. It is this gap between formal teaching and its more informal application which is central to the maintenance of the Church's moral power. While a bishop may exercise control over his curates by shifting them from one parish to another, he loses this ability once he appoints a parish priest. It is often said that if the bishop is master of his diocese, he is not the parish priest of his parishes. It may be because of this relative autonomy that in the 1970s the appointment of a parish priest was, on average, delayed until he was about fifty-five years of age. [8]

In 1981, there were 3,653 diocesan clergy of whom almost eight in ten (78.5 per cent) were actively engaged in parish ministry. This means that there are approximately two priests working in every parish in Ireland. The overall ratio of Catholics per priest in 1981 was 978, which is one of the lowest in the world. Other ratios were: England/Wales 989; France 1445; Italy 1398; Portugal 2460; Poland 2200; and the United States 1422. If one expresses the Irish ratio in terms of Catholics to each priest/brother/nun, it was 174:1. [9]

The task of the diocesan priests is to preach, catechise, and administer the sacraments. They are responsible for the spiritual, and often the social, welfare of the parishioners. They are at the forefront of the institutional Church's struggle to maintain moral power in that they have most contact with the laity. It is their task to be familiar with their parishioners' spiritual condition and moral behaviour. They are the day-to-day assessors of what is right and what is wrong. In some ways they may be understood as the moral policeman whose traditional beat has been the schools, homes, halls and hedges of the parish. They respond to the needs of the laity; needs which they are partly responsible for creating and maintaining. The need for salvation can only be met in and through them. Like the ordinary policeman, the priest is there to respond to the needs of the laity if they, or others close to them, break the law. But he is also there to enforce the law. It is still difficult, if not impossible, in many parts of rural Ireland to maintain one's social prestige if one has been censured or denounced by the priest. This is the reason why many employers have traditionally sought a reference from an applicant's parish priest. His status as moral arbiter is dependent on a number of strategies and tactics which are used to maintain adherence to the institutional Church. Most of these are personal and direct, e.g. home visitation, castigation, denial of absolution, etc. The ones most feared are public denouncements—informally through the parish grapevine, formally from the pulpit or, rarely though still a possibility, full censure and excommunication.

Just as the State is ultimately founded on a monopoly of the physical means of coercion, e.g. the army and police, the Church's moral power is ultimately founded on its means of religious and social coercion, i.e. denial of salvation, excommunication, and loss of social prestige. This power has been maintained, often in opposition to that exercised by the State, through the services and care that the Church provides, especially for the weaker members of society. The exercise of moral power is also dependent upon a detailed knowledge of the behaviour of parishioners. The more a priest knows about their behaviour the more likely he will be able to control them. This knowlege is obtained in different ways: as a broker of power, as a social consultant, through house visitation, and in Confession.

The priest in Ireland is a spiritual and moral adviser who is consulted on a wide range of social, political, and economic issues. His formal status derives not just from being the head of the parish, but also from being the manager of the local school, and traditionally one of the more refined and educated members of the community. Informally he is often the most respected member of the community. Any outsider or group which becomes involved in the parish, whether at a social, political, or economic level, will usually make contact with the parish priest. There is rarely any local committee or social occasion of importance which he is not asked to attend. It is as the guardian of virtue and morality that he can have most influence. He is the one who supervises access to social and moral respectability.

Visitations are a direct supervision and investigation into the spiritual and moral behaviour of parishioners. Although ostensibly friendly and informal, parish visits have a specific purpose. As one priest put it: 'at some stage or stages in the informal chat there must be spiritual welfare business and investigation, e.g. "I suppose you have the family rosary" or "I'm sure you have all made the Easter duty." The question about the rosary should be asked only to keep them at it.'[10] In the national survey in 1973/74, nearly half of the homes in the country had been visited by a priest in the six-month period prior to the interview.[11] It is during these visitations that the priest can check up on the signs of moral laxity, lack of discipline in attending Mass or school, or other family problems. The more often the priest visits the home the better the moral supervision. As Abbot points out: '[an] advantage of regular, methodical visitation is that "black sheep" will not feel that they are being publicly singled out for visits reserved for back-sliders whose names appear on the priest's black list'.[12] It is often because diocesan priests have been able to enter freely the home of Irish Catholics, and enquire directly as to whether members of the family are adhering to the rules and regulations of the Church, that a high level of institutional adherence has been maintained. It is usual during the investigation that attention is focused on the mother, for moral discipline is regarded as her responsibility. Unless the mother feels under a moral obligation to allow such an investigation to take place, the success of the visitiation will decline, as will the Church's control of the home and the level of adherence to its rules and regulations. This moral obligation is related to the mother's education and socio-economic status, and how dependent she is on the priest and Church for status and prestige.

Because the priest is the centre of moral power in the community, he is often used by the laity as a vehicle for social prestige. The closer one is to the priest, the arbiter of morality, the more moral one will appear, thereby adding to one's social prestige. It is for this reason that parishioners will often inform the priest of misdemeanours, moral laxity, and blatant defiance of the Catholic moral code in the community. In effect, these informers become the auxiliary force of the priest. Much of the supervision of moral behaviour of Catholics in Ireland has been carried out by members of the laity acting as the priest's aides. The more the priest is informed of the misbehaviour of members of the laity, the more he is able to maintain his status as moral arbiter. Abbot describes how information should be gathered on a visitation: 'People will certainly from time to time drop useful hints or volunteer information about neighbours. If they do so, the priest need not block his ears. After a short time he should resume the conversation ignoring the hints and the information. These hints, however, may furnish reasons for vigilance and direct enquiries.'[13]

The other method by which the priest has traditionally obtained knowledge about his parishioners' behaviour is through the confessional. It is in response to the sins, worries, and concerns being announced to him in Confession that the priest is able to redirect his pastoral care towards the needs of the community. It is when people stop going to Confession that the priest and the Church can begin to lose touch with the behaviour and needs of the laity. As mentioned earlier, there is a distinction between the formal teaching of the Church as mediated by the pope and bishops, and its informal application through the priests in Confession. While the former may demand strict compliance to the Church's teachings, the latter may interpret these more as general rules rather than specific regulations.[14] But when people stop going to Confession, the possibility of a more personal, informal application of the general rule is denied. The formal teaching can then lead to disenchantment with, and alienation from, the Church. This is particularly relevant with regard to the issue of using contraceptives. In the survey of university students in 1976, six in ten of the Catholic respondents thought that using contraceptives was right, but 35 per cent rarely or never went to Confession. Furthermore, one of the main reasons disaffiliated Catholic students gave for leaving the Church was disagreement with a particular Church teaching.[15] It is precisely because of the absence of frequent personal contact with many young Catholics, either through visitation or Confession, that priests and bishops have had to rely more on the results of social surveys to find out what they are doing and thinking.[16]

The power of the diocesan priest in Irish society is, then, related directly to his level of supervision and knowledge of the moral behaviour of his parishioners. The more he supervises, the more he will know what is going on. But as more people stop confessing their sins to him, as more people revolt against his supervision, he becomes more out of touch, and his power diminishes. As this process develops, many Irish Catholics first of all no longer interpret the morality of their actions in terms of what their local priest would say, and later distance themselves from an adherence to the rules and regulations of the Church. There has been a gradual progression away from the type of Irish Catholic who believes it is bad luck to oppose or contradict a priest, to the type of Catholic who rarely or never goes to Confession. The more this process continues the more the status and power of the diocesan priest will decrease.

Clerical Religious Orders: The strength of the human resources of the Catholic Church in Ireland can be understood from the fact that diocesan priests represent less than one in seven of the men and women who have given over their lives to working for the Church. No other organisation in Irish society has as many full-time employees who work so long, so hard, for so little. If diocesan priests can be understood as the moral policemen of Irish society, religious order priests, brothers and nuns may be seen as exemplary prophets of a life dedicated to the Church. Besides any status which derives from their occupational position as teachers, nurses, etc., their power derives mostly from their prestige, i.e., the honour, respect and deference which is paid to them on account of their vows of celibacy and renunciation of possessions. It was the dedicated work of priests, nuns, and brothers in providing health, education, and welfare services for Catholics in opposition to those provided by a Protestant English State that was crucial to the development of the Church's moral monopoly during the last century. The example they showed of a disciplined, celibate, moral lifestyle dedicated to self-surrender and caring for others was crucial to the initial modernisation of Irish rural society, and the successful maintenance of population control mechanisms such as postponed marriage, permanent celibacy, and emigration. The exemplary role of clerical religious orders is also evidenced in the fact that there are over six thousand of them doing missionary work abroad (table 6).

Half of the Irish religious who are working abroad are religious order priests. The majority of missionary priests are in developing countries and are engaged mainly in 'the pastoral care of souls'. Of the religious order priests in Ireland, three in ten are actively engaged in parish work, which includes running parishes and giving missions and retreats. Two in ten are engaged in teaching, mostly in their own schools. The remainder do a variety of tasks, e.g. administration, writing, vocation work, and tending to the day-to-day needs of the order.

Over half (55 per cent) of the full-time religious personnel of the Catholic Church in Ireland are nuns. In many ways they have been the silent, solid wall behind modern Irish Catholicism. It has been the nuns who have disciplined, trained, and educated almost every Irish girl who progressed beyond primary school. They refined and polished these girls into paragons of modern Irish virtue. The occupational choices of these well-educated girls were limited in the past. If they did not become mothers, many became secretaries, teachers, nurses, or nuns themselves. It was the nuns who virtually took over the management of the Irish hospital system in the nineteenth century, and since then have run many of the hospitals, nursing homes, remedial homes, orphanages, and other charitable institutions of the country. Yet it is the nuns who, like the Irish mother, have been written out of the history of modern Irish Catholicism.[17]

Leaving aside those who are retired, or who help run the convent, the main occupational deployment of Irish nuns is in teaching and medical work. However, because of the decline in vocations, nuns are becoming more involved in the administration of their schools and hospitals than in actually teaching in the classroom, or caring for the sick in the hospital ward. This is being done more by lay people who are employed by the nuns but paid by the State.

The main deployment of religious order brothers in Ireland, half of whom are Christian brothers, is in teaching. Like the sisters, the decline in vocations has meant that they are being forced into administrative rather than teaching roles. Although the majority of the teachers in their schools are lay and their salaries, as well as

Table 6.   Human Resources of Catholic Church in Ireland, 1981

		Number	Per-centage	Parish Work No.	Parish Work %	Teaching No.	Teaching %	Medical Social No.	Medical Social %	Other No.	Other %
Diocesan Clergy	Ireland	3,653	17.4	2,869	76.6	481	8.4	60	2.6	243	2.6*
	Abroad	109	1.8	—		—		—		109	
		3,762	13.9	2,869		481		60		352	
Clerical Religious Orders	Ireland	3,551	16.9	868	23.3	559	9.8	—		2,124	22.9†
	Abroad	3,160	52.3	2,086		304		—		770	
		6,711	24.8	2,954		863		—		2,894	
Sisters	Ireland	12,332	58.6	—		3,787	66.1	2,201	94.8	6,344	68.8††
	Abroad	2,546	42.2	—		952		924		670	
		14,878	55.0	—		4,739		3,125		7,014	
Brothers	Ireland	1,490	7.1	—		901	15	61	2.6	528	5.7§
	Abroad	229	3.8	—		128		33		68	
		1,719	6.4	—		1,029		94		596	
Total	Ireland	21,026	77.7	3,737	100.0	5,728	100.0	2,322	100.0	9,239	100.0
	Abroad	6,044	22.3	2,086		1,384		957		1,617	
		27,070	100.0	5,823		7,112		3,279		10,856	

* Includes 175 (72%) retired.   † Includes 326 (15%) retired.   †† Includes 3032 (48%) retired.   § Includes 329 (62%) retired.

Source: *Irish Catholic Clergy and Religious: 1970–1981*, pp. xiii, 24,54,65,94 102,131,136.

maintenance costs of the building, are paid by the State, the brothers generally fill the key post of headmaster, and are responsible for any teaching appointments made. As with the nuns, the contribution of brothers to the maintenance of the power of the Catholic Church in modern Irish society has yet to be fully analysed. It is not that they have educated every Irish male. It is rather that they, and the priests, have educated and trained nearly every male who has attained a high position in Irish society. Moreover it was the brothers who, before the end of the 1960s when the State introduced free secondary education, brought the possibility of post-primary education to the members of the lower socio-economic groups of Irish society.

It is when priests, nuns, and brothers are no longer responsible for educating, disciplining, moralising, and caring for Irish Catholics that adherence to institutional Catholicism in Ireland will decline. Such a decline has been taking place since the 1960s as the Church loses its control of education, health, and social welfare. This is linked to the decrease in numbers brought about by a decline in vocations and an increase in departures from the various forms of the religious life. In the eleven years from 1970–1981, the total number of clerical and religious personnel in Ireland declined by 18 per cent. The decline was greatest among brothers (32 per cent) and nuns (20 per cent).[18] It was least among diocesan priests (4.6 per cent), partly because of a lowering of the educational requirements for entry into the seminaries. Of the 175 students who entered diocesan seminaries in 1978, little more than a third (37 per cent) had the equivalent of an honours school Leaving Certificate.[19] Another problem brought about by the decline in vocations is an increase in the generation gap between religious personnel and the laity. Priests, nuns, and brothers are all, comparatively, older than the rest of the population—for example, in 1971 more than six in ten (63 per cent) Irish nuns were over fifty years of age compared to just over four in ten (42 per cent) of the rest of Irish females. Between 1970 and 1981, the number of retired sisters increased from 1,601 to 3,032, an increase of 89 per cent.[20] While the situation is not so bad among religious order and diocesan priests, the future scenario is that unless there is a dramatic increase in vocations, Irish religious personnel will be mainly involved in caring for their own sick, elderly, and infirm. Even though recent figures suggest that the annual number of vocations and departures are stabilising, for every ten who entered the priesthood or religious life in 1978, seven died and eight left.[21]

Lay Organisations

Lay groups and organisations have always played a significant role in maintaining the position and influence of the Catholic Church in Ireland. However, since Vatican II and the recent decline in vocations, they have begun to play an even greater role. This is not to suggest that in terms of the hierarchical organisation of the Church the laity are not still supervised and directed by clergy and religious, but that the dividing lines have become more blurred. In fact there has never been a very distinct line between the two, and members of the laity have often been able to limit the practice and discourse of priests, especially if they deviate from their institutionally defined roles. More recently, members of the laity have taken over a number of tasks that used to be the sole preserve of the priest, e.g. giving sermons and distributing Holy Communion. Lay organisations have also taken over from the hierarchy in putting pressure on the State to amend existing legislation and to bring it into line with the Church's teachings. This, as we shall see in the next chapter, was a major feature of the abortion referendum campaign in 1983. Being a member of a lay organisation brings Catholics closer to the centre of clerical power, and bestows greater social prestige, which is important if one has little other power, or if one is trying to legitimate what political and economic power one has already. In the national survey in 1973/74, one in seven of the respondents said that they have been involved in some kind of parish work. The activity most frequently mentioned was collecting money.[22]

In 1983, there were twenty-six different Catholic lay organisations affiliated to the hierarchy's Laity Commission. The total membership of these organisations was over 300,000 (table 7).

This list includes many children's organisations, and there is probably a good deal of double counting in that members of one organisation could well be members of another. On the other hand, the list is by no means comprehensive.

Table 7.   Irish Catholic lay organisations: membership and aims

Organisation	Number of Members	Self-defined Aims
Apostleship of the Sea	150	To show Christian hospitality and concern to merchant seamen and women; to be a home outside of home.
Apostolic Work Society	3,600	To help the Missions by prayer and active work.
Catholic Boy Scouts	35,000	To promote the spiritual, moral, cultural and physical development of its members so that they become mature Catholics, prepared for leadership and service in home and community.
Catholic Girl Guides	13,000	As above
Catholic Marriage Advisory Council	1,809	To help people initiate, sustain and enrich their marriage and family relationships.
*Charismatic Renewal	10,000	The renewal of the individual, the Church and the whole body of Christ through prayer groups.
Christian Family Movement	600	To promote happy family life in accordance with Christ's teaching.
Christian Life Communities	500	Challenges Christians to an awareness of the grave responsibilities involved as Christ's witnesses.
Faith and Light	Not available	To emphasise the contributions that mentally handicapped people have to make to the Christian community.
Focolare	700	To help bring about the fulfilment of the prayer of Jesus "that all may be one".
Irish Guild of Catholic Nurses	1,650	To promote the social, educational and professional development of its members, so as to help them work effectively in the service of life.

Knights of St Columbanus	4,500	To promote by personal group action the extension of practical Christianity in all phases of life; to maintain a material order of Catholic lay leadership.
Lay Fraternity of Br. Charles of Jesus	150	To achieve the mutual understanding and living unity right and proper for Christians through practising universal charity.
Legion of Mary	10,000	The sanctification of its members by prayer and participation in apostolic works: the provision of a *corps d'élite* at the disposal of ecclesiastical superiors.
Marriage Encounter Ireland	500	To organise weekend retreats for married couples.
Marriage Encounter World Wide	500	The renewal of the sacrament of Matrimony, thereby helping to renew the Church.
*National Federation of Youth Clubs	35,000	The personal development of young people as a process of education through the experience of relationships, through social action as well as ideas and skills.
Opus Dei	700	A personable prelature (*sic*) of the Catholic Church whose members strive to live the fullness of the Christian life, each one in their own state, by sanctifying their daily work and the ordinary circumstances of their family life and social commitments.
Pax Christi	200	To work with all men for peace for all men, always witnessing the peace of Christ.
Pioneer Total Abstinence Society	170,000	The promotion of temperance and sobriety with prayer and self-sacrifice as its principal means.
St Joseph's Young Priests Society	3,500	To promote vocations to the priesthood and to assist selected students financially.

*St Vincent de Paul	9,000	To alleviate need and to discover and redress situations which cause it, mainly through helping people in their homes.
Teams of Our Lady	250	For married couples to help one another live their lives in accordance with their Christian beliefs.
Viatores Christi	135	To encourage Irish people to volunteer for missionary service overseas.
*Volunteer Missionary Movement	230	To spread awareness of the role of the laity at home and abroad and send qualified committed lay people to the third world.
Young Christian Workers	500	To train young people to educate and represent themselves, whether at work or in society, and to see to the neglected needs of young people.

* These organisations are officially non-denominational although the vast majority of their members are Catholic and the organisation is affiliated with the Irish Catholic Episcopal Commission for the Laity, which was the criterion for inclusion in the above table.

It does not include a number of organisations, e.g Catholic Women's Federation, Congress of Catholic Secondary School Parent Associations, Cursillo, Knights of Malta, Irish Guild of SS Luke, Cosmas and Damien, Macra na Tuaithe, Social Study Conference, etc., which have either disbanded, become disaffiliated from the Commission, or whose work is not specifically Catholic. The list also does not include a wide variety of lay groups, e.g. confraternities, peace groups, bible study groups, adult theology groups, etc., which often operate on a parish level, but which do not have a formal organisation. Nor does it include organisations such as PLAC (Pro-Life Amendment Campaign) and SPUC (Society of the Protection of the Unborn Child) which came together in 1983 to force through the referendum which made abortion unconstitutional.

The contribution of members of these lay organisations to the maintenance of the moral power of the Catholic Church in Irish society is enormous. They are often termed 'the living witnesses of the Catholic faith in Ireland'. They are the apostolic workers who, in their everyday lives and contact with other lay people, put forward the Church's viewpoint. It is often through their performance of charitable works that the Church is able to look after the sick and poor. For example, the St Vincent de Paul Society is a lay organisation which engages in direct person-to-person contact. Members visit 10,000 families, 7,000 elderly people, and virtually every hospital and long-stay institution in the country each week. Some of the larger organisations are secretive about their operations, e.g. Knights of Columbanus, Legion of Mary and Opus Dei. They regularly meet in private. The minutes of these meetings are not publicly available. Prospective members are instructed on the need for the preservative of absolute secrecy in regard to any matter discussed at meetings. In some ways these lay organisations resemble Orders of Masons. In fact, this was one of the reasons why the Knights of Columbanus was first established, i.e. to promote secretly Catholic social principles and Catholics in the organisations, public and private, in which they were working.[23]

Education

Control of the education system has been fundamental to the Catholic Church maintaining an adherence to its rules and regulations. It is within the schools that young Irish children have been slowly and consistently instructed in and also imbued with the Church's teachings. This instruction takes place through a rigid system of moral discipline at the centre of which is an embodiment of the Church's ritual practices. It has been mainly through these practices, including the rote learning of the catechism, that an adherence to the rules and regulations of the Church was instilled. Furthermore it is through the school that the Church can reach into the home and supervise the mother in her upbringing of her children. As each new generation of Irish parents hand over their children to Catholic schools, often because of having limited choice, those who have let the reins of the Church's moral discipline slacken are forced into taking them up again. The Church's control of Irish education has depended, as Clarke points out, on the State accepting the Church's policy on education, i.e. that each child has a right to a Christian education; that parents have a right to educate their children according to their consciences; and that Catholic parents have an obligation to educate their children the way the Church tells them to do so.[24] However, this does not explain why the State pays for and runs the system and yet allows the Church to continue to control it. Just when, why and how the State handed over control of Irish education to the Churches, and to the Catholic Church in particular, will be dealt with in a later chapter. In this section, the purpose is to document the control that it exercises at present over the education system.

The vast majority of Irish Catholics have been educated by the Catholic Church. The instruction may not have been given by a priest, brother, or nun, but it was generally given by a school-teacher who was appointed and supervised by a member of the clergy or religious. It is within the school that every day, five days a week, children are imbued with the teachings, principles, and ethos of the Catholic Church. Religious instruction is a major part of the syllabus, and is generally taught for a half hour each day. This is above and beyond any religious practice which occurs during or after school time but which is organised by the school, e.g. prayers at the beginning of each day or lesson, sodalities, missions, retreats, etc. As Murphy points out: 'In national schools religion is supposed to permeate the whole atmosphere of the class and not to be regarded as just a half hour's instruction.' The Rules for National Schools state clearly that 'Of all the parts of a school curriculum, Religious Instruction is by far the most important. . . .'[25] In primary school, children are prepared for Confession, Holy Communion and Confirmation. They are given a thorough grounding in Catholic doctrine. In the 1960s the Church spent a great deal of time and money devising a new catechetical programme of books and tapes. However, the success of the programme was brought into question, especially in terms of instilling a knowledge of the rules and regulations of the Church. Many including the former Archbishop of Dublin, Dr Dermot Ryan, called for a return to the 'penny' catechism and rote learning of prayers and doctrine.

The Church has always fought hard to maintain control of education in Ireland. It was treated as a mortal sin for Catholics not to send their children to Catholic schools. The Dublin Diocesan regulations of Dr McQuaid, which were enforced until 1971, stated that:

In the education of Catholics, every branch of human training is subject to the guidance of the Church, and those schools alone which the Church approves are capable of providing a fully Catholic education.

Therefore the Church forbids parents and guardians to send a child to any non-Catholic school, whether primary or secondary or continuation or university. Deliberately to disobey this law is a mortal sin, and they who persist in disobedience are unworthy to receive the sacraments.[26]

It may not still be a mortal sin, but it is nevertheless an unacceptable social practice for Catholics to send their children to Protestant schools. Not only is it regarded as disloyal and conduct unbecoming of an Irish Catholic, but in many circumstances it is a prerequisite to being regarded as the same as everyone else. It is the insistence on denominational education both in the North and South of Ireland which is one of the main reasons for the persistence of different cultural practices between Catholics and Protestants. It is the persistence of segregated schooling which is also partly responsible for the maintenance of traditional forms of family life, and rigidly defined sex roles.

Of the 3,500 national schools in the Republic of Ireland, 3,400 are under Catholic management. The remaining 100 are mostly managed by the Protestant Churches, i.e. Church of Ireland, Presbyterian, and Methodist. In the Catholic schools, the land on which the school is built generally belongs to the Church. The State pays for the maintenance cost of the building and the teachers' salaries. There is a management board responsible for each school. Most of these have six members: three are nominated by the local bishop (one of whom is the chairman, usually the local parish priest); two of the members are elected representatives from parents of current school-going children; and the final member is the principal teacher of the school. In 1985, the Catholic Primary Schools Managers' Association issued a set of guidelines for Management Boards on how to interview and assess candidates for new appointments. The first criterion mentioned for assessing applicants was 'a practising Catholic'.[27] In a subsequent interview, the secretary of the Association, Fr Walsh defined a practising Catholic as someone who attempted honestly to abide by the commandments and who was a very regular attender at Mass.[28]

The national school teachers are a key element in passing on the Catholic faith in Ireland. It is for this reason that the Church has fought, since the establishment of the system in 1831, for control over their training and appointment. Being a teacher has traditionally been regarded more as a vocation than a job, and although it did not require one to remain celibate, the instruction and discipline within teacher-training colleges was almost as rigorous as that for those training for the priesthood. McCarthy described the background and training of these teachers as follows:

> These young men and women were drawn from the most academically able in the country, but certainly in the case of men, from a remarkably limited social group. It appears to me that they came primarily from small farmers and small shopkeepers in the south and west, and in many cases had themselves left home as early as thirteen or fourteen years of age, attending first the preparatory colleges (which now fortunately have been disestablished) and also the diocesan colleges, all residential in character. From there they went to a residential training college which was conducted on remarkably authoritarian lines. No doubt the church authorities were anxious to secure this rigorous training knowing that ninety per cent of Catholic children would receive their education from national teachers. . . .[29]

The Church also exercises considerable control in secondary education. Of the 572 secondary schools in the Republic of Ireland in 1982, forty-six were community schools and fifteen were comprehensive. These schools are formally non-denominational. Of the remaining 516 schools, twenty-five were run by Protestants and two were Jewish. The other 491 schools were Catholic.[30] Nuns are by and large responsible for the education of girls, and administered over half of these schools. In recent years there has been some amalgamation of their schools with those run by brothers, who control about one quarter of the total. However, regardless of any other problems, traditional attitudes regarding segregated schooling die hard. The remainder of the secondary schools are run by diocesan priests, religious order priests, and lay Catholic management boards. Diocesan priests are responsible for running their own colleges which have traditionally been regarded as breeding grounds either for vocations to the diocesan priesthood, or to the national school teacher-training colleges. Religious order priests are mainly involved in running top quality schools, many of which have expensive fees and boarding facilities and are oriented towards the sons of the upper middle classes.

It was not until the 1960s that the State, as part of its programme of investment in education, made a move towards modernising the secondary school system. Many of the schools were in poor condition, and the curriculum was heavily oriented towards classical rather than technical or scientific subjects. The accumulated effect of the classical curriculum was the production of an over-abundance of students who may have known how to decline the Latin word for a table, but had no technical skills as to how to go about constructing one. The influence which the Church's control of education has had in helping to maintain an adherence to its teachings and practices, can be seen from the results of the national survey in 1974. Those who were educated in vocational schools—which were set up by the State in the 1930s, outside clerical control, and oriented towards practical, manual skills and crafts—were more likely to be underconformers in sacramental participation, less accepting of Church doctrine, and to have a less pronounced general religious outlook than others.[31]

The pervasive influence of the Church in education extends to the third level. As Whyte points out, 'Ireland is the only country...where the Catholic Hierarchy has applied the principle of separate education for Catholics at university level.'[32] Until 1971, Dublin diocesan regulations forbade Catholics to attend Trinity College because of its Protestant connections since it was founded in the sixteenth century. The National University of Ireland, with its three colleges in Dublin, Cork and Galway, and its recognised college at Maynooth, although formally nondenominational, is Catholic in its whole ethos. The N.U.I. was constituted in 1908 after almost a century of agitation by the hierarchy for a Catholic university. It was designed so that the Church would have considerable influence in its governing bodies. This has had an effect on appointments and the curriculum, especially in those faculties and departments where the knowledge produced was directly related to Church teaching.

The main principle which the Church has fought for, since the beginning of the struggle back in the 1830s, has been control of the type of knowledge that is produced within the educational system. This it has done mainly by censoring the curriculum and controlling appointments. As long as it can confine the knowledge which is produced to that which is within the limits of its teachings, it does not matter so much whether the State provides the buildings and pays the teachers' salaries. In 1985, a High Court judge implied in his ruling that a Catholic secondary school was permitted to dismiss a teacher whose private life did not conform to the norms and values which the school was attempting to instil.[33]

There have been three main reasons why the Church has placed so much emphasis on maintaining control of the Irish education system. The first, as Titley argues, has been to maintain recruitment to the ranks. The process he describes has been that young boys are 'convinced' of their religious calling in primary schools and then 'fed' into diocesan colleges. He calculates that the influence of four priestly teachers in the period 1956–60 was sufficient to secure three vocations per annum. The second main reason was to maintain an influence and moral control over the future dominant class and political elite. As a Jesuit priest, quoted by Titley, put it in 1915: 'A suitable and thorough education for this body manifestly lies at the very bedrock of Ireland's moral, intellectual and material well-being. If they are sound, the country is safe.'[34] The third reason has been what Titley calls, 'the creation of a loyal Catholic laity', or what Clarke refers to more bluntly as 'indoctrination'.[35] With control of the schools this indoctrination is easily sustained since a lack of genuine alternatives leads each new generation of indoctrinated and unquestioning Catholic parents to go along with the existing system. The schoolchildren reintroduce institutional adherence among the parents who may wish to avoid difficulties by not contradicting what is taught in school. While this argument has validity it does not take into account the crucial role that the family, especially mothers, played in passing on the faith and creating vocations. Nor does take it into account the importance which a control of Irish health and social welfare has had in maintaining an adherence to Church rules and regulations after education has been completed.

Health

Ever since the nineteenth century in Ireland, but earlier elsewhere in Europe, the Catholic Church has been concerned with the maintenance and care of people in terms of keeping them healthy and free from disease. Health and social welfare became a major point of conflict between the Church and the State, as spheres of power were at issue and, in particular, who was responsible for the care and supervision of people. It was a struggle that was vital to the very survival of the Church. The conflict culminated in the encyclical *Rerum Novarum* (1891) which was as much a dogma against the excessive interference by the State in social welfare as it was against class antagonism. As industrial society developed, the State became interested in creating the conditions of economic growth and political stability and, consequently, in disciplining and controlling people as well as keeping them healthy. It was central to the maintenance and development of the Church's power that social control be considered as a moral issue which came under its jurisdiction. One of the reasons why there is such a high level of adherence to the Catholic Church in Ireland is because the Church, as it had done in education, gained control of the health, care, and social welfare of the people. It was mainly nuns, working from the principle that it should be a Catholic doctor and nurse who looked after Catholic patients, who began to build the hospitals and homes in which Catholics were trained, and who eventually took control of what had been until then a State-sponsored Protestant system. As an indication of just how successful this process was, Ryan estimates that by the beginning of the 1970s: 'Religious personnel either owned or had charge of 46 private hospitals, 25 nursing and convalescent homes, 32 geriatric homes, 35 homes for the mentally handicapped, 11 homes for the physically handicapped, 31 orphanages, 29 industrial schools and reformatories, 15 welfare hostels, and 20 student or business hostels.'[36] It was within these hospitals and homes that the vast majority of doctors and nurses got their training and practical experience. The departments of medicine within the universities became dominated by the Catholic code of medical ethics. Religious and medical discourse became interlinked. The physical health and social welfare for the people were not divorced from their spiritual welfare. What life was, when it began and when it ended, was defined within the Church's teaching. Doctors and nurses became obliged to adhere to the Church's code of medical ethics, formally within Church-controlled hospitals, and informally in many State-run hospitals. When a person entered a hospital or home in Ireland it was often assumed that he or she was in need of spiritual as well as physical care. The process of surrendering one's body to the doctors and nurses became allied to the process of surrendering one's soul to the priests and nuns. If anything should happen, the Church was there to save one's soul. Indeed the whole hospitalisation process demands passivity and surrender. The patient is confined, monitored and supervised. Those who exercise this control over him or her often include priests and nuns as much as doctors and nurses.

Such was the Church's domination of the Irish health system that the medical profession became dependent upon it in order to develop and maintain its own power. Together they developed a virtual monopoly of the knowledge about how the body functions—how it works and should work, especially in terms of sexuality. Not only good health, but to a certain extent the very soul of modern man, has been founded on a control of bodily functions. At least until the 1960s, the Church and the Irish Medical Association were united in opposition to the State's intervention in their monopoly.[37] It is only in recent years that this unity has been broken. Yet, as we shall see in the next chapter, although the power alliance is fractured, the Irish medical profession is far from united, and the Church is still able to divide that profession's membership in terms of allegiance to its teachings.

The first major clash between the Church and the new Irish State occurred over health. Although the hierarchy was worried about the possible appropriation of the voluntary hospitals, most of which were run by religious orders, it was really a question of delineation of spheres of power and, in particular, who had the right to educate and control the health and social welfare of women. It had to do with that section of the 1947 Health Act which required local authorities to make arrangements for safeguarding the health of women in respect of motherhood, and for their education in that whole area. The issue here was the same as the one which was at the heart of the notorious Mother and Child Scheme affair in 1951: 'To claim such powers for the public authority, without qualification, is entirely and directly contrary to

Catholic teaching on the rights of the family, the rights of the Church in education, the rights of the medical profession and of voluntary institutions.'[38] It is no coincidence that the issues on which the hierarchy has entered the public arena in Ireland, and which have caused the most division between Church and State, have been those that deal with the control of women's bodies in general, and motherhood, divorce, contraception, abortion, and legitimacy in particular. In terms of maintaining its power, the danger for the Catholic Church is that once women gain control of their bodies, primarily through diffused medical knowledge and technology, the bonds that have tied them to the home and rearing children will be gradually loosened and eventually shattered. When that happens, the compensatory power which the Church in Ireland has provided for women over the last hundred years or more will no longer be necessary because they will be able to gain entry to the economic possessions and occupational positions to which they have previously been denied access. Indeed the process is well under way in Ireland.

Conclusion

In this chapter it has been argued that the high level of adherence to the rules and regulations of the Catholic Church, which is the main type of religious behaviour in Ireland, has been maintained through the enormous bureaucratic organisation that the Church has developed in Ireland since the middle of the last century. The Catholic Church has developed a virtual monopoly of Irish morality because it has a level of human resources and an organisational network which is second only to that of the State. Religious tradition is not simply a set of beliefs and values which are held within the mind and passed on from generation to generation. It involves a physical and moral control which has been mainly exercised over the Irish people by priests, nuns and brothers. This is not to argue that the Catholic Church is an elitist, hierarchical organisation in which power resides only in full-time clerical members. There are thousands of voluntary, part-time workers who are equally responsible for maintaining an adherence to the Catholic Church's teachings. It is to argue that the Catholic Church in Ireland is a diffused, pluralist organisation of power in which those at the centre, especially the bishops, are able to limit what those at the periphery, and even those outside the organisation, do and say. It is also to argue that the way in which the teachings, beliefs, and values of the Church have been maintained among the Irish has not depended on some innate appeal or spirituality, but rather on a systematic socialisation which has depended on physical control of Irish people exercised in churches, schools, hospitals, and homes. It is within these buildings that Irish people have been instructed, supervised, and disciplined within the ritual practices and teachings of the Catholic Church.

4
Power and the Catholic Church in Irish Social, Political and Economic Life

THE QUESTION which must now be answered is why, given that the Church is a coercive organisation primarily interested in maintaining its moral power, do Irish people continue to ally themselves with it, especially since membership is ostensibly based on voluntary commitment? The most obvious answer would be that they are afraid of being denied salvation. In other words, Irish people are brought up to believe that there is an eternal life after death and that the way to gain it is through following the Church's rules and regulations. But if Irish people followed the rules and regulations of the Church in order to avoid damnation and attain salvation, then one would expect that the level of belief in hell and heaven would be at least as high as the proportion, for example, going to Sunday Mass and fulfilling their Easter Duty. This is not the case. Whereas nine in ten Irish Catholic respondents in the 1974 survey went to Mass once a week and fulfilled their Easter Duty, only half fully accepted belief in hell.[1] Among Catholic university students in 1976, eight in ten respondents went to Sunday Mass, yet only 57 per cent fully accepted belief in heaven, and only 21 per cent fully believed in hell.[2] There are, then, more general reasons, other than simply being educated and coerced into a fear of being denied salvation, why the Irish maintain their allegiance to the Catholic Church. This chapter identifies and describes some of these reasons. It is argued that adherence to the Church in Ireland is not purely a religious matter, but is tied in with social, political, and economic life. It is for this reason that the Church is able to limit not just what individual Catholics do and say, but also what the State, political parties, and other national organisations and associations do and say.

In order to understand how the Catholic Church maintains its allegiance in Ireland it is necessary to remember that, from the perspective of this study, social action primarily involves a rational struggle by individuals to realise their own will, find scope for their desires and follow their interests against those of others. In other words, social life can be understood as based on a struggle for power. This is not to say that, at a more empirical level, people are in constant conflict, but that their involvement in society pre-supposes a more fundamental, calculated and selfish struggle to get their own way. Even when people appear to be acting on the basis of a non-rational commitment to a norm such as 'love thy neighbour as thyself', their actions can be understood as an attempt to gain a more immediate goal such as the moral respect of others. There are three main ways by which individuals can carry out their own will and avoid attempts by others to limit what they do and say. The first is through possessions (economic). The wealthier you are the more likely it is that you will be able to dominate others. The second way is through holding a position of command (political). The higher up your position in a company or organisation the more likely it is that you will be able to get others, not just within that company or organisation, to do as you bid them. The third way of limiting others is by gaining their respect and esteem. The more civil and moral you appear to others, particularly in terms of being more rational and effective in your actions and less controlled by instincts and passions, the more respect they will have for you and the greater your ability to limit their behaviour. This perspective on individual social action is linked to a coercive understanding of social order and institutions such as the Catholic Church. In this respect, one of the main reasons why Irish people adhere to the Church, or indeed any other power bloc or alliance, is so that they can realise their own more immediate, material interests and, in general, maintain their power over others.

Social Prestige

Social esteem and respect mainly come from doing and saying the same as everyone else. There are certain set practices, rules, regulations, traditions, and customs by which one becomes regarded as polite, civil, and moral. When an individual behaves within these set practices, he or she attains social prestige. On the basis of this prestige, and by appealing to civility and morality, he or she can then limit what others do and say. The actual practices that are regarded as civil and moral vary from society to society. Given that in most areas of Ireland the population is almost completely Catholic, the practices by which one comes to be regarded as the same as everyone else, and the criteria by which one is judged civil and moral, are strongly influenced by the Church. To be accepted and regarded as a moral member of the community, one tradition-ally has had to engage in the rituals and socially approved practices of the Church, and not publicly contravene or criticise its teachings.

Social prestige is attained through engaging in social and cultural practices. Social practices centre on being civil and moral and generally not behaving like an animal. They are rigorously enforced and are a minimum requirement for attaining the respect of others. But there are also cultural practices which are not obligatory but which, if engaged in, give people distinction, and mark them out as cultured and morally superior. Art, sports, food, dress, and certain types of religious rituals are examples of cultural practices. But cultural practices only bring prestige if the person conforms to basic social practices. Thus, for example, someone might be brilliant at art or sport but if he is a drunken, violent lecher, it is doubtful that he would be an esteemed and respected member of the community. If, on the other hand, one is self-disciplined, peaceful, sober, and moral, and also engages in cultural practices such as playing the violin or hurling, then one is likely to have a high level of prestige within Irish society.

Such is the power of the Catholic Church in Ireland that it is still difficult, if not impossible in some parts of the country, for a Catholic to attain and maintain the respect of others without going to Mass on Sundays. This social practice establishes one as part of the community and, consequently, bestows a basic minimum of social prestige on the individual and family. Sunday Mass is a prestigious occasion. It is a time when people are on their best behaviour. They wear their best clothes in order to gain the respect of others. Additional prestige can also be attained by engaging in cultural practices such as giving up one's seat in church, greeting others by their names, having one's children behave in a disciplined manner, doffing one's hat, and using a handkerchief instead of the cuff of one's sleeve. Prestigious difference can also be attained through possessions such as a new car, a new suit, or displaying a new hairstyle. Greater worldly success is often taken as a sign of moral superiority.

Another cultural practice is receiving Holy Communion. This is not obligatory but it does mark one out as being morally superior. It is not a coincidence that in the 1974 survey, Catholic respondents with white collar jobs received Holy Communion more frequently than those employed in blue collar occupations, even though there was no significant difference in their level of attendance at Confession. Having a position of command, being well-groomed, and wearing a white collar suggest that somehow one is purer and, consequently, closer to God.[3]

It is often in order to maintain civil and moral superiority— which is part of the maintenance of economic class and political position—that children are sent to schools run by priests, nuns, and brothers. Their uniforms mark them out as being different, and a stricter training in manners and discipline mark them out as more moral and civil. In the national survey in 1974, nearly six in ten respondents preferred religious-run schools for both girls and boys at primary and secondary level. The most frequently mentioned reason was that religious-run schools gave a better training in terms of discipline and manners.[4]

There is a further, more fundamental, link between social prestige and adherence to the Catholic Church in Ireland. The whole ethos of the Catholic Church is one of surrender to the institution and its rules and regulations. The basis of social prestige is engagement in social practices which make one the same as everyone else. Surrender to the institution is at the heart of Catholic morality; and surrendering to the interests and needs of others is often a successful way of attaining social prestige. Salvation and prestige come from good works and surrendering economic and political interests to those of family and community. In concluding his review of the moral values of Irish religious tales, O'Healai states that: 'The stories show a fundamental respect for things holy and above all a practical application of the Golden Rule. Any form of behaviour which is helpful to others and which leads to harmony in the community is commended, while that which is unmindful of the neighbour's needs and disruptive of peace is condemned.'[5] The importance given to social prestige and being civil and respectable in Ireland is well documented in social research. Leyton notes that:

> To be a 'decent' man is to carry out one's obligations to society in a style characterized by cheerfulness and friendliness, to pause willingly for a chat and, most importantly, to refrain— regardless of provocation—from any display of overt hostility. Esteem is reserved for those who succeed in maintaining cordial relations with everyone in the village; and the greatest con- tempt is reserved for those quarrelsome individuals who are frequently involved in disputes.[6]

We can see here how social prestige is different from the struggle to attain economic and political power. McNabb gives a similar description of 'good-stock' and the 'decent' man, and notes that neither is dependent on economic possessions (class) or power of command (political position).

> The people of 'good-stock' can transcend the class barriers, and labourers' families who have been in the community for many generations, who are known to be respectable and whose children are well cared for and neatly dressed, will be spoken of as 'good-stock'.
>
> The 'decent man' does not depend for his status on his family background. People describe him as a person who is straight- dealing and honest, who does not talk too much and who is always willing to help a neighbour. He has a reputation for sober judgement and people tend to ask him for his advice and use him as an intermediary in settling community conflicts.[7]

Attainment of social prestige in Ireland essentially involves avoiding conflict, especially through conversation, and surrendering individual interests by engaging in practices which help others. It is the individual who wants to further his own political and economic interests and who does not engage in the social practices which maintain attachment to the community who is often criticised and censured. The 'gombeen man', for example, is one who is ridiculed for putting individual interests before those of the community. This can be linked to the dominance of the social teachings and practices of the Church. Just as the Catholic Church has fought against any notion of individual faith and discouraged the individual from using his private judgment uninstructed, so too does the family and community tend ritualistically to reject any form of individual assertion, creativity, or ambition.

The central importance of social prestige and surrender to the community, rather than attaining possessions or striving for political position, is reflected in Irish farming practices. Mutual aid or 'cooring' is a traditional aspect of Irish rural life, as it is in many peasant societies. In their study of rural Irish families at the beginning of the 1970s, Hannan and Katsiaouni found that mutual aid was still practised. Thirty-eight per cent of the husbands they interviewed said it would be very difficult to manage the farm without the help of their neighbours. The type of help generally mentioned was labour; only five per cent mentioned the loan of farm equipment and one per cent the loan of money. One third of the respondents mentioned labour exchanges of a habitual nature, while just over half (51 per cent) mentioned labour in an emergency situation.[8]

The importance of an adherence to the teachings and practices of the Catholic Church as a means of attaining social prestige has been maintained within families through the mother. Once a woman got married and gave up her dowry (possessions) and possibly her job (position), her ability to limit what others, and in particular her children and husband, did and said, became dependent on being well-respected, civil, and moral. This is one of the reasons why Irish mothers have allied themselves with the Catholic Church. In almost every aspect of religiosity, i.e. in terms of religious practice, religious belief, religious experiences, and the general importance of religion in their lives, Irish women would appear to be more religious than Irish men. Children growing up tend to perceive their mother as the primary religious figure in the home.[9] In the same way that the Church has developed a monopoly of religion and morality in the wider society, so too has the mother in the home. She creates and maintains the supervision and discipline of the Church within the home. It is the mother who traditionally brings the family together to say the rosary and night prayers. It is she who washes, clothes and ushers the family out to Sunday Mass. It is she who confines what her family does and says within the rules and regulations of the Church. In this respect the mother plays a central role in the maintenance of the power of the Catholic Church in Ireland. Indeed her moral power, like that of priests, nuns, and brothers, is often maintained through caring for the sick, poor, and underpriviliged. It is through doing the dirty, menial, and economically unrewarding tasks of caring for the less powerful that she gains the honour and respect of others and, consequently, is able to limit what they do and say. It is through the civility and morality of her children and husband that she maintains her prestige within the community. As Viney points out, 'It is the women in most rural families that influence the education of their children and so improve the standing of the family by rearing a priest or a doctor.'[10] This is echoed by McNabb:

> People who neglect their children are looked down on. It is noticeable that this community judges the character of a family by the dress and general health of the children. One constantly hears some such expression as 'Mrs X is a good class of person, her children are always well fed and well dressed.' It is not incumbent on adults to be well dressed except on Sundays but it is unusual to see a child in poor or ragged clothes. The blame for neglect falls on the mother, and it is generally held that the standing of individual families in the community is due to the work and influence of the mother. 'A good mother is everything.'[11]

The Irish mother has, then, been responsible for the moral training and discipline of children within the home. She is the last but vital link in the Catholic formation of each new generation. It is often because of her, and an interest in maintaining the solidarity and prestige of the family, that children maintain their adherence to the Church in later life. This, as Gallagher points out, helps explain the difference between Mass attendance and reception of Holy Communion.[12] Due to family pressures many children may go to Mass 'to keep the peace with the mother', and may show their alienation or unbelief by avoiding Holy Communion.

Children who do not behave in a disciplined, moral manner and obey the teachings of the Catholic Church can bring disgrace to themselves, their mother, and their families. It should be remembered that in Ireland the mother is held responsible for the behaviour of her children, regardless of their age, as long as they are living at home. Consequently, she often treats her sons and daughters as children until they leave home. It is the mother, then, who emphasises the importance of social prestige to the individual and family, and an adherence to the teachings of the Church as the means towards attaining it.

Political Position

As well as attaining social prestige, individuals are also involved in a struggle to attain a power of command over others. The higher one's position in society the more likely it is that one will be able to tell others what to do and say. Positions of command often involve the direct supervision of other workers, e.g. employers, managers, administrators, professionals, etc. While a person's status is generally derived from his or her occupation, it also includes all the different, often informal, positions which he or she may hold. Thus, for example, one's overall status and power of command may be derived from being a manager in a factory, a father in a family, and a secretary in a local residents' association.

It is part of the argument of this study that it has been in the interest of those who hold positions of command over others in Ireland to adhere to the rules and regulations of the Church. It is not so much that the Church directly interferes in political or occupational appointments, it is more that the people who supervise and command others need to justify morally their position. Public adherence to the Church has been especially important for those who are directly or indirectly employed by the Church such as doctors, teachers, and nurses. Blanshard noted an example of this in his polemical study on the power of the Catholic Church in the 1950s:

> Dr X and his wife, both baptised Catholics, have long ceased to believe in the major Catholic doctrines. In private conversation they express strong criticism of priestly policy. When Dr X started to drift away from the Church openly by failing to attend Mass, he was warned by his priest. Now he attends conspiciously with his wife. 'I must live, you know,' he says. My practice would disappear if I were branded as a lapsed Catholic.'[13]

Protestants have religious and political freedom in the Republic of Ireland. Nevertheless, in the past they have been prevented from obtaining public positions which involve moral supervision of Catholics.[14] But it is the Catholic dissenter, especially when employed in health or education, who is often under the greatest threat not to go against the teachings of the Church. Religion and morality are public matters in Ireland. Teachers, nurses, and doctors can be under an obligation to behave in a manner deemed moral by the Church. If they do not, they may be regarded as potentially some kind of traitor who can undermine the loyalty of others. As an editorial in the *Irish Rosary* put it: 'We allow no claim to good will come from those who have been brought up in the Catholic faith if they abandon it, but we can admire the good faith of those born outside the Church, even while we detest their errors.'[15]

It has also been in the interest of those whose positions depend on public support, or which have a high public profile, to be openly loyal to the Church. Amongst these occupations are traders, journalists, politicians and other elected public representatives. In the past, it has not paid to oppose publicly the moral dictates of the Church. Indeed censorship has often been self-imposed; anything which was offensive or critical of the Church being hidden away. Booksellers, chemists, and other traders in some parts of the country could still run an economic risk in selling goods which go against the dominant Catholic morality. Writers and journalists have also been forced to abstain from any serious criticism of the Church and its teachings. An employee of the supposedly secular *Irish Times* noted that in the 1950s, journalists in that newspaper 'had to avoid writing about any subject in which criticism, even if justified, could be construed as criticism of the Church'.[16] The pressures on politicians to remain loyal to the Church are perhaps strongest of all. Whyte notes that 'two ex-ministers whom I have met told me that they are no longer believing Catholics. Neither of them ever avowed this in public.' Even self-confessed Catholic politicians have been afraid to criticise the Church in public. Whyte quotes a long letter from a TD to the *Irish Times* in 1955 which is critical of a speech made by a bishop. The TD did not sign the letter 'because I do not want to finish my political career before it starts.'[17] In the 1980s, there has been a small but growing number of politicians, especially those elected from urban areas, who are openly critical of bishops. But even so, this criticism is always advanced 'with all due respect to the cloth'. Whereas bishops are, and generally always have been, freely critical of politicians, they have managed until recently to keep themselves on a sacred pedestal above criticism. The power of the priests and bishops to affect the livelihood of those living in urban areas may be diminishing, but it is still quite strong in rural areas. Like most forms of religious power, it is one which survives more on the threat of its use than its actual implementation. Nevertheless it produces very real consequences. It may be that a shopkeeper does not stock a particular magazine or book. It may be that a chemist does not consider it 'worth his while' to stock contraceptives. It may be that a doctor decides that it would be best not to do a certain operation which is contrary to Church teaching. It may be that a teacher does not say what he or she would like to say at a meeting because the parish priest is there. The power of the Catholic Church in Ireland becomes evident when people are sickened and disgusted by what the Church and its representatives do and say, but do and say nothing themselves, partly because, as one fearful dissenter put it, 'you'd be destroyed—you'd be ostracised . . .' if you questioned the authority of the priest.[18]

Economic Possessions

Adherence to the Church has played a major part in maintaining Ireland as a conservative, rural society in which people have been encouraged to live in frugal comfort, and not to attach importance to material possessions. The good life is defined as a commitment and surrender to the spiritual things above oneself. The good life is always in opposition to the materialism associated with industrial, consumer society. Furthermore the Church's teaching that salvation is attained by following its rules and regulations has discouraged individuals from making up their own minds about what is right and wrong. This, combined with an emphasis on frugal comfort and a suppression of individual interests in favour of those of Church, family, and community, has been associated with an absence of a rugged, ambitious individualism which is a feature of fully developed capitalist societies. The traditional absence of entrepreneurs and people taking risks with capital in Ireland, may be linked to the practices described above and a morality propagated by the Church, in which individual satisfaction and pleasure have been subdued through an inculcation of shame and guilt.

Through its control of education the Church has also limited the type of knowledge which could have produced a more modernised, industrial society earlier in Ireland. But it would be wrong to think that the Catholic Church has had a completely negative impact on economic life in modern Ireland. As we shall see in later chapters, it provided the basic moral discipline which was associated with the initial modernisation of Irish society in the last century. But once this basic minimum of modernisation was attained, a high level of adherence to the Church's rules and regulations prevented the type of individualism necessary for further modernisation and industrialisation.

Beyond this broad limitation of economic life in Ireland, the Church has also maintained the way in which possessions are unevenly distributed. Although actively involved in redistribution, the Church justifies and legitimates the fact that some people have higher positions and more possessions. This has been done mainly through its teachings on vocationalism which were promulgated in two important papal encyclicals *Rerum Novarum* (1891), and *Quadragesimo Anno* (1941). These legitimated the positions of individuals as members of different occupational groups, and vindicated their right to fight for their own interests. It could, then, be implied that those with high positions, and as a result usually more possessions, have these because they are fulfilling their vocational duty. On the other hand, the Church provides compensation for the poor and underprivileged; first by providing a wide variety of charitable services, especially in health and education; secondly by telling them that in the next world 'the last shall be first'; and thirdly by providing magical, devotional practices such as novenas which, if engaged in, supposedly bring about material transformations in this world such as getting money, jobs, or marriage partners. The Catholic Church in Ireland, like other Churches elsewhere, consistently plays down the importance of material benefits in this world, and it suggests that people should accept their God-given position, and generally follow Christ's example in their suffering. In this respect Catholicism is the opium of the Irish people in that it maintains the status quo, and does little to reduce the economic divisions in society. The Church maintains its power and perpetuates economic inequalities by playing down the importance of possessions, by telling the poor and underprivileged to bear with their situation, and by reminding the rich that it is their vocational duty to look after the poor.

Church and State as Power Blocs

A power bloc such as the Catholic Church in Ireland exists through its ability to limit the practice and discourse of a large number of people. If Irish Catholics limit what they and others do and say to what falls within the rules and regulations of the Church, this constitutes Church power. When Irish politicians do not enact legislation which is contrary to Church teaching, this can also be attributed to the power of the Church. This, in effect, was the situation in Ireland until 1985, when for the first time the State introduced and passed a piece of social legislation (on family planning) without amendment, even though it was directly and forcefully opposed by members of the hierarchy. But the power which the Catholic Church has had over the State in modern Ireland cannot be reduced simply to the occasions when bishops have made a direct contribution to the formation of State law. This is the type of definition which Whyte uses in his analysis of the relation between Church and State in modern Ireland. He reduces Church power to occasions when social legislation has been affected by a direct input from the hierarchy.[19]

What Irish people do and say is limited and influenced by numerous power blocs and alliances which exist both inside and outside the country. Two major power blocs within Irish society are the State and the Catholic Church. The State exercises its power through laws enforced by such apparatuses as the courts, police and army. The Church maintains its power through rules and regulations enforced by priests, nuns and brothers, as well as by committed members of the laity. However, whereas the State exercises its power in a wide range of areas, the Church exercises its power mainly in relation to social and moral matters. It has been on moral issues, particularly in relation to health, education and the family that any struggle between these two power blocs has taken place. But the history of the relationship between Church and State in modern Ireland has not been characterised by struggle but rather by peaceful coexistence, each maintaining the power of the other. The vast majority of Irish politicians and civil servants have been formed and educated by the Catholic Church and, consequently, have limited legislation in matters that fall within the general ethos of the Church's teachings. On the other hand the Church has been a major source of political stability in modern Irish society. Not only does it regularly preach submission to the power of the State, it continually condemns all forms of political violence. The first fifty years of the modern Irish State may be seen in terms of a happy marriage between itself and the Church. It was not until the 1960s, when the State began to pursue rigorously a policy of industrialisation and modernisation, that the marriage began to break down. It was only in the 1970s that a formal separation was openly discussed for the first time. But even as late as 1986, there was no question of a full divorce between Church and State, mainly because this is not possible under the Irish Constitution.

This is not to say that there have not been occasions when Church and State have clashed, and when the Church has become directly involved in State matters. Confining himself to legislation which was formally enacted between 1923 and 1970, Whyte has compiled the following list of occasions in which there was a direct input from one or more bishops:

Censorship of Films Act 1923
Censorship of Publications Act 1929
Legitimacy Act 1930
Vocational Education Act 1930
The Constitution of Ireland 1937
Public Health Bill 1945
Health Act 1947
Intoxicating Liquor (Amendment) Bill 1948
Adoption Act 1952
Vital Statistics and Registration of Births, Marriages and Deaths
   Act 1952
Health Act 1953
Agriculture Act 1958
Intoxicating Liquor Act 1960
Charities Act 1961
Adoption Act 1964
Succession Act 1965.[20]

It is obvious from this list that any direct input from the bishops in terms of law creation has been confined to moral conduct in general, and family, education, and health in particular. Besides the general reasons mentioned above, this list is unrepresentative of Church power because, as Whyte admits, it does not take into account 'important policy decisions in which the bishops took an interest, but which were not embodied in statute'. Whyte mentions as examples the educational changes in the 1960s, and the Mother and Child Scheme (1951) which was the first extended debate on Church and State relations that took place in Ireland. If one includes these policy decisions, and a number of other measures where consultation between the government and the hierarchy would appear to have been probable, then there are about three or four dozen items of legislation or other questions on which State and Church have been in formal consultation. Given that there were about 2,000 statutes enacted between 1923–1980, this suggests that the impact of the Church on the State has been slight. Chubb does not agree and argues that 'the political effects of the dominant position of the Catholic Church have been immense'.[21] The reason the effects have been immense is that in maintaining its institutional monopoly of morality, the Catholic Church has been able to inoculate Irish minds against the introduction of any legislation which is contrary to its interests. It was this institutional monopoly which inhibited the rational differentiation between religion and politics, and which limited social, political, and economic development in Ireland.

The amendments to the social legislation to which Whyte refers were not so much the result of pressure by the hierarchy as independent iniatives of successive governments to maintain State power by appeasing the Church and entering into a grand alliance with it. This alliance was partly founded on the recognition that the State could not govern successfully if it were strongly opposed by the Church. The way for a political party to obtain and maintain State power became related to how it dealt with the interests of the Church. As Whyte points out, the first Cumann na nGaedhal government needed support from whatever quarter it came and, consequently, 'proved willing to use the power of the State to protect Catholic moral values'. Not to be outdone, its main contender Fianna Fáil seized any chance to appear more zealously Catholic than its opponents.[22] The situation has not changed dramatically in the last fifty years.

The process of incorporating Catholic teaching in Irish legislation, which began shortly after the foundation of the Free State, reached a peak with the passing of the Irish Constitution of 1937. The Constitution strongly represents Catholic moral teaching especially with regard to family, private property, and education. The original Constitution contained an article which recognised 'the special position of the Holy Catholic Apostolic and Roman Church as the guardian of the faith professed by the great majority of the Citizens'. This article was deleted in a referendum held in 1972. However the Preamble to the Constitution still reads: 'In the Name of the Most Holy Trinity, from whom is all authority and to Whom, as our final end, all actions both of men and State must be referred, we, the people of Eire, humbly acknowledging all our obligations to our Divine Lord, Jesus Christ, Who sustained our fathers through centuries. . .'.[23] The social legislation of the 1920s and 1930s, followed by the Constitution, set a precedent by which the hierarchy seemed to have the right and duty to limit the State when it came to legislation involving moral issues. But most legislation involves moral issues of some kind and, at the height of their power in the 1950s, some bishops came close to advocating a theocratic State. This is best illustrated by a statement from the Bishop of Cork, Dr Lucey. Referring to the Health Bill of 1953, he noted that 'their [the bishops] position was that they were the final arbiters of right and wrong even in political matters'. Two years later Bishop Lucey amended his position and stated that 'their [the bishops] power extends only to the religious and moral implications of what goes on—the Church has no competence to control public affairs itself or indicate the practical ways and means of dealing with current public problems'.[24] Since it reached its peak in the 1950s, the formal position of the Church with regard to the State has varied enormously. Some bishops have taken a rigid line and have suggested that, especially in moral matters, the State is subservient to the Church. Collectively, the hierarchy has tended towards a more liberal distinction between public and private morality. Ryan argues that there have been four distinct viewpoints:

(1) The State cannot enact something contrary to moral law: this was the viewpoint of the late Archbishop of Dublin, Dr McQuaid, when in a pastoral in 1971, he spoke of the proposed legislation on contraception as 'offending the objective moral law'.

(2) The State laws as reflective of majority opinion: this was the position of Bishop Newman of Limerick, i.e. the Catholic

majority have a political right to the provision of a social framework that supports their moral and religious principles.

(3) The appeal to the loyalty of the people: the position of the present Archbishop of Dublin, Dr Ryan, i.e. to advise Catholics that as Catholics they could not accept legislation contrary to the Church's teaching.

(4) A question of public morality to be decided by the people: the clear and consistent position of the hierarchy as a whole since 1973.[25]

In defence of his claim that the fourth viewpoint represents the hierarchy's position in general, Ryan quotes their 1973 statement: 'There are many things which the Catholic Church holds to be morally wrong and no one has ever suggested, least of all the Church herself, that they should be prohibited by the State.' This was the formal position of the Church throughout the 1970s and 1980s, which was outlined in greater detail during its submission to the all-party Forum on Northern Ireland in 1984. The main issue, however, has been whether Catholics can go against the teachings of the Church in making political decisions about moral issues. In light of a pastoral by the hierarchy in 1980, the answer is not certain since the response to the moral issues of social legislation 'must always be in accordance with the specific commandments of God, as authoritatively interpreted by the Church'. In other words, while the bishops have moved away from the extreme viewpoints adopted by Archbishop McQuaid and Bishop Newman, they strategically vacillate between the requirement that Catholics adhere to the Church's teaching as regards social legislation concerning moral matters, and the position that it is a matter which each individual decides in full consideration of the issues and their implications. During the Family Planning Amendment Bill (1985), Bishop Newman, who became a prominent spokesman within the hierarchy following the appointment of Dr Kevin McNamara as Archbishop of Dublin, reminded 'all politicians who profess to be Catholic that they have a duty to follow the guidance of their Church in areas where the interests of the Church and State overlap'. This relates to another issue which concerns the extent to which Catholics have to obey all the teachings of the Church. Again, Bishop Newman has complained of 'the way in which some Catholics manage to persuade themselves that they are faithful to their Church even though they reject some points of its teaching'.[26]

The distinction between having to adhere strictly to the Church's teaching, and assuming individual moral responsibility for political decisions, is extremely important since Ireland is virtually a homogeneously Catholic country, and because the Church has such enormous institutional power. It is this power over people's consciences, instilled in churches, schools, hospitals, and homes which make the Church unlike any other power bloc in Irish society. It is a power which the Church still holds and which, as every politician knows, can be exercised at any time with devastating consequences. It is for this reason that the main political parties have been so cautious when dealing with moral matters. It is no coincidence that in describing the relation between Church and State in Ireland up until 1970, Whyte quotes O'Faolain twice on this point:

> The Maynooth Parliament (i.e. the hierarchy) holds a weapon which none of the other institutions mentioned holds: the weapon of the sacraments. The Church of England cannot wield the power of the Catholic Church because it does not hold this weapon. If a prime minister in England were informed by the Archbishop of Canterbury that a proposed law would be condemned by the Church of England, he would deplore it, but he would not be afraid of any effects other than political effects. If our Taoiseach were informed thus by the Protestant Archbishop of Dublin he would measure the effects in the same way. And likewise with most other institutions, religious or secular. But when the Catholic Church, through its representatives speaks, he realises, and the Roman Catholic public realises, that if they disobey they may draw on themselves this weapon whose touch means death.[27]

There has been a change, since O'Faolain wrote, in the way the moral power of the Church is exercised. There are no longer direct demands from the hierarchy. What has not changed, however, is that the majority of Catholic politicians accept that the Church has power over Irish people's consciences. In some of their formal statements the hierarchy admits to there being a rational differentiation between politics and religion; between what politicians do, and what they as bishops do. But in other statements members of the hierarchy call on individual Catholics not to make this rational differentiation between their work and their religion. As the Archbishop of Dublin, Dr Kevin McNamara put it: 'For the Church a major challenge today is to help people make a closer connection between their religious practice and their daily lives, between worshipping God in church and serving Him in the world of work, recreation and culture.'[28] This applies to politicians as much as it does to any other Irish Catholic. One of the main reasons why the Catholic Church has been so powerful in Irish society is that it has been able to dissuade people from limiting religious practice and discourse to specific times and places. In the national survey in 1974, more than six in ten (64 per cent) of the Catholic respondents said that their religious principles always guided their behaviour with regard to their occupation. Moreover, seven in ten said that they would always choose their religion if its demands conflicted with their occupational demands.[29] The Catholic Church will remain a power bloc in Irish society as long as people adhere to its rules and regulations and do not make a distinction between their work, whether as politicians or otherwise, and their religion.

The Constitutional Referendum on Abortion (1983)

The power of the Catholic Church in Irish society is evident in its ability to divide the membership of any other power bloc or alliance in terms of adherence and commitment to its teachings and practices. This power was evident throughout the 1983 Constitutional referendum on abortion. A description of this referendum will provide an example of how the Church exercises its power, not just over the State but over other power blocs and alliances.

Abortion is contrary to the teaching of the Catholic Church and has regularly been the subject of statements from the Irish hierarchy. In September 1983, a referendum was held in the Republic of Ireland to decide whether to amend the Constitution by including a statement which acknowledged the right to life of the unborn. The background to the referendum lies in the rapidly increasing availability of abortion in many Western societies. Whereas countries such as the United States, England, France and Germany have had abortion services legally available for a long time, it was only in recent years that traditionally Catholic countries such as Italy and Spain made new legal provisions for abortion.

The Pro-Life Amendment Campaign (PLAC) did not formally come into existence until April 1981. The seeds of the campaign had been sown in the previous summer during a meeting of the Irish Catholic Doctors Guild and a conference of the World Federation of Doctors who Respect Human Life. The campaign was hastened into existence by the growing awareness that over 3,500 Irish women had had abortions in England the previous year and that the Woman's Right to Choose Group had begun to press for the legalisation of some kind of abortion in Ireland. The initial aim of PLAC was to pressurise the government into holding a referendum which would not only make abortion illegal, as it was under the Offences against the Person Act (1861), but unconstitutional, and therefore irreversible by any act of parliament or decision by the Supreme Court. Within two weeks of its formation PLAC had gained commitments from the leaders of the two main political parties to hold such a referendum. The reason for the rapid success of PLAC was it exerted its pressure in the weeks prior to the General Election of June 1981. It may not have been political suicide for the main political parties to say that they were against holding such a referendum, but once Fine Gael had committed itself, Irish history has shown that Fianna Fáil was bound to follow.

After a long and heated campaign which drew thousands of letters to the national newspapers, the amendment was voted on in September 1983. Two thirds of the 55 per cent of the electorate who voted, accepted that the Constitution should be amended to make abortion unconstitutional. The proportion of these 'yes' voters varied throughout the country. It was highest in rural constituencies, especially in the West. Mayo and Donegal voted four to one in favour of the amendment. It was lowest in urban constituencies, especially in those with an identifiable 'middle-class' population. Five Dublin constituencies rejected the amendment by a small majority.

The success of PLAC was that it was able to make use of the thousands of committed Catholics already involved in lay organisations and parish work to do its canvassing. It was this enormous physical organisation throughout the country, which had existed for many years but which had never previously been mobilised as a unified force, which was central to PLAC's victory. It brought Catholic moral principles to the front door of every Irish home. As one of their spokespersons stated: 'It's the ordinary people of Ireland coming out to canvass their neighbours and friends.' It was only towards the end of the campaign that the clerical resources of the Church began to be used fully. The anti-amendment campaign group had tried to argue that the decision to make something which was already illegal, unconstitutional, was strictly a political one. It complained about priests giving partisan sermons and inviting pro-life movement speakers to give their views in church. But it was obvious that advice in favour of the amendment would come from church pulpits. As a priest from Kerry put it: 'Country people need to have quite a lot of things explained to them. They are too busy and do not have the time to read the newspapers carefully.' While the bishops were careful not to instruct the laity directly as to how to vote, they were equally careful to remind politicians that morality was their sphere of jurisdiction. The auxillary Bishop of Dublin, Dr Comiskey, stated that 'when politicians concern themselves with values they are engaging not merely in stagecraft, but in soulcraft.' In certain dioceses bishops requested that either their own letters be read out, or sermons be given, urging a 'yes' vote. In Dublin, the largest diocese in the country containing nearly one-third of the electorate, the Archbishop, Dr Ryan, had a pastoral read at all Masses in the diocese on the Sunday prior to polling day, urging support of the amendment. This was above and beyond the collective statement already issued by the hierarchy. The collective statement had begun asserting that, according to the moral law, abortion was wrong in all circumstances. It noted that 'on an issue of such fundamental importance . . . everyone has a clear responsibility to vote,' but it recognised 'the right of each person to vote according to conscience'. The statement concluded by urging a decisive 'yes' vote to the amendment, and by linking an anti-amendment stance to a pro-abortion stance, that is, 'defeat of the amendment could well be represented as a victory for the abortion cause'.[30]

The Effects of the Campaign

The main effect of the campaign was that it demonstrated the ability of the Catholic Church in modern Ireland to limit political practice and discourse, and what is held to be legal and unconstitutional, to what falls within its rules and regulations. This power is dependent on its ability to divide members of other power blocs and alliances in terms of their allegiance to its teachings. What maintains the power of the Church is its ability to get members of political parties, national organisations, professional associations and other power alliances to ally themselves first and foremost with the Church, especially when there is a clash of interests.

The division in Fine Gael, which was the major party in the Coalition government during the campaign, was slow to materialise. From the outset the Fine Gael parliamentary party had decided that the proposed wording of the amendment, put forward by Fianna Fáil, was ambiguous and could lead to unforeseen and undesirable changes in medical practice. It decided that it would not support the amendment, and that its members would remain silent except for a statement to be issued by the Taoiseach, Dr Fitzgerald. However, like most other politicians, the majority of the Fine Gael TDs were committed Catholics, and even if they were not, their constituencies were dominated by such Catholics, without whose support there would be little likelihood of re-election. By the second week of the campaign the number of Fine Gael TDs who disregarded their collective parliamentary party decision and openly supported the amendment, had risen to eleven, and it was estimated it could rise to fourteen. Even the Cabinet became divided and members spoke openly about how they would vote. The chairman of the parliamentary party issued a public statement in which he criticised the Minister for Finance, Alan Dukes, and the Minister for Education, Gemma Hussey, for not keeping their views on the referendum to themselves. He stated categorically that 'if members of the Cabinet are not prepared to accept and abide by decisions of the party they should cease to be members of the Cabinet'.[31]

The medical profession also became bitterly divided during the campaign. The whole idea of the amendment was fostered originally by a group of committed Catholic doctors. The chairperson of PLAC was Dr Julia Vaughan. The professors of obstetrics and gynaecology in the country's four main universities were original supporters of the amendment. One of these, Professor O'Dwyer of University College Galway, insisted that the amendment would make no difference to current legal or medical practice. Two days later, twelve of the country's leading gynaecologists condemned the proposed amendment, and urged people to vote against it. Three of these gynaecologists were lecturers in the same institution as Dr O'Dwyer. At a press conference organised by the doctors against the amendment, the claim was made, backed by a statement from the Government Information Service, that if the amendment were passed several contraceptive methods could be outlawed. This was counteracted by the chairman of the Irish Medical Association. He stated that he intended to vote 'yes' and that '60 per cent of the doctors in the country had signed a statement to the effect that passage of the amendment would not alter current medical practice'. Nevertheless doctors throughout the country continued to sign petitions against the amendment and to urge a 'no' vote.[32]

The legal profession became divided on the same issues as the medical profession, i.e. would certain forms of contraception become unconstitutional; would the treatment of the mother during pregnancy be affected; and would there be a threat to the mother's life? It was a member of the legal profession who was responsible for the actual wording of the amendment. The chairman of the anti-amendment campaign, Adrian Hardiman, was also a lawyer. He claimed that there were over 100 barristers in Dublin who had come out against the amendment. About the same time the Irish Association of Lawyers for the Defence of the Unborn was formally launched. The division within the legal profession continued to grow, and just over a week before polling day a press conference was called at which it was announced that there were 600 lawyers, including 22 Senior Counsels, who were opposed to the amendment.[33]

The referendum also caused open dissension within the Irish Farmers Association, the largest farming organisation within the country, with over 130,000 members. Shortly after the beginning of the campaign there was report of a newly formed 'Farmers Against the Amendment Group' of which Donal Cashman, the President of the IFA, was a member. A few days later, in an attempt to prevent an open rift, seven members of the executive committee who had been linked to the anti-amendment group, issued a statement saying that they would have no involvement publicly or privately in an organised effort to influence voting in the referendum. But the damage had already been done and when the IFA council met shortly afterwards, Cashman and eleven other members of the executive were suspended from their posts for two months for attempting to set up an anti-amendment group.[34]

It would be facile to argue that the splits that occurred in Fine

Gael, the medical profession, the legal profession, and the IFA were simply a consequence of disagreement with the actual amendment. The amendment was from the beginning a lay Catholic movement which attained the full support of the Church. The issue which mainly divided these power blocs and alliances was whether the Constitution should be changed to reflect the interests of this lay Catholic pressure group and the Church as a whole. The referendum became a test of the loyalty and respect of the Irish people for the bishops, Pope John Paul II, and the teachings of the Catholic Church.

The result of the referendum may be taken as a victory for the Catholic Church in that the majority of those who voted did what the bishops had urged and voted 'yes'. However, the result may be interpreted differently. If it is accepted that the statement of the hierarchy was an appeal to the loyalty of the people and that it was, as they stated, 'an issue of such fundamental importance' on which 'everyone has a clear responsibility to vote', then the proportion of the Catholic electorate who complied with their advice and voted 'yes' was only 37.5 per cent. This is an extreme interpretation since the bishops did recognise the right of each person to vote according to conscience. The reaction of many Catholics, confused by the divisions in the medical and legal professions, might have been not to bother their conscience, especially since an opinion poll published two days before indicated that there would be a 2:1 majority in favour.[35]

However the actual results of the referendum may be interpreted, an analysis of the campaign in terms of the power of the Catholic Church in Irish society indicates that:

(1) The Irish hierarchy indirectly pressurises the State, or individual Catholics, into endorsing its teachings through social legislation.

(2) It formally accepts the principle of the rational separation of the religious from the political sphere in modern social life and that Catholics are not bound by the teachings of their Church in making political decisions. But at the same time, the hierarchy urges members of the laity to lead a holistic lifestyle and not to segregate religious practice and belief from the rest of their lives. While acting as 'the conscience of society' the hierarchy uses the full organisation of the Church to urge the laity to remain loyal to its teachings and to incorporate these into the political framework of the country.

(3) The rational separation of the religious from the political is in practice loosely interpreted by clergy and religious who are likely to give more direct advice in their moral direction of the laity.

(4) The task of maintaining loyalty to the teachings of the Church and, where possible, incorporating these within the political framework of the country may be moving from the bishops to members of the laity. This indicates a shift in the power structure of the Church in Ireland. While the referendum represented a victory for Catholic social principles and was a demonstration of the loyalty of the people to the teachings of their bishops, it also represented a victory for lay organisations within the Church, and the increasing role which they have played in Irish Catholicism since Vatican II. This is not to suggest that lay organisations had not previously played a role in the formation of social legislation, but that this was the first time that they openly initiated and directed such a campaign. It was the first time that the laity were the vanguard, while the bishops played a more covert role from behind. Thus, the full potential of a resource and strength of the Church which had previously operated quietly in the background, was shown for the first time. It was this force of committed Catholics, for a long time the pawns of the Church, who entered the centre stage of the battle for Catholic moral principles.

(5) Because of the loyalty of these Catholics, the membership of every major power bloc and alliance in Irish society, which itself seeks to reproduce its own power, and exercises strict control over the practice and discourse of its members, can potentially be split in terms of its members' loyalty to the Church.

The Divorce Referendum (1986)

In June 1986, a further referendum was held to decide whether the article in the Constitution prohibiting divorce should be removed. The coalition government of Fine Gael and Labour proposed that the original article, viz., 'No law shall be enacted providing for the grant of dissolution of marriage,' should be replaced with a new article which would allow a court of law to grant a dissolution in certain circumstances, i.e. where the marriage had failed for a period of at least five years, where there was no possibility of reconciliation, and where adequate provision was made for any dependent spouse or child.

To counteract the government proposals, the hierarchy issued a series of statements and a fifteen-page pastoral letter 'Marriage, the Family and Divorce' of which one million copies were distributed nationwide. In their final statement two weeks before the referendum, the hierarchy said that the granting of divorce on the basis of 'failure of marriage' was a 'concept of the broadest and vaguest kind', and that in country after country such 'abstractness and vagueness' had led to divorce becoming 'more and more easily available'. They were 'convinced that the proposed amendment would weaken rather than strengthen marriage and the family'. They were emphatic that the provision of civil divorce was a moral issue.

> The questions raised in this debate are not simply political. They are also moral. Each legislator and each voter is faced with a moral decision. Changes in civil law can influence moral attitudes and affect the whole moral atmosphere of society. They can make it more difficult for people to walk in the path of God's commandments.[36]

However, they concluded that 'the ultimate decision rests with the people' and they exhorted that 'each individual make a reflective, prayerful, conscientious decision'.

In a press conference at the time the statement was issued, the official spokesman for the hierarchy, Bishop Cassidy of Clonfert, insisted that 'We're not telling them [the people] how to vote on this matter.' He emphasised that 'conscience is the final arbiter', and intimated that a Catholic could vote in favour of the removal of the ban on divorce without incurring guilt.[37] This announcement, that it was permissible for a Catholic to vote in a civil referendum for something which was contrary to Church teaching, represented an interpretation of informed conscience which had not been declared during the abortion referendum. But individual bishops interpreted their collective statement differently. Less than a week before polling day, the Archbishop of Dublin, Dr McNamara, stated that the view of some Catholics that the introduction of divorce into our society would be morally good and in conformity with God's intentions 'finds no warrant, no justification in the teaching we have given. It finds no basis in Catholic social and moral doctrine.'[38]

Up to a week before the referendum, the government remained confident that the amendment to the Constitution would be carried. Opinion polls over the previous three years had shown a steady increase in the proportion who thought that divorce should be permitted in certain circumstances. This proportion reached 77 per cent in February, 1986. As late as April of the same year, 57 per cent of those interviewed had said that they would actually vote to remove the ban. However, an opinion poll conducted a week before the referendum and published the day before polling, showed that the proportion who would vote to remove the ban had declined sharply to 40 per cent and indicated that there was now a majority against removing the ban.

This dramatic shift in public opinion was reflected in the actual results. Nearly two out of three voters (63 per cent) rejected the government's proposal to remove the ban on divorce. In fact, the results of the divorce referendum were almost an exact replica of the abortion referendum, even though the turnout this time was substantially higher (63 per cent). While Dublin constituencies voted very narrowly in favour of divorce, other urban areas such as Cork, Limerick, Galway and Waterford voted against it, and in the majority of rural constituencies more than seven in ten voted against the amendment.[39]

Given the accuracy of the opinion polls prior to the referendum, the questions which arise are how and why there was such a dramatic shift in attitudes away from removing the ban in the weeks before polling. Initial consideration would suggest four main reasons:

(1) Whereas the pro-divorce lobby had been active since the 1970s and had attained widespread coverage in the media of its position and objectives, the anti-divorce lobby, although formally organised since 1983, had remained virtually silent until the referendum was announced.

(2) The anti-divorce lobby proved to be very well-organised and to have access to considerable funding and a large network of canvassers.

(3) The anti-divorce lobby, although not formally linked to the Church, closely followed its teaching and helped transform the central issue from one of minority 'civil' rights for non-Catholics to an issue about the common good of Irish society. In doing this, it made divorce out to be a personal issue since, it was claimed, the removal of the ban would be a threat to every marriage and family in Ireland, particularly in relation to inheritance and social welfare rights.

(4) In the confusion of issues, most voters seem to have been swayed by the statement from the hierarchy, and the 'personal' position of most Fianna Fáil and many Fine Gael TDs.

The referendum demonstrated the continuing ability of the hierarchy to set limits to the political sphere of Irish society. Their argument that the referendum was not simply a political matter but also a moral one was effectively followed by Fianna Fáil who held that the referendum was not a party political issue, but rather a matter to be decided by each individual legislator and voter. Their tactics were also similar to those of the bishops; they would not advise the electorate how to vote, but all their leading spokespersons were against removing the constitutional ban. The official position of Fine Gael was in favour of the amendment but, as in the abortion referendum, members became divided on the issue. The Minister for Education, Mr Cooney, as well as prominent backbenchers, spoke frequently against their own government's proposed divorce measures. In other words, their membership of a religious power bloc came well before their membership of a political power bloc even though the latter depends, as much as the former, on the solidarity of its members. It is the ability of the Church to limit the political sphere and to divide the membership of organisations and groups in terms of commitment to its teachings which demonstrates its continued powerful position in Irish society.

The results of the referendum indicate that the separation between Church and State in modern Ireland is still far from being completed. The homology between Church and State is maintained because Irish politicians, especially those in Fianna Fáil, regard many social issues, particularly those pertaining to sex and the family, as essentially religious and moral issues which belong to the sphere of religion and should be decided by each legislator's and voter's conscience. When political issues are left to individual moral consciences, most Irish legislators and voters still make decisions in accordance with the advice given by the Catholic Church which was largely responsible for forming their consciences. The only power bloc which has consistently challenged the moral monopoly of the Church in recent years and provided an alternative perspective on issues dealing with social life, the family and sex, has been the media.

The Media

Ireland has become like many other Western societies in that nearly every home has a radio and television and gets a national daily newspaper. It is the ability of the media to reach into people's homes and to get them to listen to their message which makes them a power bloc in Irish society. Their message is often in direct opposition to the teachings of the Catholic Church. It is the media which have partly fostered and given expression to the increased interest in material possessions, individuality and sexuality. But the extension of the media throughout Ireland from the 1960s did more than just extend the limits of Irish discourse. It had a profound impact on social and cultural practices. Instead of one's sameness being constituted in and through participation in a religious ritual, it now became constituted by having viewed the same television programme in the privacy of one's home. One's difference was indicated by the different selection one made from the media's offerings. Instead of the family kneeling down around the fire to say the rosary, they now sat down around the television. Instead of listening to stories and songs of their family, community, and country, people now watched the life-styles of foreigners. Initially television altered these family and community practices in Ireland and then, after years of repetitious watching it began to alter a wider range of social and cultural practices.

If the power of the Catholic Church in Ireland has begun to dwindle in recent years it is not so much that it can no longer limit other power blocs and alliances, but that its control of moral practice and discourse is being eroded by the development of mass communications. The media have lifted the veil of silence which previously shrouded moral issues. Discussions on sexuality and sexual morality, which have a major influence in the formation of the personality of the modern individual, have been removed from the dark confines of the confessional and brought to the forefront of public debate. As we shall see in the second part of this study, it was the Catholic Church which, in the last century, brought modern civility and morality to Ireland. Through a rigid system of physical discipline, Irish Catholics were able to become as civil as people from other Western societies. But once the Church became powerful, it prevented the modernisation process from developing further. Materialism, sexuality and individualism were inhibited. In the second half of this century it has been the media which have helped inculcate these practices and beliefs and push through the second stage of Irish modernisation.

The highly authoritarian, anti-intellectual strain of Irish Catholic morality was incorporated in the Censorship of Films Act (1923) and the Censorship of Publications Act (1929). These acts were rigorously enforced up to the 1960s by a Censorship Board which was vigilantly supervised by Catholic lay organisations such as the Knights of Columbanus. Bolster indicates that on many occasions the Knights dominated the actual membership of the Board.[40] Moreover, as Murphy suggests, 'Official censorship created layers of unofficial, self-righteous, busybody censorship in many a local community. In turn, this provoked evasion, and thus contributed further to the superficially conforming, furtive, under-the-counter mentality which is one of the more unlovely facets of the Irish heritage.'[41]

Although radio had been introduced since the 1930s, most of the programmes were home produced and, as with other aspects of the media, any material which went against Catholic principles was self-censored. It was the introduction of a national television service at the beginning of the 1960s and the wide dissemination of American and English produced programmes which did more than anything else to break through the iron cage of censorship. Chubb describes the changes which the media brought to Ireland as follows:

> Perhaps most immediately obvious was the enormous widening in the 1960s and 1970s of the range of topics that the mass media were prepared to treat, and the change both in the views they expressed and in the language they used. In 1966, a bishop thought it necessary and worthwhile to telephone Radio Téléfis Éireann to express immediately his protest at the television programme he was watching, which had just shown women in a studio audience being asked—and happily telling—what they had worn in bed on their wedding night. Today the episode of the "Bishop and the Nightie", as it is now known, is an old joke. Radio Téléfis Éireann has long since crossed the rubicon of full frontal nudity and by 1977 could broadcast a programme on homosexuals in Ireland.[42]

Television changed the face of Catholic Ireland because the practice and discourse of imported programmes was at variance with traditional Catholic principles. They portrayed life-styles in which religion had little or no importance. The concentration was on urban individuals rather than on rural family life. This was quite different from home produced programmes in which family life and the priest always played a significant role. A way of life was brought into Irish homes in which people were not limited in what they did and said by mothers and priests, but by police, doctors, and lawyers. Television brought the sophisticated glossy image of urban life into the heartland of rural Ireland. It provided a constant reminder of what most Irish people were not. The demand for a modern Western lifestyle did not lag far behind the advent of television. Indeed television played a crucial role in developing and maintaining consumer demand, and this stimulated increased production. Television, then, was an important factor in the second stage of Irish modernisation which brought an end to the dominance of rural life centred on small-scale agricultural production, and its replacement by industry, urbanity and individuality, all of which added to the decline of the power of the Catholic Church.

The development of the media and the decline of censorship also brought an end to the tradition that bishops and priests were above public criticism. From the middle of the last century a halo of sanctity had hung over the heads of Irish clergy and religious. People may have disobeyed them and muttered criticisms in private, but it was rare for any detailed, systematic critique of the Church and its clergy and religious to be voiced in public. 'Respect for the cloth' made almost any public criticism about the Church and its teachings appear as antagonistic. Even as late as 1984, Bishop Newman could argue that:

> There is frequently to be found a lukewarm practice which is no real faith at all. And there is certainly to be found, far too often I am afraid, a cancer of criticism and dissent, a cynicism about the faith. Sometimes it starts from the media, sometimes from elsewhere. At times it is the result of ignorance, and other times it is the result of downright antagonism.[43]

It is the media that have shattered the myth that it is bad luck to criticise a priest. It is the media that have broken the tradition of not criticising the Church and its teachings in public. It is the media that have forced the Church into giving a public account of itself. It was the media, and in particular television, which brought an end to the long nineteenth century of Irish Catholicism. The social process where moral discourse was limited to what was taught in the school, read in the occasional newspaper, heard on the radio and from the pulpit every Sunday, was changed by the little box which appeared in the corner of Irish homes. It was then, for the first time since the middle of the nineteenth century, when the process began in earnest, that many Irish Catholics stopped being limited by the moral discourse and practice of the Church.

Conclusion

Adherence to the rules and regulations of the Catholic Church has been maintained in Ireland not just because people were indoctrinated through a fear of being denied salvation, but also because adherence was necessary to attain and maintain power, especially the honour and respect of others. Through its institutional monopoly of morality, operated through churches, schools, hospitals and homes, being a good Catholic became central to being regarded as a decent moral person, the same as everyone else. For many Irish people, but in particular mothers, being able to limit the discourse and practice of others depended not on economic or political power, but on maintaining a moral superiority by over-conforming to the rules and regulations of the Church. For others, conforming to the Church's teachings and ritual practices was part of attaining and maintaining status within the community. This was especially true of doctors, nurses, and others who supervised or dealt with the public. Adherence to the Church also legitimated the rich and compensated the poor. It maintained the status quo. It inculcated conformity to family and community, and stifled individualism, creativity and ambition. With its monopoly on morality, the Church became a power bloc that was able to limit the practice and discourse of the State and other power blocs and alliances in Irish society.

Since the 1960s, however, the State has gradually pursued a policy which has undermined the power of the Church. But it was not until 1985 that the State passed a piece of social legislation, the Family Planning Amendment Act, which had a direct bearing on the whole area of morality, without first consulting the Catholic Church and agreeing to make certain changes. Prior to the 1960s, the relationship between Church and State in Ireland is best described in terms of a grand alliance in which each maintained the power of the other. Since the 1960s, the relationship has drifted into a formally separate but peaceful coexistence which has its occasional breakdown. Although formally removed from political life, the Church is still powerful because of its ability to divide the members of other power blocs and alliances in terms of their commitment to its teachings and practices. The Catholic Church will remain powerful in Ireland as long as politicians and those who are at the centre of other power blocs and alliances remain convinced that they cannot go against the Church's rules and regulations. The Church's power, then, is dependent on the laity maintaining a holistic lifestyle in which their religious beliefs and practices are not compartmentalised from the rest of their daily lives.

It has been the media that have most undermined the power of the Church in recent years. They have altered the level of practice and discourse previously regulated by the Church. Irish people now spend more time watching television, listening to the radio, and reading newspapers than they do engaging in religious rituals, and participating in those traditional practices that sustained a commitment to Church, family, and community. It was the media, and in particular television, that brought a constant advocacy for an individualist, consumerist, sexualised, urban lifestyle that broke the unquestioning 'respect for the cloth', and has forced the Church into giving a public account of itself. It has been the State and the media that have shattered the long nineteenth-century dominance of the Catholic Church in modern Ireland. To understand how that dominance originated in the first place, it is necessary to retrace some of the major social transformations in Irish society in the last two hundred years. It was within the nexus of the power struggle betwen power blocs and alliances, and in particular the English State and Rome, that the institutional power of the Irish Catholic Church was established.

PART TWO

Origins of the Power of the Catholic Church in Ireland

5
The Growth in Power of the Institutional Church in Nineteenth-Century Ireland

The common Irish will never become Protestant or well affected to the crown while they are supplied with Priests, Friars, etc., who are the fomenters and disturbers here. So that some more effectual remedy to prevent Priests and Friars coming into this kingdom is perfectly necessary. The Commons proposed the marking of every priest who shall be convicted of being an unregistered Priest, Friar, etc., and of remaining in this kingdom after the 1st May, 1720 with a large P. to be made with a red hot Iron on the cheek. The council generally disliked that punishment, and have altered it into that of castration which they are persuaded will be the most effectual remedy that can be found out to clear this nation of the disturbers of the peace and quiet of the kingdom, and would have been very well pleased to have been able to have found out any other punishment which might in their opinion have remedied the evil.[1]

WITHIN LESS than eighty years the relationship between Church and State in Ireland was to change dramatically. In 1795, the State introduced subsidised education for Catholic priests. Maynooth College, the national seminary, opened its doors. On the evening of the official opening, instead of being branded or castrated, the Catholic Archbishop of Dublin, Dr Troy, went to dinner in Dublin Castle.

To quote a Catholic pamphlet of that year: 'This was the first time since the Reformation that a Catholic Bishop was permitted to dine or sit in the company with a Lord Lieutenant of Ireland.' Four years later, ten of these (what were to become known as) 'Castle' bishops took the idea of State support for the Irish

Catholic Church to it logical conclusion and made a detailed submission to the government favouring a State subsidy for the whole of the Irish Catholic clergy.[2]

The proposed power alliance between Church and State that was discussed openly at the beginning of the century was to be thwarted by Rome and by the newly emergent Catholic bourgeoisie. By 1845, the Irish Catholic Church had become an independent power bloc to which the English State had decided to bequeath the task of civilising and socially controlling the Irish people.

The Penal Laws

The proposed bill of 1719 to castrate Irish priests was rejected by the English House of Lords. The bill represented the climax of a whole series of Penal Laws which were directed not so much at the Catholic religion and its priests, as against Catholics. The laws were an attempt by the Protestant ascendancy to maintain its position by making the Catholics a servile caste. The strategy would seem to have been to reduce and maintain the Catholic Irish as ignorant savages by depriving them of all civil life. The Lord Chancellor and the Chief Justice both ruled that 'the law does not suppose any such person to exist as an Irish Roman Catholic'. The penal laws were a crude and brutal attempt by a Protestant State to secure permanently the ascendancy of a dominant class whose interests they solely represented. They were basically class laws directed at denying Catholics ownership of the basic means of production. Lecky summarises their economic content:

> No Catholic was suffered to buy land, or inherit or receive it as a gift from Protestants, or to hold life annuities, or mortgages on land, or leases for more than thirty-one years, or any lease on such terms that the profits of the land exceeded one-third of the rent. If a Catholic leaseholder, by his skill or industry, so increased his profits that they exceeded this proportion, and did not immediately make a corresponding increase in his rent, his farms passed to the first Protestant who made the discovery.[3]

This law against production was in addition to the land confiscatory practices of the previous century. These had resulted in the Catholic share of Irish land falling from 59 per cent in 1641 to 14 per cent in 1703.[4]

The laws restricting education and religion can be understood as part of the strategy to demean and demoralise. Without knowledge and discipline there was every chance the Irish Catholic would remain an ignorant savage. As an uneducated, uncivil, disorganised alliance, Catholics might occasionally burst out in open rebellion, as they had done in the past, but at least they would not be able to engage in any organised political revolution. Bishops, clergy and religious order priests were the means towards the end of a civilised, moralised and disciplined Catholic population, and this added to the reasons why they were, in the case of bishops and religious order priests, expelled or, in the case of diocesan clergy, reduced to the role of saying Mass. If after 1698 any priests other than diocesan clergy were found, they were to be imprisoned and transported out of the country, and if they returned, 'were liable to be hanged, disembowelled and quartered'.[5] Under a further act in 1703 diocesan clergy were required to register with the State. If they did not they were to be banished. One thousand and eighty nine did so, some of whom were religious order priests. They were free to say Mass, to administer the sacraments and carry out all the functions of a parish priest. However, since priests could not be trained in Ireland, and since there was no provision for any further registration or replacement of existing priests, the notion was that they would quietly die out within a generation. The purpose behind the proposed branding or castrating of registered priests was that they could not be secretly replaced by transferring names from one to another. By this time, the vast majority of priests had become technically illegal since they had refused to take the Oath of Abjuration (1708) which denied any Catholic right to the English throne.[6] 'Magistrates were empowered to summon any papist over the age of sixteen and require him, under oath, to reveal when and where he had heard Mass, who celebrated the Mass, and who were present. . . .'[7]

The extent to which the laws were enforced varied enormously throughout the country. The absence of chapels and the illegality of priests meant that in many areas Mass attendance was literally carried out openly, often at what became known as 'Mass-rocks', which in the north of the country were the most common place of worship until the end of the eighteenth century. In urban areas, the more well-to-do Catholic merchants had sufficient wealth and

status to confront the law, and practise their religion publicly
in the back-streets. Burke notes that 'Catholic chapels usually
had neither street-frontage nor adjacent graveyard and their sites
were usually small. They were approached by narrow lanes for they
were usually at the rear of houses, occupying sites of former stables
and warehouses'.[8]

The open-air, back-street religion of Catholics was to persist in
many areas well into the nineteenth century, and stood in stark
contrast to the substantial brick buildings of the established
Protestant Church. As late as 1845, an English commentator
described the poorness of the Irish Catholic Church as follows:
'They worship in hovels, or in the open air, from the want of any
place of worship. Their religion is the religion of three-fourths of
the population. Not far off, in a well-windowed and well-roofed
house, is a well-paid protestant clergyman ... crying in the
wilderness ... furious against the errors of Popery'.[9] It is only
when one understands the enormous demoralisation which took
place under these penal laws that one can understand why it was
that Catholics of later generations gave so much of their time,
money and effort to constructing the large number of church
buildings that became monuments to their respectability.

Penal Education

A central aspect of the demoralising process was to see that the
Irish Catholic was and remained ignorant and uncouth. Again
Lecky summarises the main effects of the laws: 'The Catholic was
excluded from the university. He was not permitted to be the
guardian of a child. It was made penal for him to keep a school, to
act as usher or private tutor, or to send his children to be educated
abroad; and a reward of £10 was offered for the discovery of a
Popish schoolmaster.'[10]

It was at this time that the famous 'hedge-schools' came into
existence. These were to dominate the field of Irish education
until the establishment of the national school system in the 1830s.
Although there was a hedge-school in every parish in the country,
they varied enormously in quality. Much depended on the individual teacher. The curriculum was inconsistent and relied heavily
on Latin and Greek classics handed down over the years. They
were attended by an élite who could afford the few pence

necessary to pay the teacher. Their success rate, even in basic literacy, was highly uneven. The buildings, if any, were rough-and-tumble places. The absence of confined and defined space mitigated against supervision and the inculcation of discipline and civility. It was this educational system which gave rise to the classical contradiction of the uncivil, ill-mannered Irish peasant being well-versed in Homer and Virgil.[11]

The penal laws were instrumental in establishing an alliance between schoolteachers and priests. Although the priest was strictly responsible for catechising the people, Corish claims that a share of this work had already devolved onto the schoolmaster in the first half of the eighteenth century. He cites three instances where it was explicitly stated that school was held in the Mass-house, and claims that 'the archbishop regarded the schoolmaster as an object of his visitation equally with the parish priest'.[12]

It was the persistence and prevalence of illegal Popish schools—a survey in 1731 had revealed at least 549—which led to the State's strategy of establishing subsidised schools to Protestantise the Irish. The Charter Schools were based on the principle of the State intervening and detaching children from their ignorant, uncivil and immoral parents so that they 'may be instructed in the English tongue and in the principles of true religion and loyalty in all succeeding generations'. As opposed to the more classical orientation of the hedge-schools, the Charter Schools aimed to train children in 'labour and industry in order to cure that habitual laziness and idleness which is too common among the poor of this country'.[13] But the whole attempt to Protestantise the Irish could only be successful if the children were detached from the bad habits of their parents. Consequently, admittance to the schools depended upon Catholic parents handing over all rights to the bodies and souls of their children who, once they had entered the schools, were apprenticed out to Protestant families and were forbidden to communicate with their parents. The schools were intended, in the words of their programme, 'to rescue the souls of thousands of poor children from the dangers of Popish superstition and idolatry, and their bodies from the miseries of idleness and beggary'.[14] Nurseries were set up in the schools in an attempt to get mothers to abandon their children in early infancy. This practice of state-subsidised, Protestant societies detaching children from what was deemed to be their uncivil and immoral parents, was also perpetuated in Foundling Hospitals.[15]

The schools were a failure. They became the object of scorn and ridicule and, Lecky claims, even in bad times when they were used most, 'it is doubtful that they had more than 2,000 pupils'.[16] The Royal Commission on Irish Education (1825) stated that in the ninety years the schools were in operation a total of only 12,745 children had been apprenticed.[17] However, the social and political interest of the Protestant ascendancy in moralising and controlling the Irish population continued. Following the Act of Union (1801) which brought Ireland under direct English control, it constantly pressurised the State to do something. As the Association for Discountenancing Vice and Promoting Know-ledge and Practice of the Christian Religion noted:

> It is a melancholy truth that the Irish vulgar are in too many instances bloody and ferocious, retaining the habits and feelings of Savages, devoid of lasting gratitude, and ready at the impulse of any groundless resentment, to exercise the most unrelenting cruelty where shortly before they had professed the most affectionate attachment. . . . Should not every expedient that either honest Policy or pure Religion can furnish, be instantly resorted to, in order if possible to introduce among them the habits and principles of rational beings, and of Christians? The change from Savageness to Civilization has been too often realised to be any where despaired of. But it must begin somewhere.[18]

In other words while the Charter School system had failed, it was felt that the best way to achieve social and political stability was through education and moral discipline, especially since the Irish were making such strenuous efforts to educate themselves. But at this stage it was still seen as essential that the education be Protestant and carried out through state-subsidised, Protestant societies. Otherwise, the Association claimed, 'the pernicious doctrines of treason and rebellion' would continue to be dis-seminated among the lower classes by hedge-schoolmasters. 'The necessity of providing some remedy for an evil of such magnitude, must be as obvious in a political as in a moral view'.[19] This pressure had results. The State through various reports from its commissioners began to accept the need for uniform instruction and supervision in order to control the Irish population. The commissioners stated that it was necessary 'to substitute for the ill-taught and ill-regulated Schools which we have been describing, a systematic and uniform plan of instruction, such as should gratify the desire for information, which manifests itself among the lower classes of the people of Ireland, and at the same time form those habits of regularity and discipline which are yet more valuable than mere learning. . . . '[20]

The English State's interest in providing a national school system of education which would standardise, regulate and supervise the morality and discipline of the Irish was fostered and cultivated by various Protestant societies throughout the first thirty years of the nineteenth century. With State support these societies felt that they could quickly civilise and moralise the Irish into the true Christian religion. The interest of these societies was essentially a missionary religious one; quite similar to that which later led thousands of Irish priests, brothers and nuns to the four corners of the earth. However, while the State did have a social interest in civilising the Irish, it also had a political interest in disciplining and controlling the population. To answer the question, which Akenson raises, as to why a state system of mass education was introduced in Ireland four decades before it was introduced in England or Scotland, it is necessary to understand the background to the English interest in Ireland, and its wider policy of policing and controlling the Irish people.[21]

State Mechanisms of Political and Social Control

Throughout its history Ireland had been like no other English colony; being right next door and yet separated by a stretch of sea. It was the sea which made Ireland easily accessible to France and Spain, and its insular proximity which made England feel militarily vulnerable. It was mainly this military vulnerability which made Ireland of unique colonial interest. It was a country with no obvious natural resources, other than some reasonably good land, and the English were forced to try various methods to pacify and subdue the natives, and sustain a permanent colonial presence. The confiscation of lands and the experimental plantation system of the sixteenth and seventeenth centuries had largely failed, except in the North. The attempted 'legal' subjugation of Irish Catholics through systematic penal legislation had also failed. By the 1820s, the State had begun to show visible signs of concern, if not outright worry, about the Irish problem. The first detailed census of 1821 had shown that the Irish population had grown to 6.8 million; over half the population of England, and one third of the British Isles altogether. To have so many traditionally rebellious people living 'next door', who to all intents and purposes were regarded as savages, posed a threat to the peaceful industrial order of England. It was within the wider context of previous failures at political and social control that the English State became willing to experiment with a number of strategies and tactics in order to subdue and pacify the Irish.

The Policing of the Irish Body: It was because Irish Catholics were successfully educating themselves—and, according to many accounts, in seditious and rebellious literature—and because agrarian outrages, organised by secret societies such as the Whiteboys, were becoming more common, that the English State was forced into trying alternative methods to subdue them. One of these methods was the expansion of the existing constabulary, which in the seventeenth century had acted more as watchguards than as a custodial and investigative force. The Police Acts of 1786 (for Dublin) and 1787 (for the rest of the country) were an attempt to specify how a new police force should operate. The Dublin Act brought in paid constables endorsed with large new powers under the orders of three commissioners of police.[22] These acts represented a further experiment in the English state control of the Irish. As Maitland points out, 'down to 1856 there was no law for the whole of England requiring that there should be paid policemen'.[23] These acts were also the beginning of the modern concept of a civil police force that was to be imitated throughout many Western societies.

The early police acts were revised and updated in 1814 by Sir Robert Peel, the under-secretary for Ireland. His new act established the Peace Preservation Force (which became known as 'Peelers'). This Act gave greater control of police activities to the centralised State. Breathnach notes that 'the lord lieutenant was empowered to proclaim any county or city or portion of any country to be in a "state of disturbance", in which case he could appoint a chief magistrate, a chief constable and fifty sub-constables to such an area . . .'[24] The constitution of the police as a specific apparatus of the State was treated with suspicion by the Protestant ascendancy. The State may have been representing their interests, but according to McDowell they abhorred 'the arbitrary tendencies inherent in centralisation almost as much as they disliked the destruction of local patronage'.[25] Indeed it was partly because the State made the decision which area should be policed, but yet required each area to pay for the force as long as it remained there, that the alliance between itself and this ruling class started to deteriorate.[26] This was all part of a new period of Irish history in which the policies of the English State became distanced from the interests of the Protestant ascendancy. The concentration was on establishing peace and order in the colony, partly as an end in itself, partly as another experimental attempt at civilisation, and partly out of fear that 'savage' Irish practices and customs might spread to English cities.

By 1820, there were at least five police forces in existence in Ireland. In 1822, a further police Act was passed establishing a new force under a provincial and county organisation. This was a para-military force, uniformed and armed. Soon after its establishment there were 5,008 such constables, operating under 313 chief constables. As Brady notes:

> It throws an interesting sidelight on the nature of British administration in Ireland in the years immediately after the union that two entirely different police systems should be developed for a supposedly 'united' kingdom. Britain got an unarmed policeman, answerable not to central government but to a watch committee and depending in the last analysis on the moral support of the community to enforce the law. Ireland, by contrast, got an armed garrison, rigidly disciplined and directly controlled by Dublin Castle, operating with the backing of the Martini-Carbine, the bayonet and the sword rather than the support of the community.[27]

The principal reorganisation of the Irish police came with the Constabulary Act (1836). The Peace Preservation Force was scrapped and a new hierarchical system of inspectors and sub-inspectors established. The key difference in this reorganisation was the emphasis on surveillance and intelligence, and the structures instituted to develop State knowledge and power. Breathnach describes the new growth in the State apparatus:

Every conceivable part of the country came within the Castle's intelligence. Baronies, which hitherto occupied 16 constables, were divided into sub-districts and as many men stationed in them. Stations were made as central as possible and took the name of their respective townlands. Even to the present day ... these areas, including districts, sub-districts and stations, are the same as they were almost a century and a half ago, the older stations still containing their lonely, hideous and formidable appearance.[28]

These new organisational structures did not, as was hoped, provide for the permanent civilisation of Ireland. They were rejected by the Irish peasant, the emerging Catholic bourgeoisie, and the State's own arm of enforcement—the magistrates—who still rejected State centralisation and interference.[29] The early experimental Police Acts did not even have the short-term effect of curtailing agrarian outrage. In effect, the peasants were shut off from the most effective means of civilisation—the Catholic clergy and bourgeoisie. It was only when these forces could gain prominence in Irish society, with or without State approval, that the mass of the Irish population could become civil along modern European lines.

State Care and Maintenance of the Irish Body: A central aspect of the growth of State power from the mid-eighteenth to the mid-nineteenth century was the growth in the number of institutions (in the beginning mostly charitable) which cared for, maintained and incarcerated the Irish people. Although workhouses and foundling hospitals date from the beginning of the eighteenth century, the rapid growth in total—i.e. life-encompassing—institutions which gained complete control of those who entered them, did not begin until the first half of the nineteenth century. The failure of the early institutions, e.g. Charter schools and foundling hospitals, was not as much because they were proselytising agencies, but that they did not really care for the inmates. Robbins points out that:

The enquiry of the Commissioners of Irish Education revealed not only that the governors had failed in their efforts to fashion the children into upright, moral citizens but that the death rate amongst the foundlings was still of huge proportions. Statistics included in the report of the enquiry disclosed that of approximately 52,000 infants reared during the period 1796 to 1826, 32,000 had definitely perished either as infants in the institution or after being sent to the country; about 9,600 others who could not be ascertained for were also thought to have died.[30]

In 1828, John Douglas made a forceful argument as to why the State should begin to develop a welfare system for the Irish poor and, in particular, extend the poor laws to Ireland. 'The necessity of protecting all classes in Britain from the degrading competition of Irish pauper labour, and the consequent augmentation of the pressure of pauperism on the British soil and capital, have become too urgent to be trifled with.'[31] The movement from a direct policing of the Irish, which was obviously ineffective, to more indirect, softer forms of social and political control, had obvious advantages.

> Such a grateful common object of universal concern, as the comfortable maintenance of the poor—the substitution of industry, morals and order, for the idleness, dishonesty, profligacy and audacity of daily public begging and midnight marauding—could not but tend greatly to soothe the asperity of political and religious rancour—to calm the agitation of the public mind—to render government more easy and mild—to reconcile and restore the absentees to their pacified country, excite and reward local industry by local expenditure of the revenues of the land and the church, and gradually invite capital to establish manufacturers, by the cheapness of labour and food among a happily tranquilised population.[32]

The growth in private and State-funded health services was spectacular. By 1836, there were thirty-six infirmaries and almost 500 dispensaries. At the beginning of the century there were only eleven hospitals in Dublin, by 1845 there were thirty. It is on the basis of this phenomenal growth that McDowell concludes that 'the Irish poor enjoyed better medical services than their fellows in wealthier and healthier countries'.[33] The other system of general care and maintenance which the State introduced was the workhouse. During the first five years of the 1840s, 118 workhouses were built throughout Ireland. They were exact models of those already established in Britain under the 1834 Poor Law Act. They were total institutions founded on the famous principle of 'less eligibility', i.e. the relief to be provided was not to be made 'really or apparently so eligible [i.e. desirable] as the situation of the independent labourer of the lowest class'.[34]

The main buildings used for politically controlling the Irish were prisons and gaols. In 1839, there were 148 official prisons of which 39 were long-term county gaols. The county gaols had 2,957 cells which in that year held up to 6,117 prisoners. Of the 8,729 prisoners sent to gaol in 1839, 7,726 were sent for less than six months; 874 for 6–12 months; and 128 for 1–3 years.[35] It was also during the first half of the nineteenth century that long-term institutions, other than gaols, began to be built. Houses of Industry, originally established for the destitute poor and which later in the eighteenth century began to be used as asylums, became total institutions for young criminals. However it was almost another sixty years before a full system of reformatories was established throughout the country. But by that time the Catholic Church, through its orders of nuns and brothers, was beginning to establish its right to the moral jurisdiction and guardianship of all young Catholics.[36]

Emigration

The English State's policy of incarcerating the totally destitute in England and Ireland can be seen as part of an overall strategy of maintaining the environmental conditions for industrial order and the exploitation of the labour power of the working classes, which constituted the wealth of England. It is impossible to separate the political interest in peace, order and stability from the genuine, humanitarian, social interest which existed at the time. Politicians had been long aware of the dangers of a mass invasion of cheap Irish labour to the industrialised cities. In his evidence to the Select Committee on the State of Ireland (1825) Mr McCulloch stated that the 25,000 natives of Ireland operated injuriously upon the British labourers in two ways: '*first*, they operate to reduce their wages by the increased number of labourers brought into the market, and by the greater competition there is for employment; and *second*, they operate in another way, by the example they set to the English and Scottish labourers. . .'[37] These opinions were echoed by Malthus two years later, when he gave evidence to the Select Committee on Emigration.

Are you able to give the Commitee any information with respect to the effects already produced by an increased number of Irish coming over to England?—I have only understood it generally, that in western parts of England, in the manufacturing districts, in Manchester and in Glasgow particularly, the wages of labour have been lowered essentially by the coming over of the Irish labourers. In your opinion, might this emigration of Irish contribute to alter materially the habits of the labouring class in England?—I should think it might, and that it might have the pernicious effect of introducing the habit of living almost entirely upon potatoes.

What general consequences would you suppose would be the result of that change in the habits of the people in England with regard to their subsistence?—That they would be very much worse off in every respect. In their manners and conduct?—Yes in every respect, moral and physical.[38]

Between 1815 and 1826, the State had conducted six separate experiments in state-aided emigration. One of these experiments was carried out in Ireland in the spring of 1822 when, following a bad harvest, it was estimated that half the population of half of Ireland was destitute. Sir Robert Peel hesitated to supply food and instead decided that 'this was the proper moment for the government to offer to remove surplus population. . .' He made two specifications: 'first the emigrants should be recruited in Southern Ireland; second, the measure should be financed entirely by the government with no expectation of reimbursement from local assessment'.[39]

The experiment in getting potentially rebellious Irish peasants to settle in Canada produced more reports than success. Emigration was to become a private rather than a state-subsidised practice. Although most of the pre-Famine emigration was to the United States and Canada, up to half of it was to the cities of Great Britain. Politicians continued to be suspicious that the arrival of so many poor, ignorant, uncivil Irish natives was having a bad effect on the good habits of the indigenous working class. In 1833, Cornwall Lewis was directed to inquire into the state of Irish labourers in Great Britain because there was a fear that: 'the Irish immigrants have exercised a pernicious influence on the English and Scottish working classes, by lowering their wages and debasing their moral character and that certain measures ought to be introduced in Ireland with a view to preventing the emigration of the poor to Great Britain.' The testimonies given to Cornwall

Lewis suggested that the Irish were 'the first to commence riots'; were 'more drunken and idle'; and tended to 'live in squalid filth in cellars'. A Liverpool priest testified that 'an Englishman who earns 18s a week is found to have his children neatly clad and his house comfortable: whereas an Irishman on the same wages has his children ill-clad, and his room and cellar filthy'. The pragmatic Cornwall Lewis warned, however, that it would be unwise to overlook the advantages which a reserve army of Irish labour supplied at such cheap rates and short notice. 'Their irregular habits and low standard of comfort may be regretted; but it is to be remembered that the Irish have been and are, most efficient workmen: that they come in the hour of need, and that they afforded the chief part of the animal strength by which the great works of our manufacturing districts have been executed.' While many of the witnesses argued that the irregular and bad habits of the Irish injured the superior character of the Scottish and English poor, Cornwall Lewis argued that 'because the Irish lived in ghettoes and did not mix with the natives' they would not endanger 'in any material degree, the moral habits of the latter'.[40]

Cornwall Lewis's report, which was over 300 pages long, was only an appendix to one of the numerous volumes which the Poor Law Commissioners produced on Ireland. These, in turn, were only a small fraction of the total number of reports produced by other commissions, select committees, etc., during the first half of the nineteenth century. Through these reports, documentations, statistics and censuses the State accumulated an enormous body of knowledge about how the Irish people behaved, and about the environmental conditions which produced their behaviour. This knowledge became the basis of State policy in Ireland.

Unfortunately no systematic analysis has been done on the overall content of these reports and the role they played in State policy formation. However, an indication of the primary importance given to producing knowledge about Ireland can be gauged from the fact that in the *General Index to the House of Commons Accounts and Papers* there are 462 references to reports on Ireland, compared to only 210 on Scotland.[41]

The State/Church Alliance

By the middle of the eighteenth century English politicians began to realise that the attempt to abolish Catholicism in Ireland through persecution had failed. Nevertheless the Protestant ascendancy still feared for their possessions and position. Any sign of 'native unrest', or indeed any large gathering of Catholics, even if for a pattern or pilgrimage, 'struck terror into the hearts of Protestants'.[42] But it was soon realised that, as Lecky puts it, 'the higher Catholic clergy, if left in peace, were able and willing to render inestimable services to the Government in supressing sedition and crime, and as it was quite evident that the bulk of the Irish Catholics would not become Protestants, they could not, in the mere interests of order, be left wholly without religious ministration'.[43]

It was at this stage that a tentative power alliance began to be formed between the English State and the Catholic Church. As long as the Irish could be prevented from bloody rebellion and became civil and disciplined, it did not matter so much who produced the results. The Protestant ascendancy continued to press for a return to the Penal code. Throughout the first half of the nineteenth century members of this class argued and wrote at length about the necessity of expelling all forms of popery from Ireland.[44] In contrast, many English politicians, responding perhaps to pressure from the English bourgeoisie, began to realise what a powerful ally the Church could be in the pacification of the Irish masses. The constant exhortations by Catholic bishops and clergy for law and order provided continuing evidence of their good intentions.[45]

But whatever role the Church might have played in bringing modern civilisation to the Irish population, it was hampered by a lack of manpower. Towards the end of the century the population was rising rapidly, but following the French Revolution and the closure of Catholic seminaries the supply of Irish priests was stopped. The medium for putting across the message of civility, law and order was in danger of being cut off. In advocating the unprecedented notion that the State should initiate and support a college for the training of Catholic priests in Ireland, the Archbishop of Dublin, Dr Troy, coyly pointed out to the Lord Lieutenant that the moral instruction of the people 'may appear to his Majesty's Ministers a subject not unworthy of his Royal consideration and Bounty'.[46] Another consideration in favour of supporting a national seminary was that once the Catholic seminaries on the Continent were reopened, young trainee Irish priests might be imbued with the revolutionary spirit which had swept France. Indeed that revolutionary spirit had already reached Ireland.

Some of the more enlightened members of the Irish Protestant bourgeoisie had begun to argue for Catholic emancipation because they associated the rapidly increasing prosperity which had occurred since the middle of the eighteenth century with the greater freedom of Catholics. If economic prosperity was to continue, they felt it was essential that an alliance be made with the new wealthy Catholic bourgeoisie. In fact, the idea had been current for a long time that persecuting the Irish Catholic was of little use and, as a strategy, decidedly ineffective. As Wolfe Tone, the Protestant leader of the unsuccessful rebellion in 1798 argued, it made matters worse:

> Persecution will keep alive the foolish bigotry and superstition of any sect, as the experience of five thousand years had demonstrated. Persecution bound the Irish Catholic to his Priest, and the Priest to the Pope; the bond of union is drawn tighter by oppression, relaxation will undo it. The emancipated and liberal Irishman, like the emancipated and liberal Frenchman, may go to mass, and tell his beads; but neither the one nor the other will attend to the rusty and extinguished thunderbolts of the Vatican. . . .[47]

Along with the general increase in economic prosperity which was spreading throughout Europe, and the enlightened civilised approach to religious adversaries which accompanied it, there were other factors associated with the new approach by the State to the Catholic Church in Ireland. These had to do with the rational differentiation that was taking place in European civilisation between the religious and political spheres. As part of this process, Rome began to curtail the political activities of the regular clergy in Ireland. In 1751, Pope Benedict XIV issued a decree confining them to living in their community houses, and putting them under the supervision and control of the local bishop.[48] In the past it had been the regular clergy who operated closest with the ordinary people and who were most feared by the Protestant ascendancy. Within twenty years the number of regular clergy had been halved. In 1757, the bishops circulated a document to the whole of the clergy requesting that it be read at the first Sunday of every quarter. The document emphasised that 'it is not and never was a doctrine or tenet of the Roman Catholic Church that the Pope or general councils have power to depose kings, or absolve subjects from the allegiance,' or that Catholics 'may break faith with, murder, or plunder, or defraud those of a different communion or religion'.[49] Furthermore, because most of its priests had been trained on the Continent, the Irish Catholic Church had for a long time been tainted with Gallicanism, a central tenet of which was that the Pope received only spiritual authority from God.[50] The more the bishops and clergy formally denied any temporal power of the Pope and any Catholic right to the English throne, and continued to denounce riots and rebellions, the more English politicians and the Protestant ascendancy became reassured of their loyalty. Catholic Relief Acts were passed in 1762, 1774, 1778, and 1782, and Emancipation Acts in 1792 and 1793.[51]

Having gone so far as to subsidise the education and training of priests in Maynooth in 1795, the State was urged to consider providing for all the bishops and clergy. In terms of attaining civil and moral order this was desirable because the Protestant Church did not have the necessary allegiance, and the Protestant ascendancy was too small and scattered to be effective civilising agencies. However, such a consideration would only be possible if the State had a veto in the nomination of bishops. (In effect, such a veto was part of the ongoing process of the rational differentiation of the religious from the secular sphere since its purpose was to avoid the appointment of seditious and treasonable bishops. In other words, a state subsidy for the clergy would be all right as long as priests stuck purely to moral matters.) Such veto powers were in fact part of a state-subsidised clergy proposal put forward by the trustees of Maynooth in 1799. Rome was consulted and, as Gwynn puts it, 'declared emphatically against any proposal of paying State salaries to bishops, [and] asserted that no Protestant sovereign could be allowed the power of nominating Catholic bishops. . .'.[52] This opposition can be understood as an attempt to maintain its own centralised power and to avoid any alliance between the Irish Church and the English State. But six years later Rome changed its ruling when the Congregation of Propaganda admitted that a veto might be accepted as part of a bill emancipating Catholics.[53] It was at this stage that O'Connell, the leader of the Catholic Association, who had already criticised the bishops for supporting the Union, denounced any links either between the bishops and the State in terms of a subsidy, or between the State and Rome in terms of a veto. Soon afterwards the bishops expressed their opposition to both a state subsidy and a veto. This was the beginning of a shift away from any possible alliance between the bishops and the State, and a move towards a new and eventually permanent alliance with the emerging Catholic bourgeoisie.

Even before Catholic Emancipation (1829) there was a harden-ing attitude among Catholic bishops and clergy against the idea of a state provision, and a conviction that 'the voluntary system was an essential part of the bond between them and the people'.[54] Although the Church never became a subsidised apparatus of the State, many of the bishops favoured strengthening any power alliance that existed. Others, led by Archbishop MacHale of Tuam, were adamant that any alliance must be with the laity, led by the emergent Catholic bourgeoisie and Daniel O'Connell.

When the State failed to get the hierarchy to enter into an alliance with it, it did its best to ensure that there was no alliance between the Church and the Catholic bourgeoisie. In their anxiety to control Irish Catholics, especially in their movement towards repeal of the Act of Union, English politicians attempted to counteract any unified Catholic alliance. This they did by sending an agent to Rome and offering appeasements to the hierarchy. This caused a split among the bishops and clergy, and a split between the Catholic Association and the Church. The State, in fact, was attempting to exercise power by dividing the hierarchy, setting its members against each other, the clergy and religious order priests against the bishops, and the laity against the clergy and hierarchy. When Peel appointed Heytesbury as Lord Lieutenant, he told him about 'the absolute necessity . . . of dis-uniting, by the fair legitimate means of a just, kind and conciliatory policy, the Roman Catholic body and thus breaking up a sullen and formidable *confederacy* against the British connexion'.[55] However, what was really happening was that despite the efforts of the State, the Irish hierarchy was emerging as a major, organised power bloc in Irish society.

Although the bishops may have been divided they were, unlike at any other time in their history, communicating and regularly meeting each other. With constant advice from Rome, especially from Cullen, the then Rector of the Irish College, and his vice-president (and later Rector) Tobias Kirby, the hierarchy was being moulded into a body which was increasingly able to limit successfully the actions of the State, especially in matters of morality. It was a constant fear of many members of the hierarchy, clergy and laity that not only was their destiny being moulded by Rome, but that this was being done in and through a concordat with the English State.[56] Moreover, insofar as it was primarily interested in gaining moral control of Irish Catholics and remained unsupportive of their economic and political struggles, Rome operated in the political interests of the English State. From the time of his appointment as Rector of the Irish College in Rome, and his becoming the official representative of the Irish bishops, Cullen was groomed to the main task of bringing the Irish Church under Roman control. This he was able to do by first, building up a detailed knowledge of the situation in Ireland, and then secondly, granting favours and fixing episcopal appointments. An effective tactic was to get the new nationalist Gallicans to supplant the old State-supportive Gallicans, and then to supplant the new Gallicans with his own Ultramontane appointees. Cullen promoted the cause of Roman first and foremost. According to Bowen he was against the nationalist struggle because it promoted religious indifferentism. Indeed Bowen goes so far as to argue that Cullen was so intent upon rectifying the religious malaise of the Irish Church that 'he showed little interest in the temporal needs of the people'.[57] What the strategies and tactics employed by Cullen and the other Ultramontanes achieved, was to slowly reconstitute the Irish Church as a united body directly accountable to and regulated by Rome. What it did not achieve was to stem the involvement, particularly of priests, in the economic and political struggles of the new class of substantial Catholic tenant farmers. But, as we shall see, the growth in the organisation and size of the Church can be linked to a gradual shift away from open rebellion to democratic parliamentary procedures as a means of gaining both control of the land and Home Rule. It was within a complex web of relations between London, Rome, and mainly Dublin that the Catholic Church in Ireland began to emerge as a power bloc. The end result, which was of most interest to the administrators in Rome and London, was that a civilising and moralising force was being exercised over the Irish.

The Growth of the Institutional Church 1750–1850

The attempt to eliminate Catholicism through the repression of the institutional Church was a failure. Instead of detaching the people from the bishops and clergy it had the opposite effect of uniting them in a struggle against the State. The penal laws failed because they did not stop the formation of a Catholic urban bourgeoisie which, in its search for civility, morality and legitimated status, allied itself with the Catholic Church. The new urban merchant class was to become a social model for the tenant farmers of the nineteenth century. When the English State attempted to control the Catholic bourgeoisie and the Church, it was too late. This formidable alliance was already well established (to be fully cemented in the Irish State). Moreover the fight for a Church independent of the State had been encouraged and partially directed by Rome as part of its own multinational power consolidation process. Such a process was not new and had been rigorously pursued in Ireland throughout the seventeenth century, even though the Church and Catholic population were often in the depths of religious persecution. The Tridentine reforms which Rome sought to introduce involved the establishment of a parish system of pastoral care operated in and through the Church rather than the home; the pursuance of a catechetical programme to produce a uniform, orthodox doctrine; and the constitution of the priest as a man of Roman precept and morality rather than a mere religious functionary. The penal laws brought a temporary halt to this process of Tridentine reform. Nevertheless even in the period of active enforcement of the laws, Rome continued to exert considerable power over the Irish Catholic Church.[58]

The growth in the discipline and bureaucratic organisation of the Church can also be linked to a general explosion of discourse and communication in Irish society which was made possible by the physical development of the infrastructure of communications, e.g. printing, road, postal service, etc. The growth in the popular press, for example, was associated with an increase in the actual reporting of the activities of the Catholic Church.[59] This, together with the fact that much of the reporting was of a favourable nature, did much to give the Church a legitimate position, especially among the more literate Protestant community. It was not that Church organisation and discipline were new. Instructions regarding clerical discipline had been laid down since at least the eleventh century. What was new was the extent to which bishops began to communicate with each other and reform their dioceses. Much of the discourse and practice of bishops in the first half of the nineteenth century was taken up with tightening clerical discipline. There was a general clamp down on public disorders and scandal-giving practices of the clergy, especially insolence, drinking and cavorting with undesirables. Larkin concludes that 'what happened between 1800 and 1845 is that the character and conduct of the clergy, which certainly left a great deal to be desired at the beginning of the period, was gradually and uniformly improved. By 1830, the worst was over since the Irish bishops with the help of Rome finally secured the upper hand over their priests.'[60] He notes that the improvement was greatest in the east, especially in the Archdiocese of Dublin, and in the towns where better mannered, better informed priests were generally placed. Throughout the rest of the century, this growth in manners, discipline and civility was to spread westwards, being instilled into the homes and bodies of most Irish Catholics through the organisations and buildings supervised by priests and religious.

But the creation of the Catholic Church as a power bloc in Irish society did not occur simply through increased communication and the greater exercise of Roman bureaucracy, discipline and control. It was also rooted in changes in Irish economic and social conditions which, in turn, cannot be divorced from the general increase in the prosperity and civilisation which were spreading throughout Europe at the time. Greater economic prosperity had its particular translation in Ireland. For the Catholic Church it meant a large increase in the size of its flock without a concomitant increase in the number of priests to administer to them—a situation which only the Famine was to rectify. In 1731, the ratio of diocesan priests to Catholics was 1:1587, which is not very different from the present-day European average.[61] However, the ratio deteriorated rapidly, not because of a decline in vocations but because of a rapid rise in the population. Among the lower classes, where the population increase was concentrated, the effects of greater economic prosperity resulted in more births, more marriages, and a greater subdivision of already small holdings. The moral discipline that was needed to forgo gratification in order to accumulate and reproduce wealth did not exist. Priests, nuns and brothers, and the institutions of discipline that were to become the principal means towards such ends, were not generally available. The temporary closure of the continental seminaries had not helped the situation. Even if these colleges had remained open, it is difficult to imagine that the vocation rate would have been much higher. Sending one's son to be trained as a priest in a continental seminary, or indeed to Maynooth, was an expensive practice which could only be supported by the better-off.

Once Maynooth opened, and the new class of tenant farmers became established, the number of vocations to the priesthood began to rise. This should not be taken to mean cottiers, landless labourers, or small tenant farmers on holdings of less than five acres—all of whom made up seven-tenths of the rural population—but rather the large Catholic tenant farmers. It was only they who could actively seek the social prestige to be gained from having a son a priest, and who could afford to send him to be educated in Maynooth. The cost of sending a son to Maynooth for the first year was £40–£50.[62] Given that the average agricultural wage was not much more than 1s. a day, this would mean that the cost of educating a son to be a priest was more than double the annual income of most people at the time.[63] In 1808, of the 205 students in Maynooth, 159 (78 per cent) were the sons of farmers.[64] From the beginning of the nineteenth century, the heart of Irish Cathlicism shifted gradually from an urban merchant class to a rural tenant farmer class.

Catholic priests may have worked among the poor laity but they were always from a different economic class. Indeed, given the low earnings of the majority of the laity it was quite an exploitative relationship. The average income of a parish priest in 1750 was about £30 to £35. By 1801, this had increased to £65. In the next twenty-five years it doubled and continued to improve.[65] The main cause for this rise in income had less to do with increased contributions from the successful bourgeoisie—which may have been directed more towards funds for church building—and more to do with the greater number of fees and dues received for services rendered.

The rise in population meant more marriages and births, which necessitated employing the services of a priest. These services were not cheap, and all the evidence goes to show that the money received for them, especially marriage offerings, was among the principal resources of the clergy, particularly in the southern half of the country.[66] Although the fees charged for marriages, baptisms, etc., were in theory 'offerings', they were socially obligatory with standard rates charged. The amount charged depended upon the service rendered; whether it was a rural or urban parish, and the economic class of those receiving the service. To get married in 1825 could cost as little as five shillings, but the general figure was from half a guinea to a guinea. In the Dublin province in 1831, the bishops jointly fixed the fees as follows: 'Five shillings to be paid after the celebration of baptism, forty shillings after the celebration of marriage: ten shillings for letters of freedom to marry, two shillings for private masses'.[67] Given an average agricultural wage of not much more than 1s. a day, the cost of the services of the priest was very high by present day standards. It is no wonder that many couples resorted to clandestine marriages performed by 'couple-beggars' (mostly ex-priests) in the cities.[68] Voluntary offerings were also expected for funerals. The amount given ranged from five to fifteen shillings depending on how many priests assisted. Offerings might also be expected for visiting the sick, usually from the better-off parishioners, and for churching, i.e. the readmission of a woman to the Church after the birth of a child.[69] The other main source of income of the clergy was dues. Dues were defined by a priest in 1806 as: 'a certain sum paid by the head of every family to the parish priest for his support and in consideration of his trouble in catechising, instructing and hearing confessions of his family. The sum is greater or smaller in proportion to the circumstances of the parishioner. In the country parishes it is generally a shilling at Easter and a shilling at Christmas: some give half-a-crown, some a crown and some few a guinea a year'.[70]

Religious dues and services were one of the main items of expenditure for the lower classes in the first half of the nineteenth century. But the services of the priest were matters of 'life and death', and of all things, including food, an absolute necessity. Because of the high prices for their services, especially for the cottiers and landless labourers who so rarely dealt with actual money, it is not surprising that there were often rebellions against them.[71] All of the agitation was local and often depended on the character and charges of the particular priest, and whether or not he had been denouncing his parishioners for their involvement in secret agrarian societies. However, besides occasional conflicts most accounts indicate a general reverence and affection for the priest, and an eager willingness to hand over their hard-earned cash to support him in a life-style which, Connolly claims, was 'somewhere, but not very much, above that of the more prosperous members of their congregations'.[72] As Murphy points out: 'It was part of a resurgent Catholicism that the priest should be seen to have a social position and residence which would compare favourably with that of his Protestant counterpart'.[73] If having a son a priest gave moral legitimation to the new class of tenant farmers, having a well-housed, well-heeled, and well-mannered priest as your representative, raised the prestige of the whole Catholic community.

The general increase in the support of the Church was also reflected in a substantial growth in capital. The days of inconspicuous mass-houses down back-alleys were superseded by the building of new monumental, if not ostentatious, brick churches. Much of this building took place after Emancipation (1829) and was, at first, confined to the east and to the towns where the wealthier Catholic merchants, traders and farmers were able to afford monuments to their respectability. Between 1823 and 1852, i.e. during the time Murray was Archbishop of Dublin, ninety-seven new churches had been built.[74] The buildings were large and costly, but eagerly subscribed to. They were featured on the front covers of popular Catholic magazines, e.g., *The Catholic Penny Magazine*, which went into great detail about the opulence and ornateness of their interiors. The German traveller Kohl remarked in 1844: 'In many parts of Ireland the Catholic churches are now beginning to tower over those of "the establishment" . . . and all over the country the Irish Catholics are vying with the English Protestant in the zeal with which they build new churches and repair old ones'.[75] In reviewing the progress of Catholicism in the nineteenth century, O'Reilly estimated that:

In twenty-five of the twenty-eight dioceses of Ireland, embracing 944 out of the 1,085 parishes into which Ireland is divided, there have been built in the sixty-three years since 1800:

1. 1805 Churches which have cost	£3,061,527
2. 217 Convents	£1,058,415
3. 40 Colleges or Seminaries	£308,918
4. 44 Hospitals, or Asylums, or Orphanages	£147,135
making a total expenditure of	£4,575,995.[76]

If the Catholic church was the largest building to be built in the towns of Ireland in the first half of the nineteenth century, the convent was often the second largest. Not only were the nuns responsible for one-third of capital expenditure in the first sixty-three years of the century, they were also responsible for diversifying the institutional Church into hospitals, asylums, and orphanages. The above figures do not take into account the other significant growth in Church organisation, which was much less costly but of lasting importance, i.e. the development of schools. O'Reilly estimated that between 1800 and 1863, 2,990 national schools were erected 'without any government aid, and under Catholic management'.[77] This does not include the many schools such as those of Christian Brothers which O'Reilly estimated at being sixty-eight for the period, or the number of schools established by nuns, which Fahey claims to have been the same as the number of convents.[78]

Education

One of the important aspects in the emergence of the Catholic Church as a power bloc in Irish society was the control it gained of the education and discipline of Irish children from 1750. By 1846, the Church had won decisive battles which made it clear that it, rather than the English state or the established Protestant Church of Ireland, had moral jurisdiction over Catholic children and how they were to be educated. It had begun to exercise control in the state-subsidised, and supposedly non-denominational, national school system. It had vetoed State proposals to establish 'godless colleges', and was preparing to establish its own voluntary Catholic university. At the second level of education, orders of nuns and brothers, especially the Mercy and Christian brothers, had already built a reputation as the providers of a relatively cheap, well-disciplined, moral education which was to become all-important in the creation of a new rural Catholic middle class. By the middle of the last century, State supervision of education had given way to a situation in which the Church was about to take control of Irish education—and without much disapproval from the State. The main transformation in education in the last century was not just the dramatic expansion in the number of well-built schoolhouses, but that the State paid for them and, by and large, handed its supervision and control over to the Church.

The origins of the Church's domination of Irish education can be traced back to the penal laws. The numbers of hedge schools had increased rapidly in the latter half of the eighteenth century. The Relief Act of 1782 restored to Catholics the right to teach in schools. From then on, most of the hedge schools became known as pay schools and were linked into the parish system. The school was either set up and run by a priest who appointed a teacher, or if set up by a private teacher it was under his authority and supervision.[79] It is difficult to estimate how quickly the pay schools proliferated. However, by 1807, it appears that a Catholic system of education was fully established, even though it may have been under the roughest conditions. In that year, the Bishop of Cloyne and Ross reported that there were 316 schools in the diocese with a total of 21,892 pupils attending them.[80] In 1824, official returns estimated that there were 10,453 schools with a total of 522,016 pupils, 397,212 of whom were Roman Catholics.[81] Dowling estimates that the total number of schools under Catholic teachers was over 8,000, and of these no fewer than 7,600 were independent pay schools under lay teachers.[82]

It was the growing success of the pay schools which brought evangelical Protestant agencies and societies into the field of Irish education. Their aim was to spread Protestantism throughout Ireland by disseminating bibles into every Irish cottage, and by eliminating 'poisonous hedge schools' which, they constantly reminded the State, were hotbeds of sedition and treason.[83] These Protestant societies were the forerunners of the Society for Promoting the Education of the Poor in Ireland. From 1812, their Kildare Place Schools were part of a new State policy aimed at controlling hedge schools. They were based on standardised buildings, school-rooms and fittings, as well as standardised timetables and curricula. These models of time and space were intended to be the institutions in which Protestant practices and doctrines were to be inculcated into Irish children. But the Kildare Place Schools were based on the principle of teaching scripture without note or comment. It was this insistence which led O'Connell to break with them.[84] He was the first snowball in an eventual avalanche of Catholic opposition. By 1824, the Society had become, in Akenson's terms, 'just another Protestant agency'.[85]

The following year, a Royal Commission recognised that the

Kildare Place system had failed because the religious and moral instruction was not compatible with the principles and discipline of the Catholic Church. Nevertheless the Commission came out against denominational education because it felt that many of the evil habits and ideas which divided Catholics from Protestants would continue. It was then that the Catholic Church made its boldest move. In 1826, the bishops issued a unanimous declaration which stated that while they accepted the principle of a national school system, they insisted that: 'in order to secure sufficient protection to the religion of the Roman Catholic Children . . . we deem it necessary that the master of each school, in which the majority of pupils profess the Roman Catholic faith, be a Roman Catholic'.[86] The bishops also demanded that the masters who taught Roman Catholic children should be trained and supervised by people of the same faith, and that they (the bishops) should select and approve of the books to be used. What was remarkable about this declaration by the bishops was that it was unanimous. Secondly, it challenged the system advocated by the Established Church and the State's own commission. Thirdly, it occurred before Catholic Emancipation, and at a time when the Catholic bishops were not legally recognised as holders of their sees. The declaration indicated clearly, for the first time, that the Catholic Church had emerged as a power bloc in Irish society, and was willing to define and defend its sphere of power over and against all others. Most remarkable of all was that within the next twenty-five years many of their demands had been granted.

When it came to the actual formation of the national school system in 1831, the State recognised that the principles of the Kildare Street Society were totally at variance with those of the Roman Catholic Church and that: 'the indiscriminate reading of the Holy scriptures without note or comment, by children, must be peculiarly obnoxious to a Church which denies, even to adults, the right of unaided private interpretation of the Sacred Volume with respect to articles of religious belief'.[87] Their solution was a formally non-denominational system with religious instruction one or two days a week, either before or after ordinary school hours. What made the system denominational in practice was, firstly, that individual managers were not strictly controlled and, secondly, that because the vast majority of the school population was Catholic, the manager generally turned out to be the local parish priest. Akenson lists three main effects of the national school system on the Irish religious situation.

1. The Church was saved, in comparison, for example, with America, an enormous amount of money.
2. It placed control of a considerable amount of money in the hands of the local clergy. It provided financial patronage for clerical use, and brought control over valuable local preferments, such as the positions of principal, assistant, and monitor in national schools.
3. It reinforced the walls between the denominations.[88]

The national school system was a major blow against the Established Church from which the latter never recovered. It heralded the decisive and last battle with the Catholic Church for moral control of the Irish population. It was a battle that the Catholic Church won easily. In effect, the State deserted the cause of Protestantism in Ireland. Political and social control was of primary importance. It did not matter who did the moral training as long as it was done effectively. Even if the growing alliance between the Church and bourgeois nationalism became increasingly obvious, the State through various political strategies such as appeasements, threats and sanctions was at least able to stem the tide of change for many decades, and most of all, to shift the political struggle in Ireland from bloody rebellion to rational discourse.

Indeed it was partly because the Catholic Church proved so capable of educating and caring for the poor that English politicians became more willing to hand over social control of the Irish people to it. Caring for the sick, poor, and uneducated has always been a major source of the Church's moral power. In the nineteenth century it was the zealous efforts of priests, who came increasingly from the expanding middle classes, as well as the dedicated and materially unrewarded work of nuns and brothers, which was to prove crucial in the struggle to establish moral control. By the middle of the century, glowing reports were coming of the civil and moral revolution being achieved among the Irish by the Catholic Church. Fahey quotes many reports from those of school inspectors to that of a House of Commons Committee (1864). One of these concerned a school run by nuns in Enniskillen:

The nuns belong to the order of the Sisters of Mercy in which capacity they frequently visit the sick and dying belonging to the most destitute classes. During these visits they turn to good advantage the opportunities which occur of inducing parents, hitherto careless about the education of their children, to send the latter to school. But these poor children must generally be supplied with some articles of clothing before they can attend school, this the nuns accomplish by means of their industrial school.[89]

As well as their important contribution to education, the nuns also played a crucial role for the Church in gaining control of the health and social welfare of Irish Catholics.

Health

Institutional health care of the Irish population was not to become a central practice of the Irish Catholic Church until the latter half of the nineteenth century. When it did it was mainly operated by nuns. It was their pioneering work in caring for and nursing the sick poor which was to become the basis of the medico-religious jurisdication of the Church over the Irish population. It was orders such as the Irish Sisters of Charity and the Sisters of Mercy who, from the 1830s, began to establish hospitals and other institutions. The system of health care extended into areas such as special schools for the deaf and blind, asylums, industrial schools, etc. The efforts were emulated by various religious orders of brothers such as the Brothers of Charity, and St John of God.

There had existed in Ireland at the beginning of the nineteenth century a number of charitable institutions and hospitals.[90] The charitable institutions were small in number and predominantly Protestant. The hospitals, of which there was a large number, were mainly for those who could afford them. There were no institutions which provided systematic health care for the Catholic lower classes, and which attended to their spiritual as well as health needs. The 1838 Poor Law Act established a tightly organised administration for the relief of the poor, and subsequently became responsible for the development of a number of health services. The workhouses established under this act could not be described as hospitals in the ordinary present-day meaning of the term but, as time went by, hospital services were developed in them. There was, then, no general health, nursing and medical care for poor

Catholics beyond committing themselves to the workhouse. This gap was filled by the Sisters of Charity who, under Mother Mary Aikenhead, opened St Vincent's Hospital in Dublin in 1834. One could be sick and in need of medical care and nursing without formally having to declare oneself destitute, or committing oneself to a Protestant hospital. The prospectus of St Vincent's stated: 'They [the Sisters of Charity] have been, in fact, for nineteen years, visiting a class of sick persons who will not go to common hospitals; and they have constantly had the painful trial of witnessing their best exertions, though aided by occasional advice from medical gentlemen, defeated by the unpropitious circumstances of the patients, the want of wholesome air, and of those comforts and accommodations which are strangers to the abodes of the poor'.[91]

Although the hospital was formally for every sect and every creed, Mother Aikenhead was fully aware that in the public hospitals many poor Catholics were dying without the help of the last sacraments. She had in fact founded the first Catholic hospital run by Catholic nuns, staffed by Catholic doctors, and with Catholic priests in regular attendance. In other words, it was a specifically Catholic institution and although, as was made clear to one nun, 'prayer and little practices of piety were to be interwoven with the day's routine, the patients were on no account to be fatigued or harassed with too many devotions'.[92]

St Vincent's filled a gap, but long into the nineteenth century Irish hospitals continued to be dominated by Protestants. In many of the hospitals, positions were filled by friendship or the highest bidder rather than by merit; both of which militated against Catholics. Even when Catholics were trained as doctors, they were trained by Protestants in Protestant establishments. As one of the few well-known Catholic doctors at the time testified: 'There is no use in Roman-Catholics in Dublin pursuing the [medical] profession, unless they have a chance of getting those situations [medical officers], because if they do not hold hospitals in a large city, they have no chance of acquiring character; and, therefore, as long as such a system of exclusion exists, you keep Catholics from entering the profession.'[93] This was one of the reasons why Newman's Catholic university concentrated on opening a medical school, and why the urge to have a specifically Catholic system of health care persisted even though Dublin was already well endowed with public hospitals.

In 1861, the Sisters of Mercy opened the Mater Misericordiae Hospital in Dublin which in its accommodation and design was one of the most modern in Europe at the time. The nuns, through their dedicated and economically unrewarding work, provided institutions for the care of the Catholic poor in a Catholic manner, as well as places where Catholic doctors could be trained. The health and care of Irish people was to become a thoroughly denominational practice, and it was St Vincent's and the Mater which struck the first blow against the Protestant domination of the medical profession. The domination was to last a long time. The Dublin Hospitals Commission (1867) concluded that:

> In the hospitals which we have mentioned, with again the exception of Jervis Street, the medical staff are, we believe entirely of one creed, Protestant, and this is so, not because there is anything in their constitutions which requires that the medical officers should profess that religion, but because having been founded in the days when it was the dominant creed, the traditional practice was always in favour of selecting Protestants, while it must be admitted that until lately Roman Catholics did not possess the educational advantages enjoyed by the Protestants. It is not surprising that such institutions as the Mater Misericordiae and St Vincent's should have sprung into existence, for although the influence of religious zeal must not be overlooked in accounting for their origin, it is almost certain that the need for such institutions, as places where Roman Catholic medical men might look for the means of acquiring professional reputation, lent an impetus to the movement in favour of starting them which would have been weaker, if not ineffectual, without this propelling cause.[94]

The care of the nuns did not extend merely to hospitals. In 1819, the Sisters of Charity had opened a house for the training of girls for domestic service and an industrial school for wayward girls. The same order had an asylum in Donnybrook, Dublin and in 1866 they opened a home for the blind. In 1856, the Sisters of Mercy began a refuge for female prisoners of Mountjoy Jail, Dublin to conclude the last part of their sentence. At the same time, the Sisters of St Vincent de Paul opened an orphanage and a lunatic asylum in Dublin. Orders of Brothers also expanded their socio-medical activities. The Carmelite Brothers started a blind asylum for boys in Dublin, while the Christian Brothers opened a home for the deaf and dumb.[95] Robbins indicates that by 1864, in the Dublin area alone, there were twenty-four Catholic lay bodies or religious communities operating orphanages or boarding-out arrangements and that there were similar arrangements being made throughout the rest of the country.[96] In 1877, Frederick Falkiner, Recorder of Dublin, described the scene at Artane, the largest industrial school being run by the Christian brothers:

> Seven hundred children, happy, healthy and busy as the bees: with its dozen trades taught in the best methods by the best practical farmers: its youthful brass band playing national and imperial airs in a fashion which would be creditable in a regiment: its one hundred or two hundred tiny knitters making socks for the large household instead of festering in the slums: its groups of glee singers chanting the national anthem . . . instead of listening to ribald howlings in the Liberties—before such scenes political economy stands touched and silent, if not convinced.[97]

Conclusion

In this chapter I have begun to trace the origins of the institutional power of the Catholic Church in modern Irish society. This power developed as the result of the conjuncture of numerous processes and events of which, at the level of power blocs and alliances, the most important was the struggle for control of the Irish population by the English State, Rome, and the newly emergent Catholic bourgeoisie led by O'Connell. The penal laws can be seen as an unsuccessful attempt at the subjugation of Irish Catholics through State legislation. It was their failure that led the English State to attempt various experimental strategies to pacify and control the Irish population. A rigorous form of policing, state-subsidised emigration, and a decent system of Protestant education had all failed before the State realised, mainly through knowledge produced by various parliamentary commissions and committees, that neither it, nor the established Protestant Church, could ever carry through successfully the pacification and civilisation of the Irish people. It attempted to come to an agreement with the Irish Church to extend the newly introduced system of state-subsidised education for Catholic priests to a fully subsidised clergy. It was thwarted in this strategy, first by Rome which was extending its multinational control throughout various European states, and then by the emergent Catholic bourgeoisie, and finally by the Irish Church itself as it began to realise its new power. This meant that when the State came to implement its most successful system of pacification and civilisation, the national schools, it was persuaded to hand over much of its operational control to the Church. Although the institutional power of the Church had been growing since the end of the previous century, partly as an equal and opposite reaction to the degradation and demoralisation caused by the penal laws, and although the Church gradually began to gain control of the systems of health and social welfare, it was the fact that the State gradually conceded control of education to the Church which was to prove decisive in the moralisation of the Irish population. It would be wrong, however, to consider that Irish population as a mere pawn which the State handed over to the Catholic Church. The interest in modern civility was part of a much wider process that had been spreading across Europe since the sixteenth century. It was because an adherence to the Catholic Church became the means towards modern civility that the Irish became and remained legalistically religious rather than secularly civil for more than a century afterwards.

6
The Irish Civilising Process

Early Beginnings

It is necessary at this stage of the argument to move outside Ireland and locate the change in what Irish people began to do and say within the space and time of modern Western civilisation. Being an island off the north-western mainland of Europe, Ireland has been slow to incorporate many social and economic changes. St Patrick did not arrive until 432 A.D. However, he made an immediate impact and not only did Ireland become a major centre of the Christian movement in the sixth and seventh centuries, but it sent out missionaries to reform continental Europe. More important, it became a centre for the development of penitential practices. It was through these practices of private body mortification that guilt, conscience and the soul of the modern ascetic Christian were slowly defined. The penitentials introduced three processes which were later, in nineteenth-century Ireland, to attain a major significance:

(1) A tarrified system of penance which, as Spear points out, became the basis of a legalistic mentality which later dominated Western moral practice.

(2) A shift from Canonical, or public confession and penance, to a private relationship between confessor and penitent which increased the power of the priest, and inculcated individual shame and guilt.

(3) An emphasis on celibacy and virginity that made second-class citizens of married people who pursued the ordinary way of life because they did not have a higher calling.[1]

Controlling sex was not just another problem with which the Church had to deal. Its regulation was central to the Church maintaining its power. The penitentials were an attempt to regulate sexual activity among lay persons and to eliminate it from the lives of clerics, monks and nuns. This regulation was enforced through the systematic classification of sins operated through private confessions. The basis of the penitentials was to devise concrete rules of actions and a suitable punishment for each moral offence. Although the penitentials were placed in the hands of clerics rather than the laity they became, through the ministry of confessors, general guides for Christian behaviour. But it would be wrong to assume that penitential practices and sexual morality were imposed upon an unwilling pagan people. Engagement in these practices was undoubtedly part of the overall struggle to attain social prestige by appearing to be morally superior. Chastity was a means of controlling animal passion, and as Spear states 'a dynamic way of separating oneself from the surrounding pagans and proclaiming the superior character of Christianity'.[2]

Penitentials were to play a crucial role in the civilisation of Western society. It was in and through penitential exercises, among which the confessional was to achieve the greatest importance, that the Christian's soul and conscience were discovered. It was through a systematic classification and analysis of bodily, especially sexual, functions and activities, as well as traditional penitential practices such as praying, kneeling and fasting, that sexual instincts were controlled and regulated. The penitentials of Irish monks made a major contribution to the Christian Church. With them the Church was able to combat the magical, pagan practices which dominated Europe. But because the Irish monks' effort was a missionary one oriented to an export rather than a home market, and because the Church lacked any rationally developed organisation, penitential practices became intermingled with the pagan practices which preexisted them. This compatible mixture of penitential practices and more traditional pagan ones survived in Ireland until the last century when the Catholic Church, as part of a rigorous process of moralisation, set about controlling the practice and discourse of sex, and eliminating everything that was instinctive and pagan. In the intervening centuries, the Irish penitentials had been transformed and developed in continental Europe from a specifically religious practice into a more general, secular civilising process.

The Western Civilising Process

The Western civilising process was not simply some cultural movement in which people became more refined and behaved less like animals. It had to do with the end of the Middle Ages in which warriors and knights were the real rulers. From the thirteenth century onwards, there was a centralisation of power all over the Western world and the gradual formation of states. Instead of battles between warriors, there were now long drawn out wars between these states. But internally these states became pacified, and instead of power being a monopoly of the aristocracy and the Church, it became diffused among the lower orders.[3] The improvement in communications, especially the invention of printing, allowed the bourgeoisie, and later other classes, to behave in a civilised manner, very similar to that of the higher classes. The internal pacification of states, then, came about through a new, differentiated, rationally ordered struggle for power that was based on being civil as much as physically powerful. Being civilised and mannerly became associated with a disciplined control of the body. For a long time in human history this control was attained through external mechanisms based on physical punishment. Western civilisation and manners became most rationally developed when mechanisms of control were internalised, and physical control became based on self-discipline. This self-discipline was mainly attained through a supervision of the body similar to that developed by Irish monks in their penitentials.

The modern civilising process was essentially a secular movement which began when chivalrous society and the unity of the Christian Church began to disintegrate. It was associated with the growth of cities and the development of an urban bourgeoisie who imitated aristocratic courtly behaviour, not merely as means of legitimating and maintaining their own power, but also as a practical means of regulating commerce. As towns and commercial life expanded, the need for civilised, regulated and disciplined behaviour extended first beyond the aristocratic court, and then beyond the confines of bourgeois family networks. With the differentiation of the work and domestic spheres, trust—the yeast of capitalist development—became dependent not merely on who one was, but on a series of practices and conventions which convinced the people with whom one was dealing that one was a trustworthy person. A manifestation of this was the extent to which one was able to regulate and internally control irrational, animalistic drives and behaviour. To sell anything in the open market, even one's labour, began to necessitate a demeanour of civilised behaviour. The structure of power began to expand beyond a traditional dependence on possessions and position and involve a new element, the prestige that came from civilised behaviour. It was through social prestige that possessions and positions could be maintained and augmented. But social prestige was also a powerful end in itself in that it allowed the possibility of limiting what others did and said. Elias describes the process as follows:

> People, forced to live with one another in a new way, become more sensitive to the impulses of others. Not abruptly, but very gradually the code of behaviour becomes stricter and the degree of consideration expected of others becomes greater. The sense of what to do and what not to do in order not to offend or shock others becomes subtler, and in conjunction with the new power relationships the social imperative not to offend others becomes more binding, as compared to the preceding phase.[4]

With the beginning of the modern civilising process in the sixteenth century and the centralisation of state power, there was a gradual but relentless shift from direct, external forms of body control such as slavery, execution, torture and beating, to softer indirect forms centred on a control and confinement of the body in schools, asylums, and prisons.[5] Within the Catholic Church there was also a shift from more extreme forms of physical penance such as flagellation, to softer forms such as prayer and charitable works. Nevertheless in the same way that magical practices have persisted within the church, so too have direct assaults on the body as a form of penitential practice. Wearing hair shirts and body chains were still practised in Ireland until quite recently. (Blessed Matt Talbot who lived in Dublin at the beginning of the century was renowned for engaging in these practices. He was found dead on the street wearing a hair shirt. Body chains were found in his room.) Irish penitential practices still contain a high level of self-imposed pain. Every year pilgrims climb Croagh Patrick and walk through the rock beds of Lough Derg in their bare feet.

The modern civilising process was not merely a change in the way in which power blocs such as the State and the Church exercised control. It was a complete diffusion of power and the strategies and tactics by which it was attained. Once the bourgeoisie began to imitate the behaviour of the aristocracy, as a means of socially differentiating themselves from the lower classes and morally legitimating their possessions and position in society, there was an explosion of etiquette and manners. First the aristocracy sought new means to differentiate themselves socially from the bourgeoisie, and then the lower classes began to imitate the behaviour of both of these classes. In Western societies today this process of imitation has been accelerated, and mass production, communications and education have made it very difficult for the upper classes to maintain a different type of language, dress and manners from the lower classes.

There are three aspects of the modern civilising process which are important in understanding how it spread throughout Europe and the Western world and how, and in what form, it reached Ireland in the nineteenth century. Firstly, because modern civilised behaviour was essentially a new type of ethical behaviour based on internal control and an inculcation of shame and guilt about the body, it never lost its religious associations. Secondly, there arose a socio-religious interest, as well as a political interest in disseminating it as widely as possible. Not only did the upper and middle classes of society, as in England want to civilise other nations such as Ireland, they also wanted to disseminate civilised behaviour to the lower classes of their own society. Thirdly, the Catholic Church played a major role in popularising and disseminating civilised behaviour throughout Europe and the rest of the world. The Catholic Church proved to be, what Elias calls, 'one of the most important organs of downward diffusion of behaviour models'.[6] Restraint of the emotions and disciplined behaviour, which were a major characteristic of the civilising process, have always been a major characteristic of ecclesiastical institutions.

The French Connection

It is at this point that the French connection with Ireland becomes important. Although there can be little doubt that modern

Western civilisation came into Ireland on the back of Catholic morality, an innocent reading of Irish history would suggest that this morality was Jansenistic and came via France. In effect the situation was a little more complicated.

In the eighteenth century, a good deal of the education of French children was carried out by nuns, brothers and priests. Civil and religious training were seen as synonymous. What had started out as a secular movement was reintegrated into Catholic life in eighteenth-century France. Numerous books on civility and morality were written during this time, and were printed and distributed together with first instructions on reading and writing. Many of these books were translated and disseminated throughout Ireland. One of the main guides for the civil and religious behaviour of Irish priests in everyday life was a translation from a book by a Frenchman, Benedict Valvy. The Christian Brothers translated De La Salle's *Christian Civility* for use in their schools. Finally, and most important, most of the philosophy and theology books used in the national seminary in Maynooth were French. But the French connection extended beyond the dissemination of moral and civil literature for, as we saw in the previous chapter, during the seventeenth and eighteenth centuries, the majority of Irish priests were trained in French seminaries. Many of the nuns who came to Ireland in the late eighteenth and nineteenth centuries were of French origin, e.g. Presentation Sisters and the Sisters of Charity. Moreover, when Maynooth College was founded there was a strong French influence in its teaching and administrative staff. All but three of the founding professors were either French or else had been educated in France, and French became the customary language of the professors' dining-table.[7]

The importance of the French connection for modern Irish Catholicism is in terms of whether Jansenism was exported along with the personnel and the literature. There is little doubt that Gallicanism, both in its old and new Irish nationalist variety, dominated Maynooth until 1850 when Cullen arrived from Rome to push through his Ultramontane campaign. However, one of the questions which has beset modern Irish historiography is whether or not Jansenism was also imported. Connolly argues that the historical evidence shows clearly that the theory that Irish Catholicism had come under the influence of the Jansenist movement is without foundation.[8] Clark insists that at no time beyond a few isolated incidents, were Irish clerics influenced by Jansenism.[9] Keenan states emphatically that there were no Jansenists in Ireland.[10] Healy, the official historian of Maynooth, concludes that, 'although so many of our Irish ecclesiastics were educated in France during the eighteenth century, none of these who came to Ireland ever showed the slightest traces of Jansenistic influence, either in their writings or sermons. Nor has any respectable authority asserted, as far as we know, that the French professors of Maynooth were in any way tinged with the spirit of Jansenism.'[11]

With such clear enunciations about the course of Irish history one might wonder why anyone ever thought that Jansenism had been imported into Ireland. There are two reasons. First, there is a confusion of Jansenism with Gallicanism and, second, a confusion of Jansenism with rigorism or Augustinianism. Bowen states that Paul Cardinal Cullen, the man who dominated Irish Catholic church affairs in the nineteenth century, used the labels Gallican and Jansenist as almost interchangeable terms. Other bishops at the time also made this association. What emerges from Bowen's analysis is that the Ultramontane Cullen, along with his newly recruited allies such as Slattery, either unconsciously or as a deliberate strategy, lumped together all deviations from Roman orthodoxy. Cullen regarded Gallicanism and Jansenism as equally heretical because they were anti-Roman. Bowen explains further:

> The French Jansenists of the eighteenth century had long abandoned their early theological speculations, and from the standpoint of Rome their concerns were increasingly political. Like the Gallicans, they believed that bishops should have immediate jurisdiction independent of the papacy, that spiritual authority rested with the whole body of the faithful and not merely with the hierarchy, and that temporal governments should have complete authority in their own domain.[12]

Besides the confusion on a more political level with Gallicanism, there is still, nevertheless, confusion as to whether the moral spirit of Jansenism was imported into Ireland. Keenan claims that there was a Jansenistic ethos within nineteenth-century Irish religious practice.[13] Turner, however, argues that it is essential to differentiate between rigorism and the Jansenism which has been associated with Maynooth.[14] Healy admits that the tendency of the early moral teaching in Maynooth was towards rigorism. He describes rigorism as 'the moral system of those who draw too tightly the reins of law in restraining man's liberty of action: those who are inclined to make precepts out of counsels and mortal sins out of venial sins'.[15] Turner argues that this rigorism was not specifically related to France but was part of Roman orthodoxy. In 1796, the Congregation for the Propagation of the Faith warned Maynooth against 'the excessive and wanton liberalism of some in laying down rules of morals . . .'. On the other hand, Aidan Devereux, an Irish priest trained in Rome, wrote to Cullen in Rome and referred to a 'spirit of rigorism which has been introduced into the national seminaries by French Professors and their disciples'.[16] Larkin follows yet another line, and argues that rigorism was something instigated by the Irish bishops themselves.

> The rigorism that pervaded the teaching at Maynooth was also the result of the growing awareness on the part of the bishops of the need to meet the requirements of the Irish mission. The geometrical increase in the population after 1800 obviously required more priests, but given the arithmetical nature of the supply they must be better disciplined and more attentive in their pastoral duties. Given the launching in 1820, moreover, of the New Reformation in Ireland by the Protestant evangelicals or Biblicals, a more learned and articulate clergy was also required. Maynooth responded to the challenge, and the result of providing a better-educated, disciplined, and pastorally attentive clergy was to produce a morally rigorous one as well.[17]

On the other hand, Connolly argues that the severe discipline and rigorist doctrines imposed in Maynooth were not radically different from those which had shaped priests educated elsewhere.[18]

Accepting the theological and historical confusions and distinctions that exist between rigorism and Jansenism, it nevertheless seems reasonable to conclude that the former was an institutional adaptation to the latter. Connolly and Turner are both in agreement that the discipline and doctrines taught at Maynooth were, in Connolly's words, 'of a kind calculated to foster the most severe moral attitudes and a puritanical outlook on life in general'.[19] Turner notes that 'the priests who emerged from Maynooth, especially in the first half of the 1800s are credited with inducing an ascetic chill on the previously uninhibited and often Rabelaisian ardours of the Irish peasants'.[20] Connolly agrees with Humphreys that the Augustinianism, i.e. the religious outlook laying stress on such themes as the sinfulness of man and the innate corruption of human nature, can be detected in the religious attitudes of both clergy and laity in the nineteenth century. The whole debate regarding rigorism, Jansenism and Augustinianism comes full circle when Connolly insists that practices associated with these intellectual movements were to be found at a much earlier time in Ireland and in places beyond where the movements reached. He links the popular tradition of extreme asceticism to the penitential tradition. It was this tradition, he argues, which made the Irish priests particularly receptive to rigorist influences from England or the Continent.[21]

The rigorism which, with the new physical growth and discipline of the institutional Church, began to be disseminated throughout Ireland in the nineteenth century, was based on a far more rational and complete system of practices than that found in the early Irish penitentials. Regardless of its theological background, rigorism was constituted by a systematic discipline, surveillance and sexualisation of the body. It was these practices which transformed the Irish into a modern civilised people. The majority of the practices were instituted in and through the Catholic Church. Many of them were similar to the Puritan ones which achieved prominence in other Western societies in the nineteenth century. In 1849, Sir William Wilde wrote that 'the tone of society in Ireland is becoming more *Protestant* each year; the literature is a Protestant one, and even the priests are becoming more Protestant in their conversation and manners'.[22] This is a confusion of Protestantism with the modern Western civilising process. It was peculiar to Ireland, and it was to have a lasting effect, that the whole civilising process took place in and through the Catholic Church. Due to the absence of a native rural bourgeoisie, the priests and later the nuns and brothers, were the most accessible and acceptable models of modern civilised behaviour. Catholic tenant farmers wanted to be as civilised and well-mannered as the Protestant ascendancy which had dominated them for so long. But from an inherited hatred they were loth to be deemed Protestant by imitating their behaviour. McRedmond makes the same mistake as Wilde, i.e. he conflates the modern Irish civilising process, which was essentially European in origin, with an embodiment of British Protestant Puritanism.

> The God of the latter-day Irish was not in fact the God of Catholic tradition in Ireland or anywhere else. He was the God of Victorian puritanism, a British and Protestant God most unnaturally superimposed upon a Latin Church which, while unIrish in its externals, was unquestionably Catholic. In straight historical terms what happened . . . was that the stringent social norms of nineteenth-century Britain became entangled with a fervent and essentially non-intellectual form of Catholicism.[23]

The Irish may have wanted to be as moral and civil as the English; they may have wanted to speak, dress, eat, and generally live as they did, but they firmly rejected the latter as a means towards that end. This is the dialectical process within the civilising process; i.e. by using different means to become civilised, the Irish avoided becoming Protestant and fully anglicised.

The civilising process was delayed in coming to Ireland not merely because of its insular position on the north-west coast of Europe, but also for a number of economic, political and social reasons. Chief among these was the absence of any security of tenure for the majority of Irish farmers. It was only from the beginning of the nineteenth century that a substantial body of settled tenant farmers, i.e. with 31-year leases, began to emerge in Ireland. Although these farmers gained greater control of the means of production, it was the absence of a sense of security that prevented them from becoming disciplined and industrious. Another reason was the absence, due to the penal laws, of decent schools to which farmers could send their children. Finally, there was a lack of human and physical resources on the part of the Church, together with a lack of discipline and organisation among its own members. Once these inhibiting factors began to be removed and, in particular, once the English State developed a social and political interest in civilising the Irish, the process developed rapidly throughout the nineteenth century.

Civil Order and Social Control

The modern civilising process was a transformation in what people did and said. It was a transformation of life-style, customs and manners. It was a transformation of the body in terms of the mechanisms by which it was controlled. It involved changes in the space in which the body operated; from one-roomed mud cabins to multi-roomed brick houses, from sleeping with animals to sleeping only with humans—first with the whole family, later with one's brothers and sisters and, finally, on one's own. It involved a change in the manner of eating—from wooden bowls on the floor to pottery, knives and forks on the table; and in diet—from one consisting mainly of cereals, milk and potatoes to a more varied one including bread, meat and other vegetables. It involved a transformation of space—from open fields to the confined spaces of school-desks, from mass rocks and houses to ornate churches with pews. It involved changes in dress and language—from coarse woollen garments to manufactured clothes and shoes; and in language—from Irish to English. It was above all a transformation from open, passionate bodies to closed, moral bodies. In Ireland, priests, nuns and brothers were the main agents responsible for bringing about these transformations.

In summarising the decades before the Famine, Connolly describes it as a period in which a clear conflict arose between the code of conduct which the authorities of the Catholic Church were seeking to impose, and the attitudes and standards of behaviour of their congregations. Connolly sees three main areas in which the Church sought to impose changes: (1) traditional practices of the pattern and wake, (2) marriage and sexual behaviour, and (3) the problem of public order, particularly in relation to the activities of secret societies and local feuding factions. In effect, the three areas were closely interlinked, and involved a new supervision and control of instincts and passions. Wakes and patterns began to be supervised because they involved submission to passion, the former in terms of sex, the latter in terms of fighting (usually after drinking). The changes which the Church sought to impose on marriage and sexual practices were not prompted by high levels of adultery and illegitimacy but rather by an interest in instilling shame and guilt about the body. Not only was this a means towards the discovery of the soul, as the early Irish monks had found out, but it led to internally controlled bodies which, in terms of public morality, were highly desirable. Connolly notes that Irish rural society in the early nineteenth century placed little emphasis on physical modesty or on verbal reticence. There was an unambiguous sexual symbolism in wake-games and May Day festivals. However this openly ribald sexuality was accompanied by a remarkably high level of chastity. Connolly estimates, from a sample analysis of parish records between 1759 and 1860, that the proportion of Irish brides who were pregnant at the time of their marriage was about one in ten. In rural England in the eighteenth and early nineteenth centuries the proportion was two out of every five marriages. Official statistics became available from 1864. These show that the proportion of illegitimate to total births was 3.2 per cent, which was nearly half the European average.[24] But although the level of chastity in Ireland may not have changed greatly from the eighteenth to the twentieth century, this does not mean that there was not an inculcation of shame and guilt about sex during that time.

Aries gives an example of the transformation from what he calls immodesty to innocence. 'One of the unwritten laws of contemporary modesty, the strictest and best respected of all, requires adults to avoid any reference, above all any humorous reference, to sexual matters in the presence of children. This notion was entirely foreign to the society of old'.[25] Elias gives a further description:

> In the civilising process, sexuality too is increasingly removed behind the scenes of social life and enclosed in a particular enclave, the nuclear family. Likewise, the relations between the sexes are isolated, placed behind walls in consciousness. An aura of embarrassment, the expression of sociogenetic fear, surrounds this sphere of life. Even among adults it is referred to officially only with caution and circumlocutions. And with children, particularly girls, such things are, as far as possible, not referred to at all.[26]

In nineteenth-century Ireland sexual ribaldry was reduced from the physical to a verbal level. Sex became a serious subject and the Church developed a monopoly of knowledge about it. Shame and guilt about sexual practices were instilled in each individual, privately, in a hushed manner, in the dark isolated space of the confessional. Sexual morality became a major issue, but it was wrapped up in a veil of silence. When it was talked or written about, it was in a vague abstract formal language which prevented the laity from developing any communicative competence about it. The control of sexual knowledge was crucial to the maintenance of the Church's power. The humorous references and asides about sex and breeding may be understood as unconscious relief mechanisms from a rigid system of sexual supervision and control. Verbal sexual ribaldry, like some of the pagan practices, is a cultural residue of past practices. It appears, like many other aspects of Irish life, as ambivalent, and yet relieves tension from rigid norms of social conduct which regulate the relations between men and women.

The other area in which the Church sought to impose changes was in terms of what Connolly calls 'vile and wicked conspiracies'. It was not that the Church was uninvolved in political matters. As Nowlan points out: 'Politics remained sectarian and the chances of the clergy withdrawing from politics remained rather theoretical.'[27] The Church was, however, against the passionate, violent rebellious activities of secret societies such as the Whiteboys and Ribbonmen. The activities of these societies were an attack on its own political strategies and tactics, which were essentaily populist and democratic. Ever since 1825, when the Catholic Association had become a mass movement, the clergy had proved of enormous importance in the hard, slogging work of organising the people, collecting funds, arranging meetings, and acting as the literate interpreters of O'Connell's mass following. This was when the new Gallican nationalism began in earnest. There was a notable change in doctrinal emphasis; the sinfulness of particular crimes replaced the duty of unqualified obedience to temporal authority.[28] These particular crimes had often been directed as much against the Church as against the forces of the State. Attacks on priests were related to denunciations by them of the secret societies, as well as to the high prices which they charged for their services.[29] Garvin notes that the Defenders, another secret society, 'had a noticeable anticlerical tinge and was receptive to the ideas of the French Revolution . . .'.[30]

Secret societies such as the Ribbonmen were the violent tip of an iceberg of class, nationalist and sectarian sentiment which was floating in an ocean of Irish discontent. The struggle between the Church and the Ribbonmen, who were the forerunners of the Fenians, was one of obtaining control of the form and content of political activity. Even though there may have been class solidarity between the leaders of the Church and the secret societies, many bishops were opposed to the societies not just because of their violent tactics, but also because they were not sectarian enough.[31] This is the reason Bowen gives for Cullen's opposition to Fenianism. 'Religiously it promoted indifferentism, tolerating the faith of a Thomas Davis or a Charles Gavan Duffy, while it deplored the kind of sectarian division between Catholic and Protestant which Cullen so assiduously tried to foster.'[32] The Church, like the State, wanted to shift the struggle for the land and Home Rule away from passionate, violent rebellion to orderly, peaceful, legal and parliamentary means. The suppression of vile and wicked conspiracies was only part of a much wider effort to civilise the Irish. This gap between savagery and civility was clearly described by Dr Kinsella, Bishop of Ossory, in 1835:

> I must admit that it is in part true . . . The people has some of the characteristics and, unfortunately, some of the defects of savage people. This people has all the virtues dear to God: it has faith: there is no better Christian than the Irishman. Their morals are pure: premeditated crime is very rare. But they basically lack the civil virtues. They have no foresight or prudence. Their courage is instinctive: they throw themselves at an obstacle with extraordinary violence and if they do not succeed at the first attempt, give it up.[33]

Mechanisms of Social Control

There were three methods by which the priest acted as a civilising agent in Irish society. The first was his mere physical presence as a civilised, disciplined and well-mannered Catholic being. He was a model of morality and civility, a shining example of what could be produced from a tenant farmer background. He interacted with the poorest of people, bringing civility and morality into their humble abodes. The second method had to do with the transformation of the priest from a religious functionary who officiated at major rites of passage, e.g. birth, marriage and death, into a rigorous disciplinarian who through pastoral visitation and confession began to supervise and control all aspects of social life. The third method was the dissemination of a detailed body of Catholic doctrine and practice, first through confraternities and book societies, and later through schools, hospitals and homes.

The Church also had formal mechanisms which it employed to moralise and civilise the Irish body. The main one, in terms of the ultimate threat (in the same way that execution was the ultimate threat of the State), was denial of the sacraments and excommunication.[34] Excommunication as the ultimate penalty was effective in two ways. It made the victim into a social outcast which could have disastrous effects on a person's social and economic life. Secondly, it was a threat held over people which could be enacted at any time. To understand the power of this threat, which may have been as much feared as that of execution itself, it is necessary to realise the faith of the Irish in terms of their acceptance of the priest as the mediator between God and man. As God's delegate, the priest could practically ensure eternal damnation. Congregations were reminded of the pains of hell. Liguori provides an example of a hell-fire sermon:

> This fire shall torment the damned, not only externally but also internally. It will burn the bowels, the heart, the brains, the blood within the veins, and the marrow within the bones. They are tormented not only by the stench of their companions, but also by their shrieks and lamentations... The damned must remain for ever in a pit of fire, always in torture always weeping without ever enjoying a moment's repose.[35]

It is not possible to document how often these hell-fire sermons were given. However, Turner indicates that the moral theology textbooks used to train priests in Maynooth were those of Scarini which were modelled on the works of Ligouri.[36]

The method by which the Catholic Church in Ireland sought to impose the new morality and civility among the people was to foster a formal, rigid adherence to its rules and regulations. Priestly censure was to be avoided by a strict adherence to Church rules. It was these rules, and the legalist manner in which they were complied with, that became the foundation of priestly power. Garvin points out that various ploys were used by members of secret societies such as the Ribbonmen to avoid being excommunicated. One was to attend the sacraments of Communion and Confession after the passwords had lapsed at the end of a quarter and before accepting the passwords for the subsequent quarter.[37] Such strict adherence to the letter of the law was reflected in other cultural practices. Mr and Mrs Hall in their literary description of Ireland recollected:

A man swearing he would not drink for a month—he soaked bread in spirits and ate it, another; who swore he would not touch liquor while he stood on earth, got drunk amid the branches of a tree; another, who vowed not to touch a drop indoors or out, strode across his thesbold, placing one leg inside and the other outside—and so, persuading himself he did not break his oath, drank until he fell.[38]

While these anecdotes should not be taken to have been common practices, they do indicate   that aspects of legalism are closely allied to a ritual fulfilment of magical formula in which intentions and consequences do not play a part in the evaluation of conduct.

To constitute itself as a power to be obeyed, the Church had to break away from all informalities with the laity. This depended on preventing the priest from mixing religious ceremonies with social occasions held in the homes of his parishioners. From the beginning of the nineteenth century in Ireland there was a general differentiation of space, and power exercised within spaces. There was a differentiation of the religious from the domestic space. The ability of the priest to limit what his parishioners did and said came to depend upon him operating in and through his church rather than their homes. When Dr Walsh of the Cork diocese, writing in 1806, discussed the disadvantages arising from the custom of having stations in private houses, one of the objections, which in his view was of no small weight, was that the clergyman, 'by his uninterrupted intercourse with the lower orders of the community, may lose that polish which by education or observation he may have attained, and be by degrees totally unfitted for more select society'.[39] House visitations were to become a formal practice rather than a social occasion. The obedience of the laity to the priest came to depend on him getting them to come to his church once a week, and to confess their sins to him in church at least once a year. The transformation of space, from the home to the church, was a crucial feature in the new exercise of clerical discipline. This may be one of the reasons why so much emphasis was given to church building in the first half of the nineteenth century. But it must always be remembered that it was the laity who built the churches, and it was ultimately they who wanted to go to church and to be disciplined. The civilisation process was carried through not simply because of the new rigorous discipline which began to emanate from Maynooth, but because of the construction of churches and schools which provided the space in which moral discipline could be exercised. There is, in other words, a very close link between the construction of churches, schools, and houses, and the moralisation of Irish society in terms of adhering to the church's rules and regulations. But it was in church that most Irish people first learnt to control their bodies, and to behave in a civil as well as a legalistically moral manner. Etiquette and good manners became associated with going to church and fulfilling rules and regulations. Indeed, there were rules as to how people were to behave when in church:

1st. Persons whilst in the Church should as much as possible avoid coughing, spitting and all manners of noise.

2nd. Should be remarkably clean in their dress and person and avoid the slightest appearance of foppery and indiscretion.

3rd. They should look only at the altar or on the priest and recollect that it is to speak to God and not to man that they appear there.

4th. Whilst they appear in a respectful posture they should avoid any ridiculous gestures or forms.

5th. All who can read should use prayer books, unless when meditation may be preferable.

6th. Mothers should take care not to disturb the congregation by bringing children under the age required.

7th. On Ash Wednesday each should approach the priest in a respectful manner to receive ashes, and on Palm Sunday act in a similar manner to receive palm.

8th. Catholics should take care never to turn their backs to the altar when the Blessed Sacrament is exposed, but kneel in a respectful posture.

9th. Children serving at Mass should not be allowed to answer the priest in a hurried manner, but in an edifying way.

10th. Communicants should approach to and proceed from the altar, in the most recollected manner and also to and from the confessional in a similar way.

11th. It is an edifying sight to see all stand when gospel and creed are read and kneel together at the same time when they come to the words, 'And God was made man, etc.'

12th. Communicants should take care to hold the communion cloth in a proper manner and on no account run out of the church in haste after approaching the holy altar.[40]

Miller has shown that the overall attendance at Sunday Mass in 1834 was about 40 per cent, but that this varied enormously, from as low as 20 per cent in rural areas (especially Irish speaking ones in the West) to near 100 per cent in some towns (especially in the East). He argues that the low attendance had partly to do with a moral laxity, and says that in the West of Ireland there were obviously enough priests to say Masses if there had been sufficient demand.[41] Larkin, on the other hand, has argued that the reason why the attendance was so low was because there were not enough churches to accommodate those who might be inclined to attend to their religious duties.[42] However, these two explanations for low Mass attendance are not contradictory. Even if there were sufficient priests to say Masses, a regular, disciplined adherence to the rules and regulations of the Church depended on the availability of a church. The devotional revolution, and the development of a legalistic adherence to the Church cannot be divorced from the building revolution which preceded them. It is no coincidence that weekly Mass attendance in 1834 was lower in rural areas, especially in the poorer Western region, where there were fewer churches. It was only when the churches were built that the process of getting the people into them on a regular basis could be achieved. In this respect the devotional revolution, as described by Larkin, could only have been consolidated in the decades after the Famine when the building revolution had reached its peak. Once the churches were built, the people began to flock to them, not just for Mass, Communion and Confession, but for a whole host of devotional activities.

To encourage the laity, missions were held in nearly every parish in Ireland in the decade of the fifties. Pastoral gains thus made were consolidated by the introduction of a whole series of devotional exercises designed not only to encourage more frequent participation in the sacraments but to instil veneration by an appreciation of their ritual beauty and intrinsic mystery. The spiritual rewards, of course, for these devotional exercises were the various indulgences, which shortened either the sinner's or the sinner's loved one's time of torment in purgatory. The new devotions were mainly of Roman origin and included the rosary, forty hours, perpetual adoration, novenas, blessed altars, *Via Crucis*, benediction, vespers, devotion to the Sacred Heart and the Immaculate Conception, jubilees, triduums, pilgrimages, shrines, processions and retreats. These devotional exercises, moreover, were organized in order to communalize and regularize practice under a spiritual director and included sodalities, confraternities such as the various purgatorian societies, the Society of St Vincent de Paul, and Peter's Pence as well as temperance and altar societies. These public exercises were also reinforced by the use of devotional tools and aids; beads, scapulars, medals, missals, prayer books, catechisms, holy pictures, and *Agnus Dei*, all blessed by priests who had recently acquired that privilege from Rome through the intercession of their bishops.[43]

Larkin's argument that (a) these devotions were only introduced after 1850, (b) they were Roman, and (c) they were introduced mainly by Cullen and the other bishops, has been criticised by Keenan. He provides contrary evidence to show that many of these devotions were in existence long before the Famine, that they were French in origin, and that they were introduced not by bishops, but by the individual efforts of priests and nuns.[44]

The successful fostering of an adherence to the rules and regulations of the Church depended a great deal on regular attendance at Confession. The evidence suggests that there was a continual improvement in confessional attendance throughout the nineteenth century. Connolly cites examples of neglect to complete the Easter Duty and attend Confession at least once a year.[45] However, evidence from Dublin Diocesan Archives suggests that by the 1830s, at least in the Eastern region, this neglect had begun to decline. Parish visitation records for Arklow in 1837 indicate that in an adult population of 5,000 probably 100 missed their Easter Duty, and most of these, according to the report, 'have since contritely applied to be admitted to Penance'. Similarly, in a rural parish such as Ballymore Eustace with a population of about 4,000, there were about 10 persons who did not comply with their Easter Duty in the previous year.[46]

Connolly emphasises the central importance which Confession had in maintaining discipline and control of the laity in pre-Famine Ireland.

It provided both for a regular and thorough scrutiny by the parish clergy of the behaviour of individual members of their congregations and for an important personal confrontation between priest and parishioner, with the former in a position of unquestioned authority, able to interrogate, exhort or reprimand the penitent as he saw fit. To conceal an offence in the confessional invalidated the whole process, while a person who had not received absolution could not receive the other sacraments without committing sacrilege and risked damnation in the case of sudden death.[47]

Confession played a crucial role in sexualising the body. The confessional was where the activities of the body were examined and suitable penances distributed. The modern Irish Catholic soul became constituted through a discipline of the body created and maintained by a rigorous system of examination, supervision and punishment. The body was seen as a major source of evil. Under examination in the confessional, it was confined in a dark space, hidden from public view, from the confessor, and from the penitent himself. Sex became problematical and privatised. A sense of private guilt and public shame was inculcated through a thorough investigation of the penitent's sexual practices. It was through such an examination procedure that 'ignorant savages' were made to feel self-conscious about their bodies and, thereby, became constituted as moral human beings. Alexander Irwin provides a translation of the instructions issued to priests regarding Confession in the *Treatise on the Decalogue*, a textbook used in Maynooth in the first half of the nineteenth century.

Since the confessor acts the part both of judge and a physician, he ought to become acquainted with the diseases and the offences of the penitent, in order that he may be able to apply suitable remedies, and impose due penance, and lest a sin that is mortal should be accounted as venial, or the foul viper lurking in the deep recesses of the heart should not venture to put itself forth to view, he ought to therefore sometimes to question the penitents on the subject of the 6th (7th) commandment, where he suspects that they are not altogether pure, especially if they be rude, ignorant, bashful or agitated. . . . A prudent confessor will, as far as in his power, advance from more general statements to more particular: from the less shameful to those which are more so; nor will he take his commencement from the external acts, but from the thoughts. Has not the penitent revolved some improper ones in his or her mind? Was this done advertently? What kind of desire was it? Has he or she felt unlawful passions? But if the penitent shall declare that he, or she, has not felt them, the confessor ought usually to stop there, unless the penitent be very ignorant and dull. But if the penitent shall answer that he, or she, has had improper thoughts or irregular desires, the confessor shall ask whether any improper actions followed. But if the penitent shall confess this, the confessor shall ask again, what were these actions. If the penitent be a girl, she should be asked whether she has adorned herself in order to please the men? Whether for this purpose she has used paint, or stript her arms, shoulders or neck? Whether she has spoken, or read, or sung anything immodest? Whether she is not attached to somebody with a more peculiar affection? Whether she has not allowed herself to be kissed?[48]

We can see here how sexual shame and guilt, which were to become the basis of the modern Irish Catholic soul and the mainstay of the civil and moral revolution of the last century, were dependent on the construction of churches, and within those large, awesome buildings the construction of small dark spaces in which the penitent was confined and interrogated. But, as can be seen from the above quotation, the sexual moralisation process became centred on gaining control of women's sex. Sex was portrayed as a disease which lurked deep within the recesses of women's bodies. Unless it was controlled, it would awaken the most grotesque animal passions. It was only when it was controlled that the refined, delicate nature of women could be revealed. If the sexual vipers within women were awakened then all delicacy and civility would be lost. The Church was presented as the only means by which women could be saved from themselves. Sex was a sickness that could never be cured. It could only be monitored and controlled by the priest. It was such a dreadful disease that the penitent, like the modern patient under a doctor, could only be told about it in vague terms. Any detailed knowledge of the condition would destroy an innocence which held the disease at bay. It was through this detailed knowledge of sex, and the means by which it could be controlled, that the priest maintained his power, especially over women.

There were other methods besides Confession by which the priest helped instil a new morality and civility in the Irish Catholic. Sermons were an important method. The priest was one of the most literate people in the parish. Newspapers, while more prevalent from the beginning of the nineteenth century, only found their way into the better-off households. Consequently, the priest's sermon, which was usually given in English, would have been one of the main talking points in the local community. The priest talked about the meaning of life and its obligations. He developed a monopoly of ethical ideals. Through the sermon he transferred these ideals into rules and regulations. Liguori gives a sermon, which in terms of civilisation and sexualisation, is indicative of the new discipline and sexual morality which priests began to demand in Ireland at this time. In *The Education of Children,* Liguori gives a long and detailed account of the obligations of a father in raising his children. He ends with some disciplinary practices for removing the occasion of sin from the children:

> Fifthly, a father should remove from his house romances, which pervert young persons, and all bad books, which contain pernicious maxims, tales of obscenity, or of profane love . . . Sixthly, he ought not allow his children to sleep in his own bed, nor the females and males to sleep together. Seventhly, he should not permit his daughter to be alone with men, whether young or old . . . Eighthly, if he has daughters he should not permit young men to frequent his house . . .[49]

It may be noticed that the moral education of children in this sermon is taken to be the responsibility of the father. This was to change. By the end of the nineteenth century, and throughout the twentieth century in Ireland, the moral supervision of children became the sole preserve of the mother.

Sermons could also be used in a more direct manner to attain adherence to church rules and regulations. A strong sermon could be a public warning against an individual or group. It might take the form of a public damnation or make an indirect reference such as 'there are some here among us'. But the priest did not always have to enforce discipline and morality. What happened during the nineteenth century in Ireland was that priests, who increasingly came from tenant farmer backgrounds were, after a strict and rigorous training in Maynooth, sent back to their dioceses as exemplars of civility and morality. A priest may not have had the same manners as the top of the scale Protestant ascendancy, but he had by the beginning of the last century reached a level not far removed from that of the petty gentry, among whom he generally found acceptance.[50]

Besides the actual training received in Maynooth, manuals were written for priests which served as reminders of the duties of the religious life. One of the manuals was a translation of Valvy's, *A Guide for Priests*. This contained sections dealing with the priest's private life, and offered guidelines for: Care of the body, Rising, Retiring to Rest, Dress, Deportment, Meals, Recreation and Travelling. On deportment, Valvy noted: 'the Priest, if anyone, should be a person welcome to all good society: but to be faultlessly correct in matters of politeness before the public, he must put constraint upon himself to be so when not in company. Without noticing, we carry with us into society all the defects which blemish our private life.' Valvy strongly advocated that priests should have one or two books which dealt with the rules of manners, that they should consult these regularly, and that they should pay attention to the language and manners of those priests who passed for models of politeness and good breeding. However, the translator of his work was obviously so sure that Irish priests would not have any books on manners that he felt it necessary to include a long and detailed section at the end of the manual entitled 'Hints on Etiquette'. This contained subsections on etiquette at home, visiting, dining out, and correspondence. Attention is paid to the minutest detail.

> When conversing with others, care should be taken not to address the conversation to one only, and each one should be looked at in turn. But if one of the company be of much higher position than the rest, the eye may be fixed upon him more than upon the others.
>
> Politeness requires that, when visitors of either sex enter the room, we should arise from the chair and welcome them. It is still more polite to advance and meet them, and the compliment is greater in proportion to the distance travelled.
>
> When walking up and down with a companion in any confined space, so as to be obliged to turn every now and then, each should avoid turning the back to the other.[51]

Once these rules of etiquette are practised sufficiently, they become almost automatic actions. Indeed it is how automatically

one acts out rules of etiquette that indicates the degree of one's
civility. In Ireland, as in most other Western societies, rules of
etiquette have been learnt in the home. But mothers and fathers
must have learnt them somewhere other than from their own
mothers and fathers. Going back to the nineteenth century we can
see that a certain amount was copied from the Protestant gentry,
especially by those who acted as servants in their households.
Many rules of etiquette were also learnt in schools. But long
before then, and long after, the priest was an exemplar of good
manners and etiquette for Irish Catholics. An exemplar of
morality and civility who rose up from among themselves and with
whom they identified and regularly interacted.

Good manners were essential for the priest in the nineteenth
century if he was able to maintain respect from the lower orders
and if he was to socialise with the established Catholic
bourgeoisie. He had to maintain his status in society, and since he
may not have had many personal possessions (excluding
knowledge), he had to rely on social prestige, i.e. being a paragon
of civility and morality. It was only then that he would be able
successfully to limit what his parishioners did and said. As the
translator of Valvy pointed out:

The great majority of our Clerics come from families more or
less straitened in circumstances, and if the contempt with which
poverty and obscure birth inspire the higher circles of society be
not compensated by observance of the laws of good breeding,
and by a noble and faultless demeanour, what can we expect
from a coarse and boorish ecclesiastic save that he will be a
dishonour to the Church and an object of disdain to seculars?
And, to tell the plain truth, how can a Priest command respect,
who, even when in Church, cannot speak without shouting:
who, by his ungainly postures, whether seated or standing,
resembles a field labourer more than a cleric. . .who is untidy,
grotesque in his dress, unshaven, with his hair all in disorder?
Who is there but has a repugnance for such a person, and who
can doubt that such a one would repel the very people whom
he ought to draw to him in order to gain them to God.[52]

By entering the houses of even the most humble people,
sometimes to visit the sick or aid the dying, sometimes on parish
visitation, or sometimes on social occasions such as stations and
marriages, the priest acted as an exemplar of civility and morality

who drew out the best manners in the people. Parish visitation became a central aspect of the civilisation process in Ireland. It was through regular visitation that the priest attained a detailed knowledge of the moral behaviour and habits of his parishioners. Such knowledge was, and still is, central to the maintenance of priestly power. Valvy describes how the priest should proceed to record and organise knowledge gained from parish visitations.

> Throughout the period that you are employed in visiting the parish, take notes every evening on matters which have attracted your attention. Make a list of the ill-taught who have to be instructed, the poor who must be relieved, the afflicted to be consoled, the families to be reconciled, etc. . . . There are priests who have a complete classified catalogue of their whole flock, and who examine themselves every month as to their obligations to each of these different classes.[53]

A detailed knowledge of the behaviour of his parishioners became the mark of a priest who had organisational control over his parish. The modern morality and civility of the Irish people grew alongside the moral supervision which priests began to exercise over their parishes. Dr Murray, the Archbishop of Dublin, required before his visit to a parish that the parish priest 'deliver in writing . . . the names of the most obstinate Absenters—of Public Sinners in the Parish, with some account of their crimes respectively, and of Public Abuses, such as illegal combinations, drunkenness, violation of the Lord's day, Night-Wakes, or Public Dances'.[54]

The moralisation of Catholics, simply in terms of instilling knowledge of the rules and regulations of the Church, was too much for the priests, especially in a rapidly expanding population. The response to their need was the creation of a number of lay organisations to help the priest in this task. The schedules from Archbishop Murray's parish visitations give detailed information on the activities of Confraternities of Christian Doctrine in pre-Famine Irish society.

Confraternities, in the words of Dr Doyle in 1825: 'consist of young men and young females of a religious character, who assemble at an early hour on Sundays, and dispose the children in classes and teach them the rudiments of the Christian religion. . .'.[55] Besides their crucial role in moral instruction, members of confraternities also helped in assisting the dying and reading the office of the dead. Nearly all the parish returns for the early 1830s in the Dublin Diocesan Archives show at least one active confraternity, and usually two.[56] Connolly notes that the Irish Education Inquiry had found that even by 1824 confraternities existed in many of the towns and most populous parishes of the south and west of Ireland. There were strict rules laid down for the running of confraternities. Teachers had to confine themselves to the instructions contained in the approved catechisms and books, and were forbidden to give any explanations other than what were contained in them.[57]

Another method which the Church used in the moralisation of Irish Catholics was the dissemination of a wide range of Catholic literature. In 1827, Dr Doyle, Bishop of Kildare and Leighlin, established the Irish Catholic Society for the Diffusion of Useful Knowledge. It later became known as the Catholic Book Society. The objects of the Catholic Book Society were:

> First—To furnish the People of Ireland, in the most cheap and convenient manner, useful information on the truths and duties of the Christian Religion. Secondly—To supply to all classes of person, satisfactory Refutations of the prevailing errors of the present age. Thirdly—To assist in supplying to Schools throughout Ireland, the most approved Books of elementary Instruction.[58]

In its first year, the Society printed and distributed 43,000 catechisms, and a similar number of doctrinal manuals. The general agent of the Book Society, W.G. Battersby, established the *Irish Catholic Penny Magazine* in 1834–5. This was followed in 1836 by the *Irish Catholic Magazine of Entertaining Knowledge*. In 1836, Battersby published the first of what was his most successful ventures, *The Irish Catholic Directory*, which has appeared every year since then.[59] The Catholic Book Society and the *Catholic Penny Magazine* were mainly a response to the increasing number of publications on civility and morality many of which were objectionable because they were Protestant, and derived from England, e.g. *The Accomplished Youth: Containing A Familiar View of the True Principles of Morality and Politeness, Moral Essays in Praise of Virtue, A Catechism of Morality*, etc.[60] In effect, most of the civil instructions contained in the tracts were quite secular and were to find their way into the lesson books used in the national school system.

The final and most important mechanism by which the Catholic Church civilised the Irish was through gaining control of the education system. From its modest beginnings in the sixteenth century, the modern civilising process became centred on the education of children. The very early texts on manners, written in the thirteenth century, were addressed to adults. However, later treatises such as Erasmus's *On Civility in Children* (1530) were specifically addressed to children and youth. Elias notes:

> The standard which is emerging in our phase of civilisation is characterized by a profound discrepancy between the behaviour of so-called adults and children. The children have in the space of a few years to attain the advanced level of shame and revulsion that has developed over many centuries. Their instinctual life must be rapidly subjected to the strict control and specific moulding that gives our societies their stamp, and which developed very slowly over centures. [61]

In modern Western societies in which the bourgeoisie have become the dominant class, the family has become the main agent for instilling moral discipline and self-control. In nineteenth-century Ireland, the Church played a major part in the constitution and formation of a class of Catholic tenant farmers which became the dominant class in Irish society during the next hundred years. A major part of the formation of that class took place in schools where rude, ignorant and what many English commentators, considered to be 'savage' children learned to be civil and moral. In subsequent generations, when the initial phase of civil and moral conditioning had been completed in the school, the family, or specifically the mother, became the prime agent of Irish civilisation and moralisation. It was not until the 1960s, and the new dominance of a commercial and industrial bourgeoisie in Irish society, that the Church's control of sexual morality and discipline began to weaken, and the family, especially mothers, became increasingly autonomous vis-à-vis the Church and assumed greater responsibility for instilling morality and civility.

The Influence of Schools

The mass civilisation of the Irish people began in earnest with the development of the national school system in 1831. Although there were Catholic pay schools in every parish at this time, they were gradually supplanted by the national schools. The pay schools were uneven institutions. Much depended on the individual qualities of the teacher. There were few official school buildings, a lack of organised space, few desks, tables and chairs, little or no equipment, no standard texts and no rigorous timetable. Most of these defects were due to a lack of finance. When they were introduced the national schools were, in theory, non-denominational. Catholic opposition to them always remained strong, but because they were managed mostly by priests, who selected and supervised the teachers, the schools soon became to all intents and purposes denominational, even if Catholic practices and doctrine were not officially permitted. This was recognised by someone like Cardinal Cullen who remained a fervent critic of the system throughout his life. In 1869, he wrote: 'In the greater part of the country the schools are in the hands of Catholics, under Catholic managers, under Catholic teachers and conducted in such a way that they cannot do much positive evil'.[62] What was important was that the Catholic Church operated and controlled the civil and moral education of Irish Catholics. It was the priests, nuns and brothers, and the teachers under their supervision, who instilled into the uncouth, boorish Irish children of the nineteenth century all the manners and habits which we today regard as standard social practices. It was they who took over the task of making the Irish into a clean-living, orderly, well-managed, self-controlled, literate people. They were the forces which girded the bent and unruly bodies of the Irish and fashioned them into fine, upstanding, moral citizens.

Many of the original plans and objectives of the Kildare Place Schools were incorporated into the national school system. The object of the Kildare Place Society, founded in 1812, had been 'to diffuse throughout the country a well-ordered system of Education of the Poor, which shall combine economy of time and money, and bestow due attention on cleanliness and discipline'.[63] *The Schoolmaster's Manual*, used by the Kildare Place Society, noted that in order to preserve public order it was necessary

to establish those habits of thoughtfulness and foresight, which would enable the poor to add to their comforts, and thereby produce content;—to confirm habits of self-control and rational obedience, and thereby produce good order and subordination;—and by early inculcating the principles of honesty and truth, to prepare the mind to resist those vices to which they are exposed; and, in particular, to supplant that tendency to drunkenness, which is the dreadful but natural resource of unoccupied minds in the intervals of hard labour.[64]

The most important transformation which schools brought to Irish life was an organised sense of time and space. All over Ireland, these nurseries of the body began to control undisciplined children. They taught them how to operate when it was necessary to share confined spaces with others. It was that discipline and control of the body whose importance underlay anything else to be learnt, and still does to this day. The schools of the national system were of a standard design.

A more particular description. . .of the school room may be useful. . . . It was a room twenty-five by sixteen, and along the front were three latticed windows, about four feet and a half from the ground: the sashes of these turned on pivots fixed in the centre, so that they could be opened for the purpose of ventilating the room. . . . The desks and forms were each fourteen feet long, which accommodated ten children, sitting at their ease; the breadth of the desk was twelve inches—of the form, six inches; distance between plumb of desk and form was three inches; and breadth of passage behind form fifteen inches, making the whole three feet for desk, interval, form and passage. Five of them were placed so as to front the mistress's seat; besides which were two small tables with drawers, each seven feet long, where the children who worked at the needle sat; and there was also a space, seven feet wide, between the end of the desks and the wall, where the children could form in classes. All round the school room there were racks, for hanging the spelling and reading tablets. . . . In short, there was a place for everything and everything in its place.[65]

The main social transformation which was ushered in with the school system was the creation of these highly specified spaces in which young children were confined. What was central to the moral and civil revolution of the last century was that at the same time each day, and in the same type of regulated space, children gradually became disciplined by learning, saying and doing the same things. What was crucial was to produce a similarity of behaviour throughout the country. This was the essence of education as mass civilisation. It was a transformation, by way of confinement, of the space in which children operated. Given the space, the next requirement was to issue a set of regulations which governed behaviour in that space. These regulations were centred around the timetable and regular supervision:

The hours of school attendance are from ten o'clock till three, except on Saturday, when the school breaks at one o'clock.

The entrance doors are to be closed each morning at half past ten o'clock, after which no child shall be admitted.

The children are to come with hands and face washed, hair cut short and combed, and clean apparel: those who neglect this rule to be sent home and marked absent on that day.

The monitors are required to be at school a quarter of an hour before the others, to prepare their classes. They are to examine their children to see if they are clean: they are to see that they do not idle, and to instruct them to the best of their knowledge. They are never to sit apart from their class, nor to leave it unless permitted by the mistress, and they are to be accountable for all books, slates, pencils, etc., given out for the use of their class.

All play things brought to school shall be forfeited.

As the improvement of the child must depend on the regularity of their attendance, those who are absent three times in one month without leave, shall be struck off the roll of admission.

When any child has been admonished for bad conduct, the parents or guardians shall be made acquainted with the circumstance: if warned a third time, the child shall be publicly reprimanded, and, if incorrigible, shall be expelled from the school.

Every child who is considered able to assist in cleaning the school-room desks, etc., must remain when required.

The mistress is to furnish the parents of the children with these regulations, and it is expected that this paper be pasted in every room in which there are children who receive instruction in the schools, in order that these rules be duly observed.[66]

The systematic regulation of time and space was the principal feature of all schools introduced into Ireland in the nineteenth century. Schools reached out and brought the family into their

system of rules and regulations. The school required a transformation of the family. Indeed the transformation in terms of
simply getting children out to school everyday was an enormous
task and, regardless of the above rule, regular attendance was not
something attained by the majority of school-going children until
the end of the century. But it was not simply a case of getting
them ready for school.There was no let up from the rigid system
of supervision and discipline exercised in the school. Once
children entered the grounds, they came under the eye of
monitors, pupil-teachers, masters and managers. Their whole
character came in for assessment. Supervision and assessment
extended into play. It was in play that a teacher could establish to
what extent moral instruction had been successful in controlling
wild, uncouth behaviour.

> It is scarcely necessary to add, that all the educationalists of the
> present day consider the play-ground as essentially necessary for
> moral training. It is, in short, the best place for discovering the
> dispositions, developing the character, and forming the habits
> of the children.
>
>   The children, while in the playground, therefore, are never
> left to themselves. They are always under the superintendence
> of the teachers, and paid monitors; who, without controlling or
> embarrassing them by their presence, keep a strict watch over
> their words, actions and general demeanour.
>
>   Of all the regulations this is the most important. The play-
> ground is not intended as a place in which the children may riot
> uncontrolled. It is the school for moral instruction: and
> inasmuch as moral improvement is of more importance than
> mere literary information, there is even greater necessity for
> the master's presence in the play-ground than in the school-
> room itself.[67]

In effect, this strict supervision of the play-ground eventually
brought an end to play, and the rules and regulations by which
modern games are constituted were gradually introduced. How to
play the game became, and remains to this day a vertebra, if not
the backbone, of most methods of schooling. The inculcation of
morality did, in fact, extend beyond the playground into the
schoolroom. Indeed it was the central focus of the learning
process. The whole curriculum of the school was centred on moral

instruction. The Commissioners of National Education were delighted with the standard set of lesson books which they had ordered to be written and used in every school throughout the system.

> Every page of them is replete with the best and fittest instruction for those whose use they are designed. They teach children their duty to their parents, to their masters, to each other, and to their fellow-creatures generally. They teach them that they must control their angry passions, be kind to the defenceless, attentive to the aged, respectful to females, obliging to one another, and merciful to animals. They teach them that it is the will of God, that they should be temperate in eating and drinking, should avoid indecent language, and be modest in all their deportment. They teach them to be industrious in order to maintain themselves and aid their parents; to be frugal, in order that they may give to those who want, and that they may not come to want themselves. They show them that, if God has ordained they should labour, labour will make them vigorous both in mind and body: that if He sends them sickness it is intended to make them patient and pious: if He allows them to wrestle with difficulties, it is to improve their tempers and hearts: and that in all emergencies they should depend for their happiness first on God, and, subordinately to Him, on their own industry intelligence, good character, resolution and fortitude.[68]

The Christian Brothers introduced a text into their schools which was specifically designed to produce and maintain civility and morality. *Christian Politeness* was mainly a translation of De La Salle's *Civilité Chrétienne* which was one of the most extensively used textbooks on civility found in France, both at home and in schools, throughout the eighteenth and nineteenth centuries. By 1857, *Christian Politeness* was in its third edition. The book is divided into two parts. The first part deals with 'modesty in the exterior' and contains chapters on deportment, control of the head, countenance, eyes and looks, and the body. The second part deals with 'decorum of ordinary actions'. It has chapters on rising and going to rest, dressing and undressing, table manners, visiting, recreation and conversation.[69]

There is a sharp contrast between *Christian Politeness* and the book on civility written for priests. When dealing with etiquette for priests, attention was paid to the finer points of body control. It was assumed that the priest had basic control over his passions and body, but that there were social conventions which applied to higher society of which he should be aware. In *Christian Politeness*, which is for use among school-children, nothing is assumed and everything is discussed in detail. The detail has primarily to do with the body. This subject takes up the whole of the first part of the book. The layout of the book implies, as does the text itself, that it is only when the body is controlled that issues such as what is said, and how it is said, come into play. In other words, in social interaction what we do with our bodies takes precedence over what we say. Practice comes before discourse in establishing a person's civility. This is the fundamental characteristic of good manners. For example, as *Christian Politeness* points out, 'the head should be kept erect, it should not be turned giddily from side to side. . . . Putting the hand to the head, or touching the hair, particularly at the table, should be avoided. The ears should be kept very clean: but they should never be cleaned in the presence of others'. [70]

Of the first twenty pages of *Christian Politeness*, which deal with Modesty in the Exterior, twelve have to do with the head and the countenance. The soul is seen as constituted in and through the body as regulated by the head. A regulated head indicates a regulated body. The heart is seen as the centre of the body. A regulated heart is not controlled by passion but by the community. The soul is constituted in and through a sacred heart. 'The source of true politeness is the heart, in which there must exist a great degree of good will to men and a sincere desire to promote their happiness.'[71] Community and civil life are seen as founded on a non-rational commitment which comes from the heart. But the heart must be regulated in and through shared conventions of civility, otherwise it will be dictated by passion. In small isolated communities, these conventions are few and simple. In modern Western society, with enormous centres of population and increased geographical and social mobility, they have increased in number and complexity. The essence of modern civility is that the body be controlled by the heart which has been cleansed of its individual passion. This control comes from the head. Communication depends on facial expression, especially eye and head movement. It is in this sense that a civilised, controlled body reveals itself in the face which becomes the main sign of civility, above and beyond anything that is actually said.

> The countenance must, and indeed will, give expression to different sensations of the soul; but the man of sense and virtue possesses sufficient self-command to observe due moderation in any manifestation of his sorrow or joyous feelings.
>
> In Holy writ, the eyes are called *the windows of the soul*, because its various feelings and emotions are easily discernible through them. Their movements should, therefore, be regulated with special care.... To turn the eyes lightly from side to side, without fixing them on anything, is a sign of a giddy and unstable character.[72]

The body without a soul is an uncontrollable mass of passions and instincts. Through the modern civilising process it became an object of private guilt and public shame. It was to be hidden. Only the face, which is the mirror of the body, was to be revealed. Particular attention had to be paid to going to bed at night and rising in the morning for that was when the mind was dull and the body revealed. It is for this reason that morning and night prayers were necessary. One of the changes which has occurred in Ireland since the 1960s has been the control of passion in the face of a greater revelation of the body. Indeed the most modern form of self-discipline within Western civilisation involves a delicate balance between continually exciting the passions and yet, at the same time, exercising a rigid control over them.

It should be remembered that all the instructions contained in *Christian Politeness* derive from De La Salle's book which had been first published in France in 1729, over a hundred years previously. The obsession with modesty and the inculcation of shame and guilt, both played a central part in the manuals on good manners.[73] However, given the more explicit instructions which were contained in De la Salle's original French edition, one wonders if, by the time *Christian Politeness* came to be written, Irish sex had already been shrouded in a veil of silence and, consequently, the more explicit sections in De La Salle's work were deleted. In the original work, De La Salle refers openly to how one should behave when sharing the same room or bed with a member of the opposite sex. However, as the civilising process develops it becomes difficult even for educators to discuss such things without shame and embarrassment. In time this led to the practice of moralists not referring to the subject directly. Writing on chastity in 1815, Henry Tuke stated: 'I wish to say as little as possible on this subject, remembering that the vices alluded to are such as the Apostle says, should "not be once named among Christians"'.[74] Children were instructed about sex in an indirect and veiled manner. Soon a new generation of parents emerged who although subjected to the forces of sexualisation could not discuss sex since they had no communicative competence in the subject. Elias notes that

> As in the course of the civilizing process the sexual drive, like many others, is subjected to even stricter control and trans-formation, the problem it poses changes. The pressure placed on adults to privatize all their impulses (particularly sexual ones), the 'conspiracy of silence', the socially generated restrictions on speech, the emotionally charged character of most words relating to sexual urges—all this builds a thick wall of secrecy around the adolescent.[75]

This is not to say that sex was not discussed at all. In fact, there was an explosion of sexual discourse throughout the nineteenth century in Ireland. What emerged was a science of sex which became the 'sole' domain of the Church. Controlling sex, as a practice and a discourse, became one of the main strategies by which the Catholic Church maintained its power. It was not until the 1960s that a whole new public awareness, expression and discourse of sexuality began to emerge. The discourse and practice of sexual arousal contained by strict body discipline, which is at the centre of Western civilised behaviour, was mainly developed in Ireland through the media. The bonds of censorship which the Church had tied around sex were shattered, thereby allowing it to enter the market place of everyday life. However although there was a new sexualisation of the Irish body from the end of the 1960s, the communicative competence to discuss these changes in social and cultural practices did not come until the 1980s. Since then the Church's monopoly on discourse about sex has been broken; shame and embarrassment have wilted away, and many Irish Catholics are now able to discuss subjects like masturbation and orgasms, even on radio and television.

Conclusion

What priests, nuns, brothers and teachers began to instil into Irish Catholics was not much different from what had been happening to other people throughout Europe since the sixteenth century. The civilising process may have taken many different paths, and it may have changed greatly in the interim, but nevertheless one of its consequences was that eventually, even after almost three hundred years, farmers in the remotest part of Ireland, which was one of the remotest parts of Europe, began to behave in a manner similar to the aristocracy of the sixteenth century. What was different about Ireland was that the civilisation of the Irish body was a state-sponsored project, operated by the Church through schools. It was not so much that there was a native bourgeois tenant farmer in Ireland at the beginning of the nineteenth century waiting to be civilised, but rather there was a network of small tenant farmers who became bourgeois through a civility and morality fostered by priests, other religious and teachers. It was through the schools that body discipline, shame, guilt and modesty were instilled into the Irish Catholic. Through such discipline and control, successive generations of farmers were able to embody practices which were central to the modernisation of Irish agriculture, e.g. postponed marriage, permanent celibacy and emigration as well as a routine, regulated life-style which is central to maintaining production. However, because it was the Church which was the civilising force behind the embourgeoisement of the Irish farmer, and because it gained a monopoly of control over their bodies, secular civility became almost synonymous with Catholic morality. The Church, family, and community, with the priest at the head, became major power blocs and alliances in Irish society. Attaining social prestige in Ireland became reliant not so much on being secularly civil as being a good Catholic, i.e. adhering to the Church's rules and regulations. This was the foundation of the legalism which, as was seen in the second chapter, is still a major, though changing, aspect of present-day Irish Catholicism.

7
The Transformation of Irish Society

THE MODERN civilisation, moralisation and sexualisation of the Irish people in the nineteenth century was part of a much wider process which had been spreading throughout Europe since the sixteenth century. This process was delayed in coming to Ireland not merely because of its insular position but also because the penal laws, which the English State had imposed on Ireland, had the effect of keeping the Irish uncivilised and demoralised. It was not until the beginning of the nineteenth century, by which time the penal laws had become ineffective, that the State changed its policy and began to foster the civilisation of the Irish people. After the initial failure of various Protestant evangelical societies to carry this out, the State eventually began to hand the task over to the Catholic Church. One of the reasons the State was so anxious that the process be initiated and carried through successfully was the enormous growth in the Irish population. By the time of the first official census (1821), Malthusian fears had been confirmed; Irish population had grown rapidly to more than half the English population and one third of the two islands. Having a population of almost seven million uncivilised peasants living nearby, who had traditionally exhibited a violent and passionate hatred of the English, became a major concern of a state which was supervising the development of England as the core area of world captialism. It was for this reason that so many censuses, so many parliamentary committees of enquiry, so many commissions, and so many detailed reports were produced on Ireland. It was for this reason that the State tried experiments such as subsidised emigration and a national system of education, and gradually handed the job of civilising and moralising the Irish over to the Catholic Church, as soon as it was feasible to do so without raising too much opposition from Protestants, especially Puritans in England.

But the civilising process was not something which could be forced upon unwilling bodies. Regardless of the Protestant Evangelical crusade which continued in Ireland until the 1860s, and regardless of the fears which such crusades caused within the Catholic Church, the fact of the matter was that the majority of the Irish people steadfastly refused to be civilised in the same manner as the English Protestant.[1] Although one of the reasons why Cullen was sent from Rome was to stem the tide of English Protestant proselytisers, and although there were constant reports of souperism and mass defection, when the census of 1861 was published it showed no marked increase in the number of Protestants, even in Connaught where the crusade had been waged the hardest. As Bowen notes: 'If any simple answer can be given to the question of why the ICM (Irish Church Mission) crusade failed, it is that the movement was English, in origin, in design, and in the goals it sought to achieve'.[2] But the Irish did want to be civilised, not merely to show that they were as moral and civil as the English Protestants who had dominated them for so long, but as a means towards improving their standard of living. To understand why the Irish were so willing to accept the rigorous discipline of the Catholic Church, it is necessary to understand the social and economic conditions which prevailed in Ireland before the Famine and, in particular, the enormous growth in population from 1750 onwards.

In brief, Irish Catholics began to adhere to the rules and regulations of the Church as a means of restricting the growth in the size of their families and improving their standard of living. If tenant farmers were to prevent subdivision and consolidate the already meagre size of their holdings, they had to ensure that their sons and daughters adhered to the disciplined, celibate lifestyle advocated by the Church. An improvement in their standard of living became dependent on encouraging practices such as postponed marriage, permanent celibacy and emigration. This form of population control had been practised throughout Europe since the sixteenth century but, mainly due to the penal laws, the interest and means to embody them had been absent in Ireland. It was the rapid growth of the Irish population which led to the adoption of these practices and the formation of stem families

in which generally one son inherited the land and, as a consequence, three generations sometimes lived in the same household.
Coincidentally, the general abandonment of these practices of
population control was one of the causes of the growth in the rest
of Europe's population.

The Growth in European Population

The most basic fact of any human society is the number of people
who live in it. All the changes in society depend on population.
Without saying which comes first, when in the past there has been
an increase in population, there has also been an increase in the
standard of living in terms of production and trade. However,
there was a limit to the extent to which population could go on
expanding before the bubble burst. Eventually there were too
many mouths to feed. There was a gradual but general reduction
in the standard of living. The poor became poorer and unfed. But
it was usually not until disease and famine arrived that a balance
between food and mouths to be fed was achieved.

World population rose from an estimated 545m. in 1650, to
750m. in 1750, to 1,000m. in 1830.[3] In Western Europe there
were three major periods of population growth: between 1100 and
1350, between 1450 and 1650 and from 1750 on.[4] In some
countries the rise in population after 1750 was faster than in
others. In England and Wales, for example, the population rose
from 5.895m. in 1750, to 17.719m. in 1851; an increase of 200 per
cent.[5] This was higher than the growth rate in Sweden and France,
but lower than that of Ireland. The Irish population increased
from 1.690m. to 2.274m. between 1687 and 1754, but between
then and 1841 it rose spectacularly to 8.18m: an increase of 260
per cent.[6] When, how and why European population rose so
quickly has been the subject of major debate ever since Malthus
wrote his seminal essay at the beginning of the last century. To
understand the power which the Catholic Church attained in
modern Irish society it is necessary to understand some of the
causes of the enormous increase in population that took place in
the century before the Famine, and the role the Church played in
ensuring that such population growth did not occur again.

There have been two major reasons given for the growth in
Western European population from 1750 onwards. The first

emphasises the fall in the death rate which, while related to socio-economic development, was more directly linked to improvement in medical knowledge and public health.[7] On the other hand, it has been argued that the growth in population was caused by an increase in the fertility rate which was linked to an improvement in economic conditions. Habakkuk, for example, links the rise in Western European population to a dramatic shift in marriage patterns, away from the traditional one of postponed marriage and permanent celibacy, to earlier marriages and unregulated fertility.[8] This was associated with the break-up of households and the type of traditional society in which families and the Church exercised moral control. This transformation has been summarised by Peterson who identifies three main types of family in Western European history:

> In the *traditional family* typical of the pre-industrial period, the postponement of marriage plus the non-marriage of a portion of the population, constituted an onerous but efficient means of holding fertility in check. In the *proletarian family* typical of the mass of either rural or urban workers released from the prior institutional and normative restrictions, there was no effective ban either to early marriage or to procreation. Indeed, social control was often barely strong enough to compel marriage once a child had been conceived. In the *rational family* type, which arose among the middle classes during the nineteenth century and then gradually spread to the rest of society, a sense of parental responsibility reappeared, and with it a limitation of family size. The average age at marriage rose again, and later the same end was achieved with less privation by the use of contraceptives.[9]

The rise in European population from 1750 may be attributed to a decline in the rate of mortality, and a shift from 'traditional' to 'proletarian' type families in which people married earlier and did not regulate the number of children they had. Shorter claims that increased fertility was part of a wider sexual revolution which took place in the eighteenth and nineteenth centuries. This revolution was directly associated with female emancipation but had different effects among different social classes.[10] For the lower orders of society the break-up of the traditional family system led to an isolation which became associated with romantic love and, assuming that romantic love is directly linked to more sexual intercourse, this led to higher fertility. Among the higher orders of society, female emancipation became associated with women being less willing to succumb to the sexual bidding of their men.[11] Towards the end of the nineteenth century, this rise of a new order of middle-class women began to be combined with a decline in marital fertility which was associated with such factors as the increased cost of rearing children, the weakening of religious beliefs, the cult of hedonism and the spread of contraceptive technology. However, as Borrie points out, restraint from marriage continued to be a Western European phenomenon right up to the present day.[12]

The question is to what extent did these transformations take place in Irish society?

The Growth and Curtailment of Irish Population

The increase in Irish population which occurred from 1750 corresponded with a general increase in trade and prices throughout Europe from that time. The years from 1793 to 1815 were the culminating phase of a long wave of expansion going back to the 1740s.[13] Connell's explanation for the sudden rise in population is that the general, increasing prosperity led to a desire to marry early which, in turn, led to an increase in the birth rate.

> At the close of the eighteenth century, and early in the nineteenth, it was the practice for the farm to be subdivided, and for cultivation to be pressed higher up the mountain-side, and farther in the bog, so that children for whom neither Irish towns, nor overseas countries, had adequate opportunities, might settle near home. The son did not need to delay marriage until his father was disposed to relinquish ownership and control of his land, he did not need to accept his father's choice of bride as the condition for acquiring the means of livelihood that made marriage possible. If his father should refuse to give him a part of the family's land this was no insuperable obstacle to marriage: he could rent a scrap from a neighbour, and marry whom he pleased when he pleased.[14]

The desire to marry early arose, according to Connell, because there was an increased demand on the world market for grains.

Landlords, in order to increase rents and profits, actively encouraged subdivision of farms, and a shift from pasture to arable farming. This increased the amount of labour required in farming and, by producing a greater yield, allowed larger families to survive.[15] The potato could be cultivated easily in lazy beds in poor quality soil, and since a pig or grain could be raised to pay the rent, cultivation began to be extended into wasteland with peasants content to live in mud-cabins which were easily constructed in a matter of days. As Clarkson describes it: 'so enduring was poverty in pre-Famine Ireland, and so hopeless the future, there was little point in postponing marriage to more propitious times: two could live as miserably as one and children were both a comfort to ageing parents and labour for tilling the potato patch'.[16]

This explanation for the growth of Irish population based on a decrease in the age of marriage would appear to fit in with the general Western European model. Cullen, however, argues that there was no dramatic shift from late to early marriage in Ireland in the eighteenth century. Ireland, he claims, was unaffected by the demographic revolution which had affected Western Europe in or before 1500, in which the marriage age rose progressively to around twenty-seven for males and twenty-five for females.[17] He argues that the Irish marriage age had been around twenty-one years since the early seventeenth century. O'Grada has found supporting evidence from literary sources which indicates that a relatively early age of marriage was common in Ireland from the seventeenth century on.[18]

This is where the potato enters the scene. Even if the switch from pasture to arable farming, along with the greater subdivision of holdings and the adoption of the potato, did not lead to any dramatic increase in early marriages, eating potatoes did mean that the Irish were not only better fed but healthier.[19] Drake argues that a highly nutritious and regular diet of potatoes so improved the health of Irish women that their fecundity increased markedly. Moreover the dramatic increase in the use of the potato between 1740 and 1780 led, according to Drake, to a once and for all drop in the level of mortality.[20] Cullen, on the other hand, has argued that the potato was not used extensively in Ireland until after 1780 and that, consequently, its adoption did not lead to the growth in population, but that rather its use was a response to population increase. In Cullen's perspective, the growth in population from the mid-eighteenth century was due to an expansion in domestic industry and trade which helped to maintain a high birth rate. It was this expansion, combined with a decrease in mortality, which caused the population to grow.[21] Mokyr, in a more detailed survey of available data, argues that large amounts of potatoes were cultivated even before the 1740s, and that while population growth would probably have occurred in the absence of potatoes, they nevertheless allowed the Irish to marry younger and have more children.[22] However, a decline in the death rate is the key factor. Regardless of whether the Irish started to marry younger, if the reduction in the death rate were concentrated on the young (0–5 years), then a sharp rise in the number of marriages would have followed some twenty years later.[23]

In broad terms it may be said that up to 1750 the Irish married comparatively early and had a high level of fertility. Population was regulated more by famine and disease than by postponed marriage, permanent celibacy, or emigration.[24] When economic conditions began to improve, there was an increase in the birth rate. People, especially labourers and cottiers, continued to marry at a comparatively young age. They began to cultivate the potato more and rely on it as a stable diet. The change in diet was associated with a decline in mortality and an increase in fertility. There was a decline both in major famines and in outbreaks of disease.[25] This situation continued among the majority of the population until the Famine which, in three years, eliminated more than one and a half million people through death and emigration.[26] Most of these were from the labourer and cottier classes. The devastating effects of the Famine brought about harsh changes. The potato could no longer be relied upon; landlords who had been trying to push through consolidation of farm holdings prior to the Famine now found that the small tenant farmer was himself reluctant to subdivide. Commercially viable farms on compact holdings were the only hope of survival, let alone a decent standard of living. There was a growing tendency to pass the farm on to just one son. His marriage was delayed until the father died, or was ready to surrender possession of the farm. The dowry obtained from the incoming bride allowed one daughter to marry. The remainder of the brothers and sisters had the choice of remaining single or leaving the land.

This general description of Irish demographic history hides a number of sub-currents which are crucial to an understanding of the transformations in Irish society in the nineteenth century. The population did grow until 1841, but the rate of growth had been declining for some time. In the period 1753–91, the rate of growth of population was between 1.6 and 1.9 per cent per annum which, as Clarkson indicates, is very high and difficult to match elsewhere in Europe.[27] Between 1791 and 1821, the overall growth rate had declined to between 1.3 and 1.6 per cent; between 1821 and 1831 it was 1.4 per cent; and, finally, between 1831 and 1841 it had dropped dramatically to .63 per cent.[28] There is even some evidence to suggest that the population had actually begun to decline in the 1840s before the Famine struck. From his analysis of the population changes in the Trinity College Estates 1841–1843, Carney concludes that the population slightly decreased in absolute terms before the onset of the Famine.[29] If the rate of population growth declined between 1821 and 1841 and, possibly, actual numbers declined in the years immediately before the Famine, this indicates that, notwithstanding minor outbreaks of famine and disease, some measures of population control began to be exercised in Ireland from 1820 on. I will now examine how those practices of population control, traditionally associated with the stem-family system, came to be embodied and maintained within the Irish population.[30]

Emigration

The Battle of Waterloo (1815) and the end of the Napoleonic wars were the whip which forced many Irish into changing their habits. The decline in economic prosperity, associated with the end of a war economy and the inability of a cottage-based industry to compete with the factories of Britain, prompted many Irish people to do what the English State had tried to force them to do, i.e. to emigrate *en masse*. More than one and a half million people emigrated from Ireland before the Famine.[31] There were 801,000 emigrants reported during the Famine, and over a million in the five years following it.[32] Emigration continued to be Ireland's main form of population control right up to the 1960s. In the 120 years from 1841 Ireland had the highest rate of emigration in Western Europe. Without emigration there would have been a natural increase in the population during this time, when in fact it was declining rapidly. Between 1871 and 1901, 1.5m. people left Ireland, and a similar number (1.6m.) left between 1901 and 1966.[33]

Kennedy has made some important points concerning the pattern of emigration. Overall, but especially from 1885, there were more female emigrants than male. Female emigration occurred in a steady stream, mainly to urban areas in America in the nineteenth century, and Britain in the twentieth century. There were greater fluctuations in male emigration which increased when the switch from tillage to pasture farming gathered momentum; when labour-saving devices such as the horse and the tractor were introduced; and when there were no wars to be fought. In other words, it was a more common and expected practice for females to emigrate. Males were inclined to wait around more. This was linked to the practice of the father not naming the inheriting son until quite near the end of his life. Consequently, because emigration among females was higher, permanent celibacy was more common among Irish males. Both of these trends are the reverse of the general Western European pattern.[34]

While this interpretation of the emigration data for Ireland is acceptable, Kennedy assumes, under an implicit rational economic model of man, that all those who emigrated did so voluntarily as a means of raising their standard of living. This is an over-simplified explanation. It was in the economic interests of those who were to remain on the farm that all unnecessary labour, especially daughters, emigrate if they did not intend to remain single. This was crucial both for those smaller farmers who wanted to sell up, and the bigger farmers who wanted to raise their standard of living by introducing labour-saving techniques. This is not to suggest that sons and daughters were thrown out. It is to argue that emigration did not always occur spontaneously, and that in many cases those who did go, had to be persuaded or coaxed into doing so. As we shall see in the next chapter, present ethnographic evidence suggests that mothers raised many of their children, especially daughters, in the expectation that they would emigrate. In this respect, the traditional notion of Irish mothers raising their children for emigration is correct. It could be that the objective was to obtain emigrant remittances—the money sent home by sons, daughters and relatives who had emigrated. However, the question that Irish historiography has to answer is not only why did mothers continue to engage in the practice of rearing children for export but, when necessary, how did they manage to persuade most of their children to emigrate or, if they stayed at home, to delay marriage or not to marry at all?

Even if sons and daughters decided not to emigrate but to stay on the farm, the interest in raising the general standard of living and developing the practices associated with the stem-family system meant that the inheriting son, and the daughter who was to get a dowry, would have at least to postpone marriage, while the others who resisted emigration could not marry at all. Again it should not be assumed that postponed marriage and permanent celibacy were practices which were chosen voluntarily. It would be naïve to think that the urge to marry early, so common among the Irish in previous generations, was suddenly and easily transformed into an urge not to marry. The successful acceptance of postponed marriage and permanent celibacy were dependent on the new discipline and sexual morality which were brought to bear on the body externally through surveillance and schooling, and internally through the creation of shame and guilt about sex. Without the new rigorism of the Catholic Church, imported by the priests into schools and homes, there could not have been the successful embodiment of postponed marriage and permanent celibacy which characterised social life in Ireland in the generations after the Famine.

Postponed Marriage and Permanent Celibacy

It was not until after the Famine that delaying marriage and remaining single became common practices among the Irish. However, this does not mean that such practices, as well as stem families, did not exist prior to 1845. They clearly did. The overall or 'crude' marriage rate fell from 6.0 per thousand in 1830, to 3.8 per thousand in 1844. This is the opposite to what one would expect, for as Crotty notes: 'In a population growing younger with a large number of people in the marrying age group, it is to be expected that the crude marriage rate would be increasing, and that possibly the average age at marriage would be falling.'[35] Drake claims from an analysis of 1830 marriage statistics that the age of marriage in the generation preceding the Famine was much higher than previously supposed.[36] Lee points out that it is a mistake to generalise from a particular class to the whole of pre-Famine Irish society, and that the age of marriage among cottiers and labourers continued to be low right up to, and even after the Famine.[37] In other words, from a couple of decades before the Famine, although there may have been a shift to postponed marriage among a new middle class of tenant farmers, nevertheless labourers and cottiers, who formed the majority of the population, continued to marry early as they had always done.

By 1841, the level of postponed marriage among males in Ireland was 43%, which was 6% higher than it was in England and Wales in 1851. The level among Irish females in 1841 was 28%, which was 5% higher than it was in England and Wales in 1851. Although the Irish were new to the practices of postponing marriage or not marrying at all, they became so good at them that within the space of a hundred years that they had become the most extreme example of the general European pattern. In 1936, 74% of males and 55% of females aged 25–34 years were single. In the same year, 29% of males and 24% of females aged 45 years and over were single. This compares, for example, with a postponed marriage rate (for the same year) of 17% for French males and 15% for French females; and a permanent celibacy rate of 8% (males) and 10% (females).[38]

In his explanation of why the Irish delayed marriage, or did not marry at all, Kennedy rejects the notion, which he associates with Connell, that rigorous Catholic practices and beliefs instilled a fear of sex and degraded the status of marriage compared to celibacy. He argues that the Church never condemned sex as immoral and that during the nineteenth century early marriage was encouraged by the Church as a deterrent to immorality. Moreover, he argues, history shows permanent celibacy to be equally prevalent among non-Catholics.[39] His own thesis is that postponed marriage and permanent celibacy were the means which individuals, mainly men, chose to raise their standard of living. 'These persons did not marry because they could not support a family *at the same level of living* which they shared as a member of a landholding family'.[40] He points out that the Catholic Church was strongly opposed to married women working, and since there was a permissive attitude to single working women, marriage often meant two adults living together on one income where, previously, two had been living separately on two incomes.[41] When Kennedy tries to explain why the Irish disregarded the Church's teaching on early marriage and yet adhered to its teaching about married women working, he points to dominant cultural beliefs, e.g. a working wife is an indication of the failure of the husband, and available jobs should go to married men first.[42] This is where Kennedy's argument that the special character of present-day Irish Catholicism is the result and not the cause of a high proportion of single persons in the Irish population, breaks down. It is not a question of whether one caused the other, but rather, in a reproductive process, how one maintained the other. The family is at the heart of Irish social reproduction. If mothers had not stayed at home and had gone out to work, the very means by which postponed marriage and permanent celibacy were maintained would have been threatened. The mother staying at home was central to getting the sons and daughters to adhere to the rules and regulations of the Church, and at the same time to preventing them from getting into situations in which they may have had to marry. For, as Kennedy notes himself: 'if one of the unmarried relatives married and set up a second household on the same farm, he would be in effect reducing the standard of living of the other persons dependent on the holding to a level below the acceptable minimum'. The Catholic Church's teachings, especially those on sexual morality, were the means by which the emergent stem family kept its sons and daughters from marrying, and thereby increased its standard of living. The Protestant Church provided similar means for Protestants.[43]

Finally, Kennedy's claim that the Church encouraged early marriage throughout the nineteenth century needs investigation. The only primary source which he cites for this claim is the twentieth-century bishop of Cork, Dr Lucey's statement that 'late marriage, particularly if so late as to entail a small family or none at all, is undesirable and in a very real sense unnatural as a population practice'.[44] There is some evidence that indicates that up to 1825 the clergy might have encouraged marriage since it was among their principal sources of income.[45] However, since the number of priests from a tenant farmer background increased, it is more than likely that they too recognised the detrimental effect that early and prolific marriage was having on Irish rural life. Connell suggests that 'many a priest's attitude to marriage, whatever its veneer of learning, was that of the peasant society from which he sprang'. He goes on to argue, from a survey of late nineteenth-century literary sources, that for most priests' parents, the purpose of marriage was seen mainly in terms of ensuring labour for the land and an heir for the family. Thus 'barring a parent's premature death or incapacity, every child was wise to postpone it [marriage] and not a few to forgo it altogether'.[46] The moral rigorism which the Church brought to bear on nineteenth-century Ireland was the most persuasive and the most pervasive of the agencies which stemmed the passions of the Irish and reconciled the young to non-marriage. It is important in this respect to realise that, contrary to what Kennedy suggets, Connell did not see the Church as the cause of delayed marriage and non-marriage, but rather as an agency, i.e. a means to the end of consolidating the size of the farm and improving the standard of living.

The question still remains as to how postponed marriage and permanent celibacy were maintained in everyday life. It is too simple to think that a new economic man or woman rose automatically like an invisible hand within Irish families, and was maintained by adopting existing Catholic practices and beliefs. Postponed marriage and permanent celibacy involved dramatic changes in lifestyle which were unlikely to have come easily. These practices required a whole new discipline of the body which began to be learnt among Catholics from the beginning of the nineteenth century. It was first introduced in the Catholic pay schools and confraternities, but these were ineffective because they had no systematic organisation and regulation of time and space. It was more successfully inculcated in the thousands of schools which sprang up around the country during the rest of the century. It was maintained through a system of surveillance which extended beyond the school, into the family, and, finally, into the wider community. The school, the family, and the community began to supervise the activities of girls and boys.

Even allowing for the possibility that the Church and school did an excellent job in instilling sexual morality and discipline into Irish bodies, and that the process spread slowly throughout the country, there is still the problem of how conformity was ensured in everyday life. It was not that the Church just poured beliefs and practices into the minds and bodies of Irish children and that they were then set on the right path for life. The shame and guilt about the body, created through confession, sermons, and in the schools, needed to be maintained in everyday social relations. The primary mechanisms undoubtedly operated within the family. But if these strategies of power which limited what boys and girls did and said were to be maintained successfully, there needed to be mechanisms of control within the wider community. Young men and women had to be discouraged from marrying. Marriage had to be portrayed as something to be avoided. Just how successful the community became in fostering such a perspective is difficult to assess. However, some insight can be gauged from McNabb's description of Limerick in the 1950s and 1960s:

> The concensus of opinion seems to be that in the course of time one marries, just as in the course of time one grows old, and that as old age is a limitation of life, a narrowing of one's sphere of activity, so marriage is also an inevitable limitation. The community is not opposed to marriage ... but each individual avoids it as long as possible, just as one tries to avoid old age. Where such an attitude to marriage reigns, the institution has low status. It may be a personal necessity but it is not a social ideal, nor is it a positive goal for the majority of the community.[47]

This indicates how successful the community became in reinforcing a negative perspective on marriage among young people, but it still does not tell us anything about the practices or mechanisms by which this perspective was maintained. While this area of Irish social history has yet to be investigated, there is some evidence about one of the major mechanisms—the bachelor drinking group.

The Bachelor Drinking Group

It is not certain when the bachelor drinking group first emerged in Ireland. Stivers, who has given a detailed account of the group, suggests that it arose between 1840 and 1870. The male drinking group is not peculiar to Ireland. It has a long history and is strongly linked to traditional European marriage patterns and the stem-family system. However, like permanent celibacy itself, once it took root, the Irish became the most extreme example in Western Europe.[48]

The bachelor drinking group was a power alliance which grew up among Irish males as a means of maintaining their independence of marriage and women. It was an alliance often founded on the relationship between sons and their maternal uncles, and equally often fostered if not directed by the mother. Since, from 1840 on, more and more males had to postpone or delay marriage, it was in their interests, as well as the interests of their family, that they ally themselves with this group. Consequently, the all-male group, in Stivers's terms, 'functioned to make palatable the system of single inheritance, few and late marriages, and chastity to young males not naturally inclined toward delayed gratification. Older males socialised younger males into the bachelor group traditions, attitudes and norms that served to elevate the unmarried state at the expense of the married'.[49]

As much as the Church and school served to develop a rigid system of sexual morality, the pub, in later life, served to maintain this morality, albeit in a more convivial but nevertheless highly ritualistic and disciplined manner. The pub became the place where men displaced their sexual frustration through a repetitive compulsive pattern of drinking. If the school was the penitential house which characterised the transformation of Irish society in the first half of the nineteenth century, the pub became a type of perpetual secondary school for males. Even to this day, Irish towns are characterised by the number of small pubs dotted along their main streets. Pubs were traditionally male sanctuaries. It has only been in the last ten years, with the spread of the sexual revolution and female liberation, that women are to be seen in these dark holes. Throughout the last century, as the differentiation of the work and domestic spheres took place, and as women through their alliance with priests took control of the home, men—not just bachelors—began to congregate in pubs. Stivers argues that this was crucial to maintaining the religiously inspired segregation of men and women which even marriage did not break down. Moreover, to make the celibate state attractive it was necessary that married men continue their bachelor group activities. It is important to realise that the male drinking group was not some spontaneous functional response to new needs. It arose in and through a struggle for power. Inasmuch as the home became the space in which women exercised control, the fields and the pub became the spaces in which males exercised their power. As much as there was, in the increasing rationalisation and differentiation of the spheres of Irish social life, a time and place for everything, there was a time and place for males in the pub.[50]

As Irish life became routinised and disciplined, it also became ritualistic and legalistic. The shift to institutional religious behaviour was a major characteristic of the nineteenth century. This was reflected in other aspects of social and cultural life. Drinking in the pubs became not so much a festive event as a ritualistic, almost dutiful activity. It came to involve a type of ethical behaviour in which there are general rules which may vary from group to group and which are open to interpretation—for example, whether or not singing or card-playing is allowed. But there are also specific regulations to which everyone is expected to conform. Irish pub life has been traditionally associated with the rounds system of drinking. There is a highly complicated but unwritten code of regulations pertaining to this system.

Drinking became a ritual practice that many males embraced in order to be considered and treated the same as other males. Buying a round of drinks, in the order of one's turn, was the social practice by which the male drinking group was established and maintained. Buying out of turn, whether it was to get home, to go to work, or because one had a higher position or class, was unacceptable. Once a drink was offered, there was an obligation to accept it.[51]

Now while much of the rounds system corresponds to the intricate rules and regulations which pertain to all gift relationships, a full understanding of the system can only be attained by placing it within the overall Irish social context. The bachelor drinking group is not constituted solely in and through a social exchange of drinks.[52] It is developed within a much wider network of social relations; not simply in terms of women and the home, but also in terms of the Church—since, while in the pub, men escaped from the moral supervision of priests and women. Moreover, even within the group, social exchange is not so much an end in itself as a means by which individuals can attain social prestige and, thereby, limit what other members do and say.

It is only by fully accepting the social and cultural practices associated with drinking that a member can attain social prestige within the group. This prestige is quite independent of a member's formal position or occupation (political power) in the outside society, or his possessions (class). Male prestige is often attained by what a man does and says within the legalistic confines of the round system. There is, for example, the need for self-control. A man who cannot hold his drink, in terms of either being physically sick, or losing control of his passions, will rarely attain social prestige within the group. As Stivers points out, prestige accrues with the ability to consume alcoholic beverages frequently, for extended periods of time and with little outward display of intoxication.[53] Peillon has indicated that the highly legalistic pattern of Irish drinking, in which extreme control is exercised over the body and the passions, is in contrast to the general European pattern in which drinking is associated with festivity and letting go; with mocking and breaking the rules by which people are limited and controlled.[54]

But although this analysis helps to explain how a male power alliance was maintained within the pub, it does not explain how the alliance limited the practices of its members outside the pub. This is particularly important in terms of maintaining its members as desexualised beings, both inside and outside of marriage. This process of desexualisation was linked not just to a surrender to the group, but to the establishment and maintenance of an inhibition of creativity and achievement. Just as the group depended on its members staying together and not going off with women, it also depended on its members not getting high and mighty notions that they were above the group, or capable of being independent of it. Such notions would be a threat to the survival of the alliance. One of the mechanisms by which they were suppressed was through a ritual put-down of those members who were perceived as being above and beyond the group. McNabb refers to this practice. He notes that when men drink heavily and their tongues loosen, they engage in an unfortunate habit of taking a rise out of some person. In this way, 'a group of men when over-confident by drink may chafe one of the company on his shortcomings'. But what McNabb refers to as 'an unfortunate habit' is not so much a social problem but rather a practice by which the drinking group is maintained. The ritual put-down through 'taking the mickey', slagging, and teasing, etc., is a strategy by which members strengthen the alliance. Again it is important to remember that these shame-producing practices did not arise spontaneously within the home. Another more direct strategy by which the alliance is maintained is overt criticism of its members. But this overt criticism takes a particular form which can be linked to other more general religious social practices, i.e. silence and excommunication. One of the mechanisms by which shame is inculcated is to make out that the subject is too grave to be discussed—this as we saw above is a major practice in reproducing sexual morality. The offender is excluded through silence. McNabb describes the process:

> The groups in bars have developed an interesting method of community criticism and ostracism. The offending party is allowed to sit on his own. The men are polite but restrained. On such occasions there is always an air of tension in the public-house. Later in the night, a group of men will begin to talk in stage whispers (loud enough to be heard by the offender), in general terms and in a derogatory manner about people who commit offences similar to the one which he has committed. The offender may choose to ignore the indirect criticism. If so, he loses face. It is more common for the offender to challenge the group to say what's in their minds. Here we have the very essence of expression in this community: the fear of giving direct offence even to one who by his actions has merited exclusion, and the inability to step outside accustomed behaviour without the support of the group.[55]

As indicated earlier, the drinking group is constituted as a power alliance in and through a wider network of power which is centred around the family and the Church. It is no coincidence that the strategies by which the group is maintained are similar to those by which the family and the Church maintain their power over the individual. Stivers has given a plausible explanation of the relationship between the drinking group and the family. He argues that in Ireland the father-son and husband-wife relationships have tended to be cold and formal, while the maternal uncle-nephew and brother-sister relationships have tended to be warm. This has been crucial, he claims, because it has often been the maternal uncle who has tied each new generation of males to the bachelor drinking group. Unfortunately while there is some ethnographic evidence to support the claim that the relationships between fathers and sons, and husbands and wives, have tended to be cold and formal—although the relationship between brothers and sisters has tended to be warm and strong—there is little or no evidence about the uncle-nephew relationship.[56]

There is much that is appealing and reasonable about Stivers's structuralist analysis, but it does not explain why the father-son and the husband-wife relationships came to be cold and formal. Moreover, it does not describe the conditions and mechanisms which prevented the relationships from becoming warm and informal. In fact, the cold relationship between father and son can be linked with the rise in the new stem-family practices whereby sons were prevented from marrying by being denied plots of land subdivided from the family holding. The farm began to be handed over intact to just one son. But which son that would be was not made clear for years. This was a strategy by which postponed marriage and permanent celibacy were maintained. While none of the sons knew which one would inherit, there was little point in courting women. When the father eventually made the announcement, the inheriting son was usually in his thirties or forties and had little or no experience with women other than his mother. If he decided to get married, which his widowed mother may often have actively discouraged because of her reluctance to hand over the home and her son to another woman, he arranged through a matchmaker to get a wife in the same way that he might arrange to buy a cow.[57] This helps to explain why the initial relationship between newly married couples would be cold and formal; above and beyond members of one's own immediate family, there was simply no experience or competence in relating to the opposite sex. But how was this cold relationship maintained in everyday life? One might argue that a man not able to interact freely and competently with his wife sought refuge in the drinking group. But not even Irishmen could spend all their time in the pub. It is here that the Church, and in particular the priest, enters the network of power relations.

For a number of reasons, some of which are dealt with in the next chapter, the priest came between the husband and wife and formed a power alliance with the woman. It was through this power alliance that the mother gained moral power in the home, not merely over her children but also over her husband. It is this moral power, and the ensuing control that the Church gained over women, which helps explain why, from the end of the nineteenth century, Ireland developed a higher level of marital fertility than any other country in the Western world. In 1960–64, Ireland had an annual married fertility rate of 195.5 legitimate births per 1,000 married women aged 10–49 years. This was higher than other traditionally Catholic countries such as Portugal (148.9), Spain (142.1) and Poland (130.1). In 1871, the Irish rate had not been significantly different from that of England and Wales. However, whereas the latter's rate dropped to 111 by 1935, Ireland's rate was 248 in 1950.[58] Efforts to control Irish fertility not only appear later than in other European countries, but even today they are still either less extensive or ineffective.

In trying to explain why so many Catholic women accepted the Church's teaching on a large ideal family size, Kennedy is forced, in the absence of a general theoretical model, to suppose that the women who remained in Ireland and married young were more conservative and willing to accept Catholic Church teaching. He argues that those who postponed marriage to a late age, or who remained permanently single, were less influenced by the Church.[59] Even if this were true, which appears unlikely since single middle-aged women have often had the highest levels of religiosity in Ireland, it does not explain why women who married late had a high level of marital fertility. In effect, a reason why Irish women had so many children, no matter at what age they married, was because not only did the Church demand such behaviour but their mothers and other married women also demanded it. Just as hard drinking was the ritual practice by which men allied themselves with the bachelor group, bearing numerous children was the ritual practice by which mothers became allied to each other and the Church. To understand why and how this occurred it is necessary to understand some of the changes that occurred in Irish rural life in the first half of the nineteenth century, e.g. the end of home employment for married women, the rational differentiation of the domestic (women's) sphere from the work (men's) sphere, the growth of a substantial class of tenant farmers, the constitution of modern motherhood and its responsibilities in and through churches and schools, and the mother's dependence on the Church, through which she would attain moral power in the domestic sphere.

Conclusion

The growth of the Catholic Church in nineteenth-century Ireland cannot be divorced from the growth in population which began towards the end of the eighteenth century and the means that were employed to stem that growth. As the Church grew in strength, many Irish Catholics—in particular a new middle class of substantial tenant farmers—began to adopt population control practices which had become common in many parts of Europe in the two previous centuries. Postponed marriage, permanent celibacy and emigration were central features of the stem-family system in which one son inherits all the land. It was the Church which provided the moral discipline and supervision necessary to incorporate this new system. To some extent the breakdown of the stem-family system in Europe, and the growing inability of institutions such as the Catholic Church to control sexual behaviour, were associated with a growth in population. That growth in population was checked not so much by redeploying stem-family practices, but by wives saying no to their husbands and, later, using contraceptive devices. What makes Irish demographic history interesting is not that the Western European stem family and its associated practices were embodied by the majority of the population after the Famine, but that marital fertility grew to be the highest in Western Europe. The reason for this is that adherence to the Catholic Church, which had helped bring about the moral discipline necessary to introduce and maintain the new stem-family system, prevented the adoption of strategies and practices which might have reduced marital fertility. The development of the Catholic Church in modern Ireland went hand in hand with the attempt to control the growth in population and improve the standard of living. But as the power of the Church grew, especially over women, there was little or no attempt to control fertility once they did marry. This maintained the need for postponed marriage, permanent celibacy and emigration and, in turn, the need to adhere to the Church's rules and regulations, especially on sexual morality. It also institutionalised patterns of emotional relationships within families, especially between husbands and wives, and mechanisms of control within the wider community such as the bachelor drinking group.

8
The Irish Mother

I see that little mother, and hear her as she pleads.
Now it's getting on to bedtime, all you children get your
beads.
And she lit our drab existence with her simple faith and
love.
And I know the angels lingered near, to hear her prayers
above.
For her children trod the paths she trod, nor did they later
spurn
To impress her wholesome precepts on their children in
their turn
Ah those little Irish mothers, passing from us one by one.
Who will write the noble story of the good that they have
done?[1]

WOMEN HAVE been written out of Irish history. It is men, we
are told, who have shaped the course of Ireland's development.
O'Connell, Cullen, Parnell, Pearse, and de Valera are put forward
as the heroes who took Ireland by the scruff of the neck and led it
reluctantly into the twentieth century. Great men, it would seem,
make great history; women make only beds and dinners.

There are three main reasons why women, and in particular
mothers, have yet to gain the recognition they deserve in Irish
history. First, men have written most of the history. Second, Irish
historiography has concentrated on politics and personalities as
the causal factors in Ireland's development. Third, because they
had no jobs or incomes of their own, women were considered to
be powerless. Since the 1960s, historians have begun to rewrite
Irish history and to take into account the position and role of
women. There has been a concomitant shift away from politics
and personalities as the key explanation of historical change and a
greater emphasis placed on economic and social factors. A social

history of Irish women has yet to be written, and until such a time we are working in uncharted territory. Nevertheless there are some paths that can be discovered, even through a mere exploratory study.

A central argument of this study is that far from being a nonentity, the Irish mother has played a crucial part in the social and economic development of Ireland. It was the mother who, from the middle of the nineteenth century, became the organisational link between the Catholic Church and the individual. It was she who carried through the new moral and civil code from the church and school into the home. It was she who, through a variety of social and cultural practices which were handed down through generations from mother to daughter with the support of the priest and Church, produced the Catholics of modern Ireland. Indeed it was the continuous bearing of children, once she got married, that necessitated the inculcation of strict discipline and sexual morality.

It was this rigorous moral training which helped in the subordination of individual interests to those of family and community. But it was the mother who enforced the necessary moral discipline. It was she who, through a variety of subtle strategies and practices, persuaded her children to emigrate, postpone marriage, or not to marry at all. It was she who, through inculcating these practices and a rational regulation of life in her family, provided the vital force necessary for the restructuring of Irish rural life in the late nineteenth and early twentieth centuries. It was she who, through the changes she helped introduce in Irish lifestyles, became the impetus behind the creation of homes, the consolidation in the size of Irish farms, and the general social maintenance of a class of tenant farmers which was at the centre of the initial modernisation of Irish society. However, the mother was created as a moral power in and through the Church. Her ability to get her husband and children to do what she said, depended heavily on the moral support she received from the priest. The effect of this powerful alliance between priests and mothers was that once the initial modernisation had been attained, Ireland became a highly conservative society in which the Church's definition of the good life held sway. It was through this alliance, and the practices by which it was maintained, that the Church became a dominant force in economic and social life. For it was through a continual demand for surrender to the family, and its ally the Church, that inhibition and shame were nurtured, and ambition and creativity—the necessary ingredients for a fully mature capitalist society—were impeded.

Women and Change in Nineteenth-Century Ireland

To understand the role which the mother has played in modern Irish society, it is necessary to understand the transformation that took place in agriculture and, consequently, in the position and occupation of women in Ireland from the beginning of the nineteenth century. Unfortunately, compared to other European countries and regions, very little is known about the Irish family and in particular the role of wives and mothers in social and economic life in previous centuries. Nevertheless it would appear that the institution of motherhood, i.e. the specific occupational position of women, whose sole task it was not just to feed and clothe their husbands and children but to instruct and supervise them morally, did not flourish until the beginning of the last century. Modern Irish motherhood developed in association with the differentiation between the work and domestic spheres of life. Until the beginning of the nineteenth century, home employment, especially the manufacture of wool and linen, was a regular feature of tenant farm production. This went into decline with the arrival of steam-driven machines in the new industrial cities of Britain, and the flooding of the Irish market with cheaply manufactured yarn and cloth. This transition mainly affected married women who did much of the spinning and weaving. It was also associated with a change in marriage formation patterns away from a free and easy system to the deployment of the matchmaking system. Hynes has described the change as follows:

> At an earlier stage the domestic textile industry provided widespread spinning employment for women, and a wife brought her labour power to her husband at marriage. As this industry declined and agriculture began to shift from tillage to livestock (both processes accelerating after the economic depression following Waterloo in 1815) the value of a woman's labour declined and, increasingly, dowries in the form of capital rather than labour skills were required.[2]

There is considerable debate as to when and where the shift from tillage to livestock, mentioned by Hynes, took place. This is important as such a shift may be associated not just with the advent of dowries and matchmaking, which were major character-istics of stem-family life, but also with the institution of practices such as postponed marriage, permanent celibacy and emigration. Crotty, in his seminal work *Irish Agricultural Production*, argues that the shift from tillage to livestock occurred in the second quarter of the nineteenth century.

> The years 1820 to 1850 span the period during which Irish agriculture and the Irish people struggled to adjust to the new conditions created by the market changes which were initiated in the years immediately following the Battle of Waterloo. Essentially the changes necessary, given the economic and institutional conditions of the time, were twofold: first to halt and then reverse the population growth and second, to halt the fragmentation of farms and to consolidate and to reorganise them on a pastoral, livestock basis.[3]

Crotty goes on to argue that under the new market conditions, capital in the form of livestock once again became a factor of major importance in agricultural production. People without capital could not compete successfully for land and, therefore, could not get maried and have families. (In fact this only pertained to a small but historically significant section of tenant farmers. In the poorer regions of the West small farmers continued to marry early, without capital, and settled on subdivided, reclaimed or rented land for some time after the Famine.) Lee, on the other hand, insists that the Famine was the watershed in Irish history, and that none of these social and economic changes, which Crotty associates with the Battle of Waterloo (1815), were established until after the half century mark. Nevertheless the trend he outlines is similar, especially the decline in women's economic power.

> Before the Famine women's economic contribution was so essential to the family economy that they enjoyed considerable independence. Growing factory competition was, it is true, sapping the strength of domestic industry, but as late as 1841 women accounted for more than half of the non-agricultural labour force.

> The Famine helped change this situation in three main ways.

First, it delivered a crippling blow to domestic industry. The numbers of spinners of wool, cotton and linen fell about 75% between 1841 and 1851. . . . Secondly, the Famine permitted a marked shift from tillage to livestock, and agriculture became less labour intensive. Women were now less necessary about the farm. . . . Thirdly, the proportion of agricultural labourers to farmers, and of smaller farmers to strong farmers, fell sharply. As women had probably enjoyed greater economic equality among the poorer orders than among the wealthier, this in itself sufficed to tilt the balance of economic power within the family in the male direction.[4]

There is, then, agreement about the nature of the social and economic transformation that took place in Irish society in the last century and how it affected women. The only question is when did it begin. There is evidence which supports the timing put forward by both Crotty and Lee. An examination of export figures indicates that in the decades coming up to the Famine, Irish farmers were already switching from tillage to livestock farming. Up to the mid 1830s, there was an expansion in the export of oats, wheat and barley, but from then on these went into decline and were replaced gradually by the export of cattle. On the other hand, O'Grada has quantified agricultural output in the period 1840–44 without referring to export figures. He comes to the conclusion that potatoes and all other crops formed 63 per cent of production in this period, and that cattle, sheep and wool output was only 13 per cent. Furthermore he contends that tillage farming increased right up to the Famine.[5] This question about the shift from tillage to pasture farming brings in a whole series of questions which has obsessed Irish demography and historiography, and which has yet to be resolved: When did the subdivision of farms end? When did farm consolidation begin? When did postponement of marriage begin? In other words, when, where, and among whom did population growth begin to decline? Did these changes occur before or after the Famine and, consequently, what role if any did the Famine play in Irish social history?

There are too many issues involved in these questions to deal with here. However, the major point that has confused the debate is that of economic class. As mentioned in the previous chapter, it makes a great difference whether or not one is talking about Irish population as a whole, or a particular economic class in the society, which adapted more quickly to the changing social and economic conditions. In effect, the shift from tillage to livestock, from free and easy marriage to postponed marriage and permanent celibacy, from subdivision to consolidation, and from the production of a bare minimum for survival to economic security and comfort, were changes which had been embodied for some decades before the Famine by a small, but significant, proportion of the rural Irish population, i.e. the medium-to-large Irish tenant farmer.

The failure of Connell, the doyen of Irish demographers, was that he did not distinguish between the various economic classes in pre-Famine Irish society, and the sharp divisions in the social and cultural practices by which these classes were established and maintained. In Connell's perspective, there were just peasants and landlords (of whom middlemen were a sub-category). The absence of a satisfactory class model led him into making three erroneous conclusions about pre-Famine Ireland. (1) Society was stagnant due to landlord exploitation and the absence of a middle class. (2) The absence of a middle class was associated with the absence of a family system which could impose the practices necessary to consolidate the farm holding and improve the standard of living. (3) Consequently, 'the desire to postpone marriage until the accumulation of capital, or the acquisition of a better farm which would allow a higher standard of living could seldom, it is clear, have influenced action in Ireland in the period under review [i.e. pre-Famine]'.[6]

It was not until Crotty pointed out that there had been a class of substantial tenant farmers in Ireland prior to 1760, which had gone into decline because of a switch to tillage farming, that a new generation of scholars began to investigate the class structure in Ireland in the decades immediately prior to the Famine.[7] Clark has argued that besides landlords and middlemen, there were basically two other classes: large landholders who after the Napoleonic wars preferred grazing livestock, and small tenant farmers, cottiers and landless labourers who preferred tillage. Taking twenty acres as a rough division between the large farmer class and the rural poor, Clark estimates that, in 1841, 25 per cent belonged to this farmer class.[8] Connolly, in a more thorough working of the figures, estimates that between 1841 and 1845, only 277,000 (18 per cent) belonged to the category of farmers having over 15 acres.[9] This still leaves us in a quandary as to what proportion of these were Catholic. If we use Larkin's arbitrary figure of 70 per cent, which is based on the fact that 80 per cent of the population at the time was Catholic and that there would be an over-representation of Protestants in the large land-holding class, then there were approximately 194,000 Catholic farmers in 1845 with more than 15 acres.[10] Regardless of the exact size of this Catholic tenant farmer class, Clark, Larkin and Connolly are in agreement that it was largely untouched by the Famine. In effect, the Famine decimated the rural poor. Clark estimates that 'the percentage of the adult male agricultural labour force comprised by labourers fell from 56 per cent in 1841 to 38 per cent in 1881, while the percentage composed by farmers and farmers' sons rose from 42 per cent in 1841 to 60 per cent in 1881'. In other words, the tenant farmers became the largest group in the class structure of post-Famine Ireland. There was a definite shift in the type of agricultural production. Between 1847 and 1876 the cattle population rose by almost 60 per cent, while the sheep population rose by more than 80 per cent.[11]

What these researchers have shown is that, contrary to what Connell argued, there was a small, but vibrant, class of substantial Catholic tenant farmers in Ireland before the Famine, who comprised up to one seventh of the total agricultural labour force. These farmers were employers both of labourers and servants. They were the mainstay of the Catholic Church in terms of providing money and manpower. It was mainly they who had the necessary capital for church building, and who could afford to educate their sons and daugthers for the religious life. It was they who united with the urban bourgeoisie to form the Catholic Association and push through Emancipation and other reforms. It was they who, in Larkin's terms, 'have not only remained economically viable and maintained their numbers, but ... have also emerged as the dominant political class in modern Ireland'.[12] But how did they do it? They did it in and through a power alliance with the Catholic Church. For just as the Church was reconstituted as a power bloc in and through the new tenant farmers, these farmers were constituted as the dominant economic class in modern Irish society in and through the Church. The Church offered these farmers the means of becoming civil and moral. Through an adherence to the Church's new moral discipline, these farmers could not only attain the same social prestige as the Protestant gentry who had dominated their lives but also, hopefully, the same economic class. Through the Church they were to become more Puritan than the Protestants themselves. But it was because these farmers became a power bloc in and through the Church that, once they had consolidated their holdings and the struggle for ownership of the land had ended, they became a highly conservative force. They were limited by the rules and regulations which had made them civil and moral. It was this limitation which inhibited the economic individualism central to the development of a fully mature capitalist agricultural mode of production. On St Patrick's day 1943, that 'great man' of twentieth-century Irish history, Eamon de Valera', who himself came from a small farming background, defined what has come to be recognised as the classical vision of Catholic Ireland:

> That Ireland which we dreamed of would be the home of a people who valued material wealth only as the basis of right living, of a people who were satisfied with frugal comfort and devoted their leisure to the things of the spirit—a land whose countryside would be bright with cosy homesteads, whose fields and villages would be joyous with the sounds of industry, with the romping of sturdy children, the contests of athletic youths and the laughter of comely maidens, whose firesides would be forums for the wisdom of serene old age. It would, in a word, be the home of a people living the life that God desires that man should live.[13]

But what were the mechanisms by which this power alliance between the new rural bourgeoisie and the Church was constituted? How did it work out in everyday life? How was the new moral discipline established? What were the micro-structures of power by which this grand alliance was maintained? In effect, it was not so much the Church's relationship with the farmer that was to turn out to be crucial, but the relationship with his wife. It was the mother who became the organisational link between the newly institutionalised Roman power bloc and the individual farming family. It was she who instilled and maintained in her husband and children all that was disciplined, moral and civil. Within the rational differentiation of the work from the domestic sphere, the home became the space within which the mother

began to fulfil herself in carrying out her new specialised tasks, and
to wield her new power. The home became central to the moralisation and civilisation of Irish tenant farmers and, consequently, to
the consolidation of their holdings and the reproduction of their
standard of living. The importance given to the home can be
gauged from the fact that in the years following the Famine, while
there was no great change in the size of farm holdings, there was a
considerable change in the type of houses in which people lived.

Table 8.   Percentage of Distribution of Holdings Above One Acre,
Ireland (32 Counties), 1841–1901

Year	Size of Holding in Acres					Number of Holdings (Thousands)
	1–5 %	5–15 %	15–30 %	30 and over %	Total %	
1841	45	37	11	7	100	691
1851	15	34	25	26	100	570
1861	15	32	25	28	100	568
1871	14	31	26	29	100	544
1881	13	31	26	30	100	527
1891	12	30	26	32	100	517
1901	12	30	26	32	100	516

Source: Kennedy, *The Irish*, 89.

The main change in the size of holdings in the nineteenth
century came with the Famine. Between 1841 and 1851 the proportion of farms over 15 acres increased from 18 per cent to
51 per cent (Table 8). However, in the next forty years there were
few changes in the size of farms. By 1901, the proportion of farms
over 15 acres had increased to only 58 per cent. The decades after
the Famine were a period of consolidation, of holding onto and
perhaps improving what had been already gained. Farms were no
longer subdivided, but there was a dramatic change in the size and
quality of houses.

In 1841, the Census Commissioners undertook an assessment of

housing conditions in Ireland. This assessment was repeated in subsequent censuses. It was based on three criteria; the extent of the
house (number of rooms); the quality (number of windows); and
its stability (material of walls and roof). They then composed a scale
compounded from these criteria: 'in the lowest, or fourth class,
were comprised all mud cabins having only one room—in the third,
a better description of cottage, still built in mud, but varying from
2 to 4 rooms and windows—in the second, a good farm house,
or in towns, a house in a small street, having from 5 to 9 rooms
and windows—and in the first, all houses of a better description
than the preceding classes'. This classification changed slightly over
the years. In 1871, third-class houses of brick and stone (which
formed approximately one third of the total) were classified
separately from those of mud. By 1891, the classification of the
two lower classes had become as follows: 'In the lowest of the four
classes are comprised houses built of mud or perishable material
having only one room and window: in the third a better description
house, varying from one to four rooms and windows. . . .'[14]

As the Famine brought a dramatic change in the size of farms, it
also brought a dramatic change in housing conditions. In 1841,
37 per cent of Irish houses consisted of one-roomed mud cabins
many of which were made in a matter of hours with sods of soil
stacked up on top of each other, often allowing no space for a
window or chimney (table 9). By 1851, these mud cabins formed
only 13 per cent of Irish houses. The majority of the population
then lived in a more defined, permanent space which may have
been made of mud and other materials, but which contained
separate rooms and windows. It was in these newly defined spaces
that the civilisation and moralisation of the Irish people began to
reach down to the lowest common denominator—the individual.
In the next forty years there was an even greater revolution in the
size and quality of houses. In 1851, almost two thirds of Irish
houses were still in the third or fourth class. By the turn of the
century (1901), 70 per cent of the population were in the second
or first class, i.e. were living in 'good farm houses' or better.

The transformation of Irish society in the last century was
essentially based on a transformation of space and time. In pre-
Famine Ireland, there was the impressive programme of building
churches and schools. Within these large, ordered spaces, priests
and teachers began to define and regulate time. In the decades

Table 9.   Percentage Distribution of Class of Houses, Ireland
(32 Counties) 1841–1901.

Class of House

Year	1st Class %	2nd Class %	3rd Clsss %	4th Class %	Total %	Number of Houses (Thousands)
1841	3	20	40	37	100	1,329
1851	5	30	52	13	100	1,046
1861	6	36	49	9	100	995
1871	6	40	50	4	100	961
1881	7	46	42	2	100	914
1891	8	54	36	2	100	871
1901	9	61	29	1	100	858

Source: Census of Population 1901, General Report, Table 49.
Census of Population 1851, General Report, xxiii.

after the Famine, this civilising and moralising process reached down to the smaller ordered spaces of houses, and within these to the even smaller spaces of rooms. It was in these new houses and rooms that behaviour became regulated and supervised by mothers. It may have been the men of Ireland who built these new houses, but it was the women of Ireland who transformed them into homes. It was by making the space in which they lived a home rather than an unregulated, undefined, badly constructed living space, that Irish mothers were able to establish and maintain the practices associated with the new stem-family system. Through the moral and civil instruction received from Church and school, Irish women began to transform the confined space in which they operated from what was in reality an animal house to a modern, civilised home. It is crucial to realise that a major aspect of the Irish civilising process was the expectation if not the demand, which was reflected in their new training and education, that Irish women become good mothers. It was the confinement of women to the house which led it to be turned into a home. It was from within the home that the practices central to the modernisation of Irish agriculture, i.e. postponed marriage, permanent celibacy, and emigration, were developed. It is in this respect that mothers became a major power behind the modernisation of Irish society, and not mere servants of their menfolk. This is the mistake Lee makes, for although he recognises the important transformation from houses to homes, and the central position of the kitchen within the home, he reduces the role of mother to that of a slave:

> Before the Famine women did not have to know much about cooking. The potato pot demanded no great culinary pretensions. The spread of stoves and ranges, and the greater variety of diet, meant that women had to spend far more time cooking after the Famine than before. As the clothes and utensils the family possessed increased, the wife had to spend more time cleaning and scouring. Making the bed and washing the sheets was a simple matter in many cases before the Famine, when the bed was often a pile of straw on the floor. Pre-Famine women did not spend most of their day isolated in the kitchen, if only because more than half the houses had no separate kitchen.[15]

Lee's argument is that after the Famine, with declining marriage prospects in an increasingly male-dominated society, women were reduced to a subservient, if technologically transformed, role in the home. Women may have been servants, but like many other Irish servants, civil or otherwise, they nevertheless wielded considerable power. Unless there is an understanding of the nature and extent of this power, of how it was established and maintained and of its consequences for everyday social and economic life, there can never be a full understanding of the power of the Catholic Church in modern Irish society.

The Constitution of Irish Motherhood

Towards the middle of the nineteenth century, reports from various parliamentary commissions began to indicate that the civilisation of Irish society depended not just on giving more power to the Catholic Church, but on the transformation of Irish women into good mothers. The Poor Law Commissioners, for example, drew an unfavourable and unfamiliar portrait of Irish mothers:

> Another circumstance, which has a powerful influence in

retarding the improvement of the Irish settlers in Great Britain, is the unthrifty and dissolute character of the women as it is on the wife that the care of the house, and on the mother that the training of the children, chiefly depend among the poor. The Irishwomen are likewise, for the most part, not only wasteful and averse to labour, but also ignorant of the arts of domestic economy, such as sewing and cooking. Hence they are unable to make the best of the plain food which they purchase, or to keep their own and their husband's clothes in order, even when they only require mending.[16]

This was one of the reasons why, when the national school system was set up, such a heavy emphasis was given to the training of girls to be good mothers. However, it was not simply a case of teaching girls the skills of household care and management which once learnt would never be forgotten. They had to be monitored and supervised within the house. This became the task of the Church. It was mainly priests and nuns who from the middle of the nineteenth century began to define the tasks of mothers and supervise them in their new roles. As we saw earlier, one of the main ways in which priests gained control of women was by gaining control of their sex. This they did by portraying women as weak, fragile beings who must be protected (by the priest) from the sexual viper which lurked within them. This was not just a strategy of the Catholic Church but was, as Taylor points out, part of a wider Puritan strategy by which 'women are forced into an exaggerated feminity, magnifying their relative weakness into complete helplessness, their emotionality into hysteria and their sensitivity into a delicacy which must be protected from all contact with the world'.[17] In Ireland, it was the knowledge and control that priests and nuns had over sex which helped maintain their power and control over women. Women especially were made to feel ashamed of their bodies. They were interrogated about their sexual feelings, desires and activities in the confessional. Outside the confessional there was a deafening silence. Sex became the most abhorrent sin. It was through the control of sex that the modern Irish mother and family was first established. The Church's strategy of keeping women ignorant about sex and their bodies was later maintained in and through a control of medical science and practice in Ireland. Just how successful this control of knowledge became over the years can be gauged from the comments of a married woman in Humphreys's study of Dubliners in the 1950s:

> I think it is really sinful that I was allowed to marry as ignorant and as innocent as I was about the whole matter. At the time the only way you learned was from the girls you worked with, but I did not work in a factory and I knew nothing. Honestly, I could surprise you with what I did not know. I used to think of marriage as a mere matter of companionship. I thought the children just came somehow, I knew not how. It never occurred to me that children or the purpose of marriage had anything to do with sex.[18]

One of the best known descriptions of how priests gained control of women was given by Michelet. He argued that the priest, like any other man, is born strong and virile, but is trained into being weak and resembling women. This androgynous being interposes in marriage between the husband and wife. Michelet argued that as an unwitting instrument of Jansenist repression, the priest through confession gains control of the woman, and in the process attains a knowledge about her sex far greater than that of her husband who, consequently, feels alienated from his wife and becomes submissive to the moral power of both wife and priest. Estranged from her husband, the wife confides in and associates with her daughters. On the priest's advice, she sends them to the nuns, and brings up her sons like priests.[19] Michelet was writing about France, but Stivers comes to a similar conclusion about Ireland. 'No wonder then that the Irish priest was sometimes referred to as "she". The priest sometimes acted just like one's mother in the rigid enforcement of the moral code. The Irish mother often desired that at least one son become a priest. The priest was the mother's ideal of manhood for her sons'.[20]

Where Michelet and others have gone astray is in describing the mother as a helpless, powerless, and isolated being. It was not simply that the Church gained control of women but that, due to their isolation within the domestic sphere, women and especially mothers were forced in their struggle for power to surrender to the control of the priest and ally themselves with the Church. For women to attain and maintain moral power, it was necessary that they retain their virtue and chastity. This was the message which mothers began to pass on to their daughters. Within the rational differentiation of spheres of moral responsibility, chastity and modesty became the specific goals for women. Temperence became the goal for men. Referring to the reform of abuses in female manners, an editorial in the *Catholic Penny Magazine* asked:

> Is it not possible that a Christian company cannot exercise themselves, or take a few hours of agreeable relaxation, without having their shoulders bare, or their bosoms uncovered? Do they ever think upon the tremendous consequences of their subjecting themselves or others to gross temptations? But it is not merely the dress, but the manners of females, that we condemn. Can a lady of the least virtue, or modesty, behold, much less take part in some of these scandalous dances, called Waltzes, in which common decency is set at defiance? ... Every lady then, of virtue, and of decency, who wishes to preserve her character pure should utterly discountenance such an invasion on the pleasures of private and public life. There is no charm in the female sex which can supply the place of modesty. ... The best preservative of female honour is female delicacy—we mean a delicacy not assumed or affected, but the delicacy of a modest mind, and a pure heart. This is the visible angel guardian of the female sex, which even the ruffian will respect—it is the handmaid of virtue which attends her coming in and going forth: without it no female is safe or beautiful.[21]

What happened, then, during the nineteenth century was that a Puritan sexual morality which maintained women as fragile, delicate creatures whose nature had to be protected began to be instilled among Irish women, first by the Catholic Church and later by women, as mothers themselves. It was the creation and maintenance of such women which was the mainstay of bourgeois Catholic morality, and the basis of the initial phase of the modernisation of Irish society.

Motherhood as Learnt in the School

A major aspect of the civilising process was the segregation of the sexes, first into separate beds, then into separate bedrooms and, finally into separate lifestyles. Such a historical pattern of events is not easily discernible in Ireland but there is evidence of segregation being an integral part of the modern schooling process. Nano Nagle, who started convent schools in Ireland, not only had separate schools but also separate curricula for boys and girls. 'I have two schools for boys, and five for girls. The former learn to read, and when they have the Douay catechism by heart, they learn to write and cypher. There are three schools where the girls learn to read, and when they have the catechism by heart, they learn to work [sic]'.[22] An examination of the texts used in national schools shows that segregated education was a key component of the system. Boys were instructed on how to run a successful small farm. *The Agricultural Class Book* which was introduced in 1850 tells in story form how a peasant transforms his land through drainage, does mixed farming, rotates crops, keeps fowl, and keeps his accounts, etc. The story goes on to relate that, while the man is busy outside tending his fields, his wife is inside preparing a varied diet of bread, meat and soup, keeping her house clean and repairing clothes.[23] Needlework was made out to be the essential skill for any woman to acquire. Indeed, as an instructional manual for teachers indicated, the development of a sense of decency and industry often depended upon it. 'To needlework she [the teacher] must be particularly attentive, for on her instructions (of course assisted by their own exertions) may depend whether many a poor, friendless girl shall or shall not have the means of supporting herself, and, if she becomes a mother, whether her children are to be in dirty rags or decent clothes, or brought up in idle or industrious habits.'[24]

The whole structure of a girl's education was towards the development of modesty and virtue and the practice of being industrious. Idleness was portrayed as the vehicle which passions used to express themselves. Consequently, if a mother was not cooking, tending her garden, cleaning the house, or mending clothes, she should be praying. These tales of domestic economy and housekeeping were also set out in the *Reading Book for the Use of Female Schools* which had been brought out five years earlier.[25] The book is best summed up by its table of contents which shows that most of the essays, borrowed mainly from the writings of contemporary moralists, were concerned with housekeeping and child-rearing practices. In 1853, the Commissioners described the lessons as forming 'a complete manual of the moral and domestic duties of females, whether in single or married life, and cannot be read frequently and attentively without producing the most beneficial results'.[26]

After the Famine, nuns began to have a major influence on the education of Irish Catholic girls. This occurred at two levels. First, the nuns went out and brought into their schools children of the destitute classes who would otherwise probably not have attended school. Second, and this was of importance to the constitution of a new bourgeois farming class, the nuns came from good backgrounds and were, in Fahey's terms, 'solid examples of middle class respectability'.[27] Not only did they teach all that was contained in the national school syllabus, but they often had knowledge of foreign languages, art and music which were essential for the constitution of good mothers and fair ladies. Tynan, writing towards the end of the nineteenth century, had little doubt that the transformation she witnessed in Irish homes was largely due to nuns: 'Housecraft is seen in its perfection in a convent. What was it that made the girls who would have been slovenly at home, fit in with the life so exquisitely neat and feat? Perhaps those who went back leavened the lump of indifference and unthrift. Certainly, coming back to Ireland after twenty years absence, I find in the Irish households an order and efficiency which were rare in my young days.'[28]

The school was more than just a place of education. It introduced a whole cycle of discipline into the family. Children had to be got up and out to school. Family life began to revolve around the school timetable. Throughout the nineteenth century the number of children attending school increased rapidly. In 1833, there were 107,042 children on the rolls. Even after the ravages of the Famine, the number continued to rise, although the population was declining rapidly. In 1852, there were 544,604 children on the rolls. However daily attendance was another matter. From 1875, when figures first became available, to 1900, the average daily attendance did not increase much beyond 60 per cent.[29]

It was through the school that priests, nuns and brothers reached out into the home. The child became the link between the moralising forces of the Church and the isolated homes of Ireland. The forces of discipline which were applied in the school began to be extended to the home. Parents, but especially the mother, began to be held responsible for the conduct of their children in school. Children were inspected for cleanliness. If they were dirty, or misbehaved, they were sent home. Throughout the nineteenth century the control of instincts, passions and emotions shifted gradually from the school to the home, where such control became the specialised task of the mother.

It is important to realise that the disciplines and control which began to be exercised over mothers and their children was not something which was inflicted by the Church and State on an unwilling people. Reluctant, lazy and uncivilised as many might have been in the beginning, it did not need much insight to realise that control of the instincts and passions through moral discipline was the key to modernisation and an improvement in the standard of living. More important, it was the care and dedication which especially the nuns and brothers brought to their work, that allowed the Church to instil into the lower orders an interest in being civil and moral. It was that care and dedication, something that the State could never attain, which was central to the ability of priests, nuns and brothers to limit what Irish Catholics did and said. A report of the National Commission on Education (1864) described this relationship:

> When the nuns find that anyone of their pupils has been from school for some days, they enquire into the cause of the absence, and generally employ the monitresses, or some of the more grown girls, to ascertain the facts. Parents, more specifically those belonging to the humbler classes, are pleased to find that persons filling a high and respected position take a deep and sincere interest in the well-being of their children. They are consequently forced, as it were by feelings of thankfulness and gratitude, to see that their children attend school as regularly as their circumstances will permit.[30]

It was in and through the national school system that Irish females were taught the basic practices of housekeeping and the moral upbringing of children. It was in the school-room that the specific tasks of motherhood were systematically defined and explained. The system was slow to get started and depended on a feedback mechanism. In the beginning not everyone got the message because going to school depended largely on the existence of a 'yet to be constituted' good mother. It would follow that it was those farmers who already had substantial holdings of fifteen or more acres, who were more successful in getting their children to school. Once mothers began to send their children to school, they and their children became more and more disciplined, regulated people, and their daughters learnt the skills and tasks of housekeeping and mothering more and more diligently.

Priests, Mothers and the Moralisation of Irish Children

Deprived of possessions, unable to contribute to the income of the household, and having no formal occupational status, the already negligible power of women went into decline during the first half of the nineteenth century. It was the priest, and later the nuns, who were the only light at the end of this dark tunnel of powerlessness. They were the only people with power who regularly visited women in their homes and took an interest in what they were doing. Priests and nuns did not have personal wealth. Their ability to limit what others did and said depended on the services which they rendered, often free of charge, and on their being more moral and civil than those with whom they interacted. The same means became those by which mothers created and maintained their own power.

The ability of the Church to limit what its members did and said, depended on the indoctrination of children into its rules and regulations. This was originally carried out through the confraternities of Christian doctrine and, later, through the schools. But the success of the indoctrination process depended upon its being followed up within the home. The home became the object of supervision and surveillance by the Church. This was part of an overall differentiation of space between the home and the church. Whereas previously the home had been the place of socio-religious practice, e.g. house stations, marriages, wakes etc., as well as a good place for priests to eat and drink, it now became primarily a private space, while most religious practices took place within the church. The way for the mother to obtain the priest's blessing and approval, was to bring up her children within the limits that he laid down. In doing so she was able to call upon him as an ally in her attempts to limit what her husband and children did and said. Moreover through engaging in the same humble tasks of moralising children and looking after the sick, elderly and dying, mothers began to attain a similar perspective on the world to that of priests and religious. This was a crucial aspect of the alliance with the Church, for it was through this similarity of practices and perspective that mothers fostered the vocations within their children on which the Church depended. Equally important, it was through an imitation of their celibate lifestyle, their body discipline and morality, that the mother inculcated a sexual and emotional repression which was crucial to the attainment of post-poned marriages, permanent celibacy and emigration. Even when they emigrated, Irish women gained a reputation as self-sacrificing, noble mothers. Diner states that women in Irish-American communities were noted not only for holding the family together but for propelling it 'out of poverty and into the respectability of the middle class'. Irish women were regarded as 'civilisers', especially in their attempts to stop men from drinking, and in this activity, Diner notes, 'wives operated in league with the priests'.[31]

We have seen how, within the new discipline and organisation of the Catholic Church in Ireland, priests and religious brought a new Puritanical sexual rigour to Irish social life. What is of concern in this chapter is how this was imparted to children. In other words, what were the practices by which first the priest and later, through imitation, the mother instilled in children not merely a sense of modesty, but an emotional and physical segrega-tion of the sexes that resulted in an uneasy and awkward com-munication between them, which became the backbone of virtuous, moral and civil behaviour in Ireland? Unfortunately, historical sources which would provide an insight into how such practices were first established are few and far between. This is related to the fact that one of the chief strategies in this moralisation and socialisation process was the institution of silence about such matters. Connell has reviewed Irish literary sources that deal with the relations between priests and young people in terms of the sexual supervision of the latter by the former. We are told of priests separating courting couples, of a priest who every night used to walk through all the lonely lanes and by-ways, threatening the lovers with his big stick; of others bursting in upon private social parties; and of how generally they brought an end to traditional courtship practices.[32] The image of what Murphy calls the blackthorn stick of the prowling priest, is a popular one in Irish folklore, but it is one which only seems to have come to the fore towards the end of the nineteenth century.[33] This was the priest at the zenith of his power which was to last, especially in rural areas, well into the 1960s. But when and where he began to exercise such power, and how frequently he did so, is something that Irish historiography has yet to answer.

The model of modesty, virtue and humility which priests and religious provided was maintained in the home through a growing devotion to Our Lady. Our Lady may have been popular in Ireland before the nineteenth century, but it was then, as part of the devotional revolution, that the rosary, novena, May and October devotions, as well as shrines, processions and pilgrimages made in her honour, became common practices. These practices reached their peak in 1879 in Knock, County Mayo, when she appeared to fifteen people. Our Lady occupies a unique position in the history of the Catholic Church because of her dominance in an otherwise patriarchical institution. Taylor argues that devotion to her was introduced as a deliberate strategy by the Church to counteract heretical movements, mainly towards orgiastic, sex-imbued pagan practices.[34] She was a mother figure who was at the same time completely desexualised. In other words, it was crucial that the pagan practices which were rampant in pre-Famine Ireland be replaced by an ideal-type figure that was fecund and female, and yet remained virgin and pure. The chaste, modest and humble virtues of Irish women and mothers grew apace with their penitential devotion to Our Lady. The rosary, those penitential beads which rarely left her hand or pocket, became the means by which the mother maintained her own soul, and those of her family. It was a penitential practice that bound the family together. Griffith painted the following picture of holy Catholic Ireland. 'Come with me some evening to, it may be a humble, but always a hospitable home in holy Ireland. The mother is there, surrounded by her family, generally a large one. She has (to use Our Lord's beautiful comparison) gathered them together around her as the hen doth gather her chickens under her wings (Matt. 23:37). Each kneels with beads in hand.'[35] The rosary was a time when the mother exercised her moral power and called her husband and children to the attention of God and Our Lady. It strengthened her position as the sacred heart of the home. It bound the family together in ritual practice. Such ritual practices were essential to the maintenance of pious devotion to the mother and family and the suppression of individual interests. It is slightly romantic, but quite reasonable, for Lockington to describe the rosary, and the devotion to Our Lady, as the girdle that lifted Ireland out of the blackness of pestilence and famine.[36] It was through such devotional practices as the rosary, that the mother retained her power in the home. It was through a devotion to Our Lady that she fostered a devotion to herself and motherhood in general. But most important of all, she developed a notion of the chaste mother. It was through a devotion of Our Lady that women gave control of their bodies to the Holy Spirit. Sex itself became a penitential practice. Just how successfully these practices and beliefs were inculcated over the years can be judged from one of Humphreys's respondents:

> I think there is something wrong with sex and nothing will ever change me. . . . And I think that is the general attitude. One woman friend of mine who is married told me that she felt that after she was married that the loss of her virginity was the greatest loss of her life. And I felt the same way about it . . . There is something repulsive about it and nothing will get that out of my system. And the women will tell you that it is the men who enjoy it, not the women—they get no enjoyment out of marriage that way.[37]

Throughout the late nineteenth and twentieth centuries, the Church, faced with the threat of an economic individualism associated with urban industrialisation, came to depend more on maintaining control of the family. This it did by developing its alliance with the mother and keeping her within the home. As part of this strategy, the Church perpetuated a notion that women had a natural vocation as housewives and mothers, and should not indulge in matters of the mind and reason, even if they were capable of such things. As a priest at the turn of the century put it: 'Let it first be supposed that girls are capable of such higher studies as Greek, mathematics, philosophy, etc., and are a success in them; is it too much to surmise that this success would be gained at the cost of other studies which are better calculated to make them good heads of houses?'[38] The Church's message was consistent: if a mother went out to work, family life would be destroyed. Worse still, as Pope Pius XII claimed, it would give bad example to the daughter and her preparation for real life, for she would not feel the slightest inclination for austere housekeeping jobs and, consequently, could not be expected to appreciate their nobility and beauty and to wish one day to give herself to them as a wife and mother.[39] But Pope Pius XII was writing about the dangers of an urban, industrial society which was to remain foreign to Ireland until the 1960s. If he had read Griffith's description of the Irish mother, he would have realised that, as regards Ireland, there was at that time little to worry about.

> You may enter, almost at random, any of the thousands of Catholic homes in the land, and there you will meet the ideal mother, modest, hospitable, religious, absorbed in her children and motherly duties. The outside world, the masculine woman and her antics, have little attraction for her. She feels herself placed in a position by God, her life and actions their model. She is the class of woman who makes her home a home in the truest sense, a house in which her children are happy, and to which they ever look back with love when they have left it for a home of their own.[40]

Irish Mothering Practices

From the above description we can gain some insight into how the power alliance between the Catholic Church and the Irish mother was created and maintained, and how the mother instilled in her children a pious devotion to the Church and Our Lady which were central to maintaining the chastity and modesty necessary for postponed marriage and permanent celibacy. But this still does not give an adequate account of how these practices were successfully maintained over the years. To gain some understanding of how this was achieved it is necessary to focus on some of the more specific child-rearing practices of Irish mothers.

In traditional Irish families, mothers are not only responsible for child-rearing and moral instruction, but also for the more general task of emotional management. In their study of the extent to which traditional family roles had changed in Ireland from the 1930s, Hannan and Katsiaouni found that in a quarter of all families the father played almost no part at all in such 'emotional management' tasks and in over half the cases played a minimal role.[41] This is supported by McNabb who noted that there is some evidence that fathers believe that the expression of too much interest in children is a sign of immaturity.[42] Scheper-Hughes has suggested that it is through the control of the moral emotional sphere that the mother not merely instils the prerequisites for postponed marriage and permanent celibacy, but through the various psychological strategies that she employs she tends to identify those sons who will do well by becoming priests, teachers, civil servants, etc., those who will emigrate, and the one who will stay on and look after her and the farm. Her daughters are reared to the tasks of mothering, but also taught a sense of independence which will allow them to emigrate. Scheper-Hughes argues that it is no longer the case that a number of sons wait around in competition to see who will get the land, but rather that the one to escape gets stuck by default with the land and saddled with a life of almost certain celibacy and self-negating service to the old people. This has led to a change in psychological strategies. 'An Irish mother has always had special endearments for her favourite child and it appears from the life histories of older villagers that, in former generations, the family pet was often the first-born son, traditionally named after his paternal grandfather and reared in order to fill his projected role of farm heir.'[43]

Today, Scheper-Hughes argues, the first-born are reared for export—for the occupations of schoolteacher, civil servant, successful emigrant, possibly the priesthood. She details the justifications and rationalisations which are used to give pre-ferential treatment to the mother's pet, and how often the last-born son, often jokingly referred to as the 'runt', the 'scraping of the pot', the 'bottom of the barrel', will be encouraged to end his education in primary school.[44] Connell has described this practice in detail:

> Many a mother, too, though happy enough to see her daughters settle down—even the sons who had left home—resisted the marriage of their heir. Perhaps with justification, she pictured herself the object of his affection over 40 years and dreaded her relegation; she dreaded, too, the daughter-in-law, scheming not only for her son, but for the kitchen and yard she had ruled so long. By rousing a sense of sin, by ridicule, even by words unspoken, she kept her boy from girl-friends, leaving him awkward with women, perhaps incapable of courtship—a bridegroom, if at all, in a match made for him when her day was done.[45]

These strategies of keeping a son on the farm are extended to the wider community. Males use 'slagging' and 'taking the mickey' as a means of cutting each other down to size, and to censure those young men who try to shake off village apathy by making an effort to get ahead or to demonstrate feelings for others. But, as Scheper-Hughes indicates, these strategies of creating inhibition through ridicule are first learnt in the family, where the mother, often purely for reasons of economic survival, has brought up one of her sons with a sense of dependency on her and an inability to survive in the wider world without her.[46] Hutchinson argues that not only is the Irish mother a stifling influence on individual initiative and innovation, but that in this respect she is an exception in Western society:

> Restrictions imposed upon the son by a father jealous of his status were not counterbalanced (as they have been in other western societies) by contrary influences emanating from the mother. If the Irish mother's influence upon her son was a powerful one, it operated, nevertheless, in a direction opposed to economic development based upon individual initiative and innovation. Her influence set limits to her son's freedom which, while different from those imposed by his father, were equally difficult to circumvent.[47]

Daughters, on the other hand, are reared to be responsible, competent and independent, which gives them a greater sense of autonomy, prepares them for early emigration from the village, and allows them to feel less guilty about severing ties with old people. More important Scheper-Hughes's research gives us an understanding of how the emotional distance and sexual 'flatness' of the Irish are maintained. She argues that both sons and daughters are reared in a harsh, unphysical, comfortless manner by the mother. Loneliness, lack of tenderness, and consequent feelings of psychological abandonment and loss have, she argues, become basic components of the Irish personality structure, and are learned at an early age through the experience of a less than satisfactory relationship to the first love object—the mother. The basic line of Scheper-Hughes's argument is as follows: The reason why the Irish are so often schizophrenic, shy, withdrawn and uneasy in the company of others, especially members of the opposite sex, is because their mothers, as part of a traditional, cultural practice, deny physical gratification and stimulation to their children whom they leave for an inordinate amount of time by themselves, unrocked, unheld, and unreassured. Besides being excessively preoccupied with controlling their children's sexuality—which they link to the ascetic Jansenist tradition of Irish Catholicism—Irish mothers tend to be schizophrenogenic because, while they are too protective and extremely possessive of their children, they are at the same time unconscious of—and ignore— their expressed needs and demands.[48]

Stivers also picks up on this ambivalence: 'A puritanical sexual code is upheld by the mother in the Irish family: in fact, sin in general comes close to being equated with sexual sin in particular. The Irish mother often functions as an autocrat in the home, although she is often gentle and overprotective toward her children.'[49] The reason for this ambivalence is that from the time they get married, mothers come under a traditional, cultural pressure from their own mothers, other women, and the Church, to have children, even though they often express resentment at having had more children than they want or need. This is the double bind that Irish women experience in their struggle for power. It is this double bind which is transmitted in terms of over-protection but emotional coldness. The lack of fondling, cuddling, and emotional intimacy which Scheper-Hughes documents as still being practised by Irish mothers today has, it is argued, its roots in the transformations that took place in Irish society in the nineteenth century. It was the domination and control of women by the Church, and the necessity for women to ally themselves with that dominating power if they themselves were to have any power, that led to their high level of marital fertility which, in turn, created the need for postponed marriage, permanent celibacy and emigration among their children. These practices were encouraged by the mother in the home through a devotion to the Church, a rigorous sexual morality, and a physical and emotional distance from her children. It is this scenario, re-enacted over generations, that is the essence of the dialectical relationship of power between the Church and family in modern Ireland.

Conclusion

When we come to explain why it was that from the beginning of the nineteenth century successive generations of Irish Catholics began to adhere strongly to the rules and regulations of the Church, it is necessary to go beyond the extension of the modern European civilising process into Ireland and the interest in consolidating farm holdings and improving the standard of living. It is also necessary to go beyond the changes that took place within churches and schools, and examine what was happening to individuals within families. It is the family which has been the continuing link between the Church and individual Catholics. More specifically, it has been Irish mothers who have produced each new generation of Catholic souls. When, as has been happening since the 1960s, Irish women are no longer dependent on the Church for power (having gained access to political and economic power), and, consequently, the Church loses its ability to control them and their sex, then one of the pillars, if not the foundation, of what has held the Church above modern Irish society begins to crumble and decay.

Irish motherhood as primarily involving the sentimental and moral education and care of children within the home, did not exist among the majority of the population at the beginning of the last century. It was constituted, like the power of the Church itself, through the conjuncture of a number of processes and events. The first of these was the termination of the economic power which women had held through various jobs, mainly involving spinning and weaving. The second was the gradual shift from tillage to pasture farming. This was part of a third process which involved the consolidation of a new class of substantial tenant farmers who refused to subdivide their farms and insisted that their offspring either postpone marriage, not marry at all, or emigrate. These practices depended upon numerous other processes, one of the most important of which was the separation of the religious from the social sphere and, in particular, a separation of Church and home. The priest became a formal, austere figure; a man of Roman precept, civility and morality who helped develop, especially among those large tenant farmers from among whom he came and with whom he socially interacted, a rigorous discipline over the body and its passions which was the key to the Irish stem-family. It was he and the Church who helped transform rough, uncouth girls into fragile, delicate colleens who must be protected from the sexual evils that lurked deep within them, and who made good Irish mothers chaste and fertile in the image of Our Lady.

A new regulation and supervision of the body and its passions also began to be exercised by teachers in schools. It was here that girls, who until the advent of the national school system were mostly illiterate and less educated than boys, began to learn not just to read and write but the specific tasks and duties of mothers. Increasingly confined to the house, increasingly losing any specific economic role, and increasingly being supervised by priests, nuns and teachers, Irish women began to take on motherhood and helped transform Irish houses from a mass of mud cabins into substantial farmhouses in which, as in the school, time and space were regulated and in which there was a proper time and place for everything, and everything was in its proper time and place. It was within the home that a new power alliance between priest and mother began to emerge; an alliance that was founded on her dependence on the Church for moral power. The result of that alliance was an embodiment of the rules and regulations of the Church among successive generations of Catholics. The price of that alliance was a chaste motherhood with unregulated fertility. Most of the children were reared for export; some as examples of local pride and joy; and some as good-for-nothings who would always be dependent on their mother, as she herself was on the priest and the Church.

9
The Influence of the Catholic Church on Modern Irish Society

IRISH PEOPLE behave in much the same way as people from other Western societies. They work at the same kind of jobs. They are taught the same things at school. They live in similar kinds of houses. They worship in the same kind of churches. They have similar manners and habits. They watch the same television programmes. They read the same articles and stories in newspapers, magazines and books. Indeed such is the similarity in behaviour that Irish people can easily communicate with Westerners from other societies, even though they might not speak the same language.

But in this vast ocean of similarity the Irish are also different. The traditional image of the Irish is of a happy-go-lucky people who have a deep devotion to their family, community and Church and who, compared to other Westerners, have a greater interest in social and religious life than material things. Irish Catholics not only strongly adhere to the teachings and practices of the Church, but their religious life is enlivened with holy water, statues, shrines and pilgrimages. The priest is treated with the same awe and reverence as a holy man from any other traditional society. His word is the word of God. It is the dominance of the Catholic Church in everyday social life which is associated with the pious humility of the Irish, their practice of self-denial and the surrender of individual interests to those of family and community. Irish mothers are seen as paragons of Christian virtue who are happy to stay at home rearing their numerous children in the love and sight of God, and who fuss and worry about their husbands who spend too much time in the pub. What makes community life in Ireland different is not so much that the Irish drink more, but that they do so in pubs where no man is powerful enough to avoid having his leg pulled hard. Like the pub, and teasing, many of the social and cultural practices which make the Irish different and yet as civil and as moral as other Western people, may be linked to the Catholic Church. Indeed it is because the Irish became the same as other Westerners in and through the Catholic Church that they have remained different.

In order to explain the position of the Catholic Church in modern Irish society, this study has posed and sought to answer three main questions. What is the nature of the Church's power in Irish society? How has this power been maintained? When and how did its power become established? In attempting to answer these questions, I have developed a particular theoretical perspective on the Church and social life in general. I have avoided looking at the Church as being founded simply on people's commitment to a supernatural faith in God and Christ. Instead, I have developed a more materialist perspective which sees the Church as a large bureaucratic organisation which, like any other organisation, is primarily interested in maintaining its position and influence in society. I have looked at the Church not as a voluntary institution to which people are freely committed, but as a coercive and dominating power to which people have become allied in their own rational, instrumental struggle to attain more immediate, worldly ends. In other words, although Irish Catholics may adhere to the rules and regulations of the Church in order to attain salvation, this can be analytically separated from the more immediate, instrumental struggle to attain possessions, positions and prestige.

This study has sought to demonstrate that a rigid adherence to the teachings and practices of the Church has been the dominant type of ethical behaviour among modern Irish Catholics. What most Irish Catholics have interpreted as right and wrong has been defined by the rules and regulations of the Church. It developed a monopoly on what constitutes good moral behaviour. This legalist ethical behaviour has been in the past, and still is, mixed with magical practices and beliefs, many of which are pagan in origin. The dominance in modern Irish Catholicism of religious legalism has been maintained by the bureaucratic organisation which the Church has developed over the last hundred years, especially its control of education, health and social welfare. In more recent times, a rigid adherence to the rules and regulations of the Church has been giving way to more individually principled ethics. Irish Catholics are now more willing to make up their own minds about what is right and wrong rather than to follow the dictates of the Church. This is not to say that the Church is no longer able to limit what Irish Catholics do and say. The high level of Mass attendance, the Church's ability to prevent the introduction of social legislation that is contrary to its moral teaching, and its ability to get people to give their allegiance to the Church before any other power bloc to which they are allied, provide sufficient evidence of its continuing powerful position in Irish society.

However, this moral power has been declining since the 1960s when many Irish Catholics became less dependent on the Church to attain power, in particular the honour and respect of others. This decline in the Church's moral power cannot be separated from the growth in the power of the State and the media. The State abandoned the Church's ideal of a self-sufficient, rural society based on small-scale production in which family, community and religious life took precedence over the aquisition of material possessions. From the end of the 1950s the State began to pursue economic growth through increased industrialisation, urbanisation, international trade, science and technology. The growth of the media brought enormous changes to family and community life. Instead of going out to the church or kneeling down to say the rosary, Irish families began to sit down and watch television. Many of the programmes portrayed rich, glossy American and British lifestyles in which priests and religion had little or no influence. Television changed the nature of social discourse and practice in Ireland in that watching television in the privacy of one's home became a major collective ritual. Increasingly, television programmes more than Church rituals became the basis of a shared experience about which people communicated and related to each other. It is now the media as much as the Church that form and inform consciences and expand or limit how people perceive the world. It was the development of television which was mainly responsible for loosening the censorship on sex, while the growth of the media in general has increasingly forced the Church into giving account of itself.

The other question which this study has sought to answer is

when and how did the Church manage to attain such a powerful position in Irish society, and how has this power been maintained over successive generations? The growth of the power of the Catholic Church in Ireland cannot be attributed to one or two factors. Rather has it been the result of numerous events and processes coming together over a period of time. One of these was a transformation in the way in which the English State sought to control the Irish population. There was a shift away from repressive penal laws and the systematic attempt to subjugate Irish Catholics, to softer, more indirect forms of control centred on policing, emigration and education. Once it was realised that the attempt at Protestant evangelisation was doomed to failure, and once the reports from various investigative commissions began to be submitted, the State started to hand the task of educating and civilising Irish Catholics over to the Catholic Church. One of the reasons which precipitated this capitulation was that the Irish Church, in and through Rome, was already emerging as a cohesive, bureaucratically organised power bloc, able to challenge and harangue the State.

But again it would be too easy to explain the growth in Church power simply as something which was imposed by power blocs, in this case the Roman Catholic Church and the English State, on an unwilling people. Hierocratic power, or the power of priestly religion, cannot be considered coercive in the same way as the power of the State, even though the threatened denial of salvation is often as effective as the threat of death itself in attaining compliance to commands. One of the reasons why the Church was able to attain compliance with its teachings and practices was because it afforded the ability, denied during the penal laws, for Irish Catholics to become the moral equals, if not the superiors, of the Protestants who had dominated them for so long. Indeed Irish Catholics are a good example of a traditional people who, in the transition to modernity, place primary importance on becoming the same, i.e. as civil and refined, as those who have dominated them, but who use a different means—in this case the Catholic Church—to attain that end. In some respects the penal laws were a failure in that they made Irish Catholics more Roman and attached to the Church than they might ever have been. On the other hand, they were a success in that once they were abolished there was such an intense interest in becoming as civil and moral as modern Europeans that, beyond the struggle to attain ownership of the land and to a lesser extent to attain the status of a nation-state, economic and political development was of secondary importance. In other words, the abolition of the penal laws helped foster the very economic backwardness which they had been intended to establish among Irish Catholics.

The interest in becoming as moral and civil as Protestants, and in worshipping in large, ornately furnished churches rather than in secluded back-streets—or worse still in the open air—was a major factor in the physical growth of the Church in the first half of the nineteenth century. But the interest in modern civility had much deeper roots. It had been spreading throughout Europe since the sixteenth century. Essentially it involved the imitation of the manners and customs that characterised the court behaviour of aristocrats, first by the bourgeoisie and later by other classes. What is coincidental is that the development of this civility involved a moral discipline over passions and instincts which was best achieved through an internalisation of shame and guilt about the body, a process which had originally been developed and exported to the Continent by Irish monks back in the sixth and seventh centuries. The most rationally developed forms of this morality were Puritanism and, in particular, Jansenism. Now while there is no evidence that Jansenist doctrines were ever preached or adhered to in Ireland, there is little doubt that a Catholic brand of Jansenist practices was imported under the umbrella of rigorism. It is a matter of debate whether this rigorism was Roman or French in origin or whether it was a development within the Irish Church itself. Whatever its exact origins, and again it was probably a combination of all three, this new morality began to be developed from the middle of the last century, first in churches and later in schools and homes.

The strict adherence to the rules and regulations of the Church became the means of halting the impoverishment which had been caused by the subdivision of farms. There was little differentiation of time and space in the mud cabins which dominated Irish housing until the Famine. There was a differentiation made between animals and humans, but the pig was often given the right to his space since he at least helped pay the rent. It was in and through the church and the school that the child began to take precedence in Irish homes, and the pig was removed to the outhouse. The new moral discipline aided the adoption of postponed marriage, permanent celibacy and emigration. These practices became the principal means of consolidating farm sizes and raising the standard of living. Homes, like churches and schools, became well-ordered, supervised spaces in which there was a time and place for everything, and everything was in its proper time and proper place. The transformation in the size, quality and durability of Irish houses during the second half of the nineteenth century involved an internal revolution of time and space centred on body discipline. It was paralleled by an initial differentiation of spaces; of churches from schools, of churches from homes, and within homes of kitchens, bedrooms and living-rooms. It was because this initial differentiation of space took place in and through the supervision of the Church, and because the Church continued to be able to determine what went on in schools and homes, that there was no rational development and, consequently, the full modernisation of Irish society was delayed until the middle of the present century.

But for all the priests and teachers, the development of the Church and a rigorous moral discipline could not have been attained without the Irish mother. She became the sacred heart of the Irish home. It was she who inculcated a ritualistic and legalistic adherence to the rules and regulations of the Church. She brought the family to prayer and enforced the Church's code of morality. She was the Church's representative in the home who supervised the moral conduct of her husband and children. She became the living embodiment of Our Lady—humble, pious, celibate and yet fecund. She gave herself to the Church, and in each succeeding generation produced the relitous vocations that sustained the Church. Her moral power in the home was sanctioned by the priests, nuns and brothers that she bore.

The mother maintained her power within the home in the same way as the Church did in wider society. She did the dirty, menial tasks involved in the care of members of the household. She looked after the young, the sick, the elderly, the weak and the distraught. In Humphreys's terms, she 'dominated by affection'.[1] She slaved, especially for her husbands and sons. She encouraged her daughters, as part of their training, to be good mothers, to do likewise. By doing everything for her sons, the mother made them dependent on her. But by limiting and controlling the physical expression of her affection, she inculcated an emotional awkwardness in her children. This denial of the physical expression of affection was a major child-rearing practice in the preparation for emigration, postponed marriage and permanent celibacy. The segregation of the sexes, the lack of physical contact between bodies, the denial of emotional expression, the ridicule and teasing about affection, especially in the male bachelor drinking group, partly accounts for the awkward distance between the sexes in Ireland. This also explains the cold and often formal relationship that has existed between husband and wife in Ireland. Whatever possibility there was of a warm, physical relationship, there was little or no possibility of any knowledge or rational discourse about sex. This helped perpetuate the high level of fertility which has continued to be a major characteristic of Irish marriages to the present day. It has only been since the 1960s that the reproductive cycle of high marital fertility, maintaining the need for postponed marriage, permanent celibacy and emigration, has begun to be broken. It has been broken because women have begun to acquire a knowledge of sex and a control over their bodies which has been instrumental in attaining economic and political power, thereby shattering the bonds that made them dependent on the moral power of the Church.

The Modernisation of Irish Society

Two questions which arise from this study are when did the modernisation Irish society take place, and what role did the Church play in the process? The answers to both of these questions are interrelated but depend on what one means by modernisation. If one means the end of magic as a dominant form of ethical behaviour; the end of people living with and like animals in mud cabins; the beginning of a new control over life and death; the adoption of many of the manners and practices of modern Europeans; and the adoption of a new discipline over the body; then Ireland can be said to have modernised during the nineteenth century and the Catholic Church to have played a major role in the process. If, on the other hand, one means by modernisaton the advent of an industrial type of society in which production and consumption have primary importance and in which individuals are no longer hide-bound by tradition, then it might be said that Ireland did not begin to modernise until the 1960s, and that the Catholic Church, because of the nature of its teachings and practices, and its opposition to materialism, consumerism and individualism, has been an inhibiting factor. In effect, Ireland has gone through two stages of modernisation and it was because the initial stage took place in and through the Catholic Church, that the Church became such a power bloc in Irish society, thereby delaying the advent of the second stage.

A different but related question may be posed about the modernisation of Irish society. If it is accepted that modern industrialisation is to a certain extent dependent on the prior and full development of agricultural production along the lines of small-scale petty commodity production, then we might ask what were the social and cultural practices that existed in Ireland which inhibited the development of this form of production, and what role did the Catholic Church play in maintaining this inhibition? In other words, accepting the existence of economic and political factors, what were the social factors that prevented Irish farmers from modernising their holdings?

In attempting to explain why more mature capitalist agricultural production developed in Northern Ireland and how, by the end of the nineteenth century, that region became one of the core industrial areas of these islands, some commentators have argued that people in the south were generally more interested in leisure than work. Black, for example, claims that 'the people of the north did devote more time and energy to their work and less to fairs and race-meetings, patterns and wakes then did the people in the south'.[2] The implication here is that in the south being sociable and attaining the honour and respect of others has an equal, if not higher, priority than attaining possessions, and that this is related to the dominance of the Catholic Church and its associated rituals which demand a surrender of individual interests, time and possessions to others.

Lee points out that there was no shortage of capital in nineteenth-century Ireland but that farmers were inclined to keep it for dowries, to give it to their children for a professional education, or simply to put it in the bank, rather than invest it in their farms. He associates this with Irish Catholics always trying to emulate their social betters, the Protestant upper classes, and says that they were more interested in the veneer of respectability than in developing trade.[3] Larkin attempted to draw a more direct link between the interest in social and moral respectability and economic underdevelopment. He argued that in the second half of the nineteenth century the Catholic Church absorbed almost 15 per cent of the surplus available over susbsistence for the Catholic population.[4] However Larkin is a better historian than an economist, for Kennedy has argued convincingly that far from inhibiting economic growth the Catholic Church made a positive contribution:

> The Catholic Church was itself a major consumer of goods and services. It had strong linkages to enterprises in the local economic context. By raising the level of economic demand for such services as building and maintenance services, as well as requiring steady supplies of food and food products—outputs which, on the whole, could only be provided by native industry—it is quite probable that the Church contributed to economic growth rather than the reverse.[5]

Whatever the merits of this Keynsian economic argument, what is more important from the perspective of the present study is that Kennedy goes on to claim that the intensive and systematic propagation of Catholic Church teachings did not have any major effect on the modernisation of Irish agriculture. He argues that although high marital fertility 'might be seen as increasing the economically dependent proportion of the population and as straining the productive resources of the country,' this cannot be linked to the Church's prohibition on forms of birth control since 'the people of 19th century Ireland possessed neither the desire nor the techniques to practise family limitation'. He also claims that there was a 'relative autonomy of the religious and economic spheres' which is evidenced by the fact that 'the growth of piety was paralleled by a growing consumer consciousness, rising material expectations, and a ruthless commitment to land possession, almost irrespective of the human costs involved'.[6] This study has argued that, contrary to what Kennedy claims, there was no absolute separation between the religious and economic spheres in nineteenth-century Ireland, and that the Catholic Church did play a major part in the initial modernisation of Irish agriculture. It was through a rigid disciplining of the body, which was propagated in and through the Church, that Irish farmers embodied the discipline that was central to increased production and that Irish mothers inculcated stem-family practices among their children which were central to the consolidation of farm sizes and an improvement in the standard of living.

But it was mainly the peripheral position of Ireland to mainland Europe, together with the increasing dependence for power of Irish women on the Church, which prevented them from embodying the family limitation practices of other European women. This, combined with a lack of knowledge or communicative competence about sex, maintained a high level of marital fertility among Irish women until the 1960s. The high level of marital fertility not only increased the economically dependent proportion of the population, but led to the persistence of a labour intensive form of agricultural production. The persistence of large families was also characterised by a need for a set of child-rearing practices which inhibited self-confidence, ambition and achievement. These became extended into practices such as teasing and ridicule which became established within the wider community. These practices prevented the development of an economic individualism that is the prerequisite for modern Western risk-capital production. The curtailment of individuality, combined with an unquestioning obedience to the Church, led to what Hutchinson has called 'a dominance of familial and social conformity'.[7] It was a rigid conformity that led to, and maintained, an interest in social prestige that was equal to, and sometimes greater than, economic and political interests. In many ways, it was because the Catholic Church was responsible for the inital modernisation of Irish society that Irish Catholics became legalistically moral rather than secularly civilised. It was not until a new urban bourgeoisie achieved dominance, and through the State broke free from the shackles of rigid moralisation, that Irish society began to industrialise and Irish Catholics unashamedly sought material rather than spiritual comfort.

The Future of the Catholic Church in Ireland

The long nineteenth century of Irish Catholicism is drawing to a close. There is a transformation occurring in present-day Irish society that is as dramatic as that which occurred during the middle of the last century. The monolithic Church which brought a holistic view to Irish social, economic and political life is beginning to fragment. The days of the unquestioned moral power of the priest are over. The awe, reverence and obedience which the priest enjoyed during the heyday of holy Catholic Ireland have begun to dissipate into general disregard if not actual cynicism. Irish Catholics are still a long way from publicly criticising and challenging priests and bishops, but they have gradually been moving away from a legalistic acceptance of the Church's rules and regulations to a more Protestant, do-it-yourself type of religious ethic in which they are making up their own minds about what is right and wrong. The official position of the Church is that members, who still form over ninety per cent of the Republic's population, have a duty to follow the Church's teachings on moral matters. In this respect the results of the constitutional referendum on abortion in 1983 are illuminating for although there was a three to one majority in favour of making abortion unconstitutional, more than four in ten Catholics disregarded the Church's exhortations to go out and vote, and almost three in ten actually went against the Church's advice and rejected the amendment. The Church in general is facing a dilemma which has been growing rapidly in recent years, i.e. how can it contain all the different, divergent trends which have appeared within it and yet maintain itself as a monolithic, multinational organisation? In Ireland, the future power of the Catholic Church will depend on its ability to reconcile the demand for an adherence to its rules and regulations as the criterion of Church membership with the more Protestant do-it-yourself type of ethic which is becoming dominant among the younger generation.

A related problem for the power of the Catholic Church in Ireland is the increasing demand for status by the laity. The shift from a legalist to an individually principled ethic has led at some levels to disaffiliation from the Church; at other levels it has led to a demand for more power by the laity. The days of a rigid, hierarchical division between the permanent, celibate members of the Church and the laity to whom they ministered, are coming to an end. The recent decline in vocations and, consequently, in the number of religious personnel, has necessitated the incorporation of some members of the laity into the inner core of power. But an increasing role for the laity threatens the organisational cohesiveness of the Church as a power bloc, especially at a multinational level. It could threaten not just an acceptance of papal infallibility, but of the rules and regulations by which the universal power of the Church has been maintained. It could lead to a Protestant-type situation of sects and Churches doing and saying their own thing. It is this threat which has led to the recent Ultramontane campaign of Dr McNamara which in many ways is similar to that waged by Cardinal Cullen in the last century. Yet the reality is that this campaign will alienate 'lapsed' Catholics even further.

The Catholic Church in Ireland is also threatened by the encroachment of the State into areas in which it previously held a monopoly, especially the provision of education, health and social welfare services. This is not to suggest that the vast organisational network of schools, hospitals and other institutional buildings will not continue to be a major aspect of the Church's power, but that the more there is a revolt by 'lapsed' Catholics against the power of the Church and the less dependent the State becomes on the Church for legitimating and maintaining its power, then the more likely it is that State financial support for these institutions will dwindle. The State, as it has been doing, will continue to set up its own schools, hospitals and welfare systems. Catholic institutions will be forced increasingly to rely on private, necessarily middle-class, support. Until now the Catholic Church in modern Ireland has received support from every economic class. The Church was able to educate and legitimate the position and possessions of the rich, and discipline and compensate the poor for their lack of possessions. In the days when the Church dominated education, when the media were there to support and not to challenge the Church, and a rigid adherence to the rules and regulations of the Church was the dominant ethic, these inequalities in wealth and power were easily explained and justified. However, the more State withdrawal of funds forces the Church to depend on private support, and the more the supporters of liberation theology side with the poor and oppressed (whose poverty and oppression is often caused by an exploitative bourgeoisie within their own Church), the more the cohesion and unity of the Catholic Church in Ireland will continue to fragment.

There was a time, until quite recently, when there was a unified, holistic view of life in holy Catholic Ireland, in which the Church put forward a vision of an ideal society of saints and scholars. It was a vision of a democratic, decentralised society in harmony with nature in which the interest in materialism and economic growth was limited by a sense of spiritual well-being centred on Church and family. The non-rational acceptance of the values on which this vision was based depended on people being content with the possessions and positions they held. It has been the State, and the science and technology by which the State has sustained economic growth, that have done more than anything else to destroy this vision. In accepting the rational differentiation between religion and politics, between what the Church does and what the State does, the Church has lost the possibility of maintaining a unified, holistic vision of Irish society. A holistic view of life may be necessary for the salvation not just of Irish society but of all human societies and living species. But for such holism to become a reality the Church needs to challenge the power of the state directly. It also needs to challenge the media which, like the Church itself formerly, are increasingly attaining the position of being accountable to none other than themselves. More importantly, the Irish Church will have to transcend its interest in an unquestioning, legalistic adherence to its rules and regulations. It must adopt an ethic of individual responsibility, leaving behind its obsession with sexual morality and individual salvation to embrace an ecological ethic of global responsibility and, perhaps, the salvation of the earth.

Notes

Chapter 1, Introduction, pp. 1–8.

1. Bishop Newman, quoted in the *Irish Times*, 29 September 1984.
2. Paul Blanshard, *The Irish and Catholic Power*, Boston: Beacon Press 1953. John Messenger, *Inis Beag*, New York: Holt, Reinhart and Winston 1969.
3. Michel Peillon, *Contemporary Irish Society*, Dublin: Gill and Macmillan 1982, 2.
4. E. Larkin, 'The Devotional Revolution in Ireland 1850–1875' in *American Historical Review* LXXVII (1972), 649.
5. L.M. Cullen, *The Emergence of Modern Ireland 1600–1900*, Dublin: Gill and Macmillan 1983, 255.
6. D. Miller, 'Irish Catholicism and the Great Famine', in *Journal of Social History* IX(1975), 81–98.
7. S.J. Connolly, *Priests and People in Pre-Famine Ireland 1780–1845*, Dublin: Gill and Macmillan 1982, 278.
8. E. Hynes, 'The Great Hunger and Irish Catholicism' in *Societas* VIII (1978), 81–98.
9. I am grateful to DBK for his help in formulating this Marxist interpretation.
10. For a more detailed discussion of the issues involved in this perspective on social action and social order, see Jeffery Alexander, *Theoretical Logic in Sociology* Vol. 1. *Positivism, Presuppositions and Current Controversies*, Berkeley: University of California Press 1982, 64–112.

Chapter 2, The Religious Behaviour of Irish Catholics, pp. 11–32.

1. Robert Kennedy, *The Irish*, Berkeley: University of California Press 1973, 110.
2. M. Nic Ghiolla Phadraig, Personal Communication. For details of the sample see M. Nic Ghiolla Phadraig, 'Religion in Ireland: Preliminary Analysis', *Social Studies* V (1976), 116–19.

3. B. Walsh, 'Religion and Demographic Behaviour in Ireland' (Paper 55) Dublin: Economic and Social Research Institute, 1970, 33.

4. Jack White, *Minority Report*, Dublin: Gill and Macmillan 1975, 130.

5. Walsh in ESRI(55), 32.

6. Kennedy, *The Irish*, 187–8.

7. Research and Development Commission, 'Students and Religion 1976' Dublin 1978, 22–5.

8. See Sean Connolly, *Religion and Society in Nineteenth Century Ireland*, Dundalk: Dundalgen Press 1985, 49–50.

9. This typology is adapted from Max Weber, *Economy and Society*, 2 vols., ed. Guenther Roth and Claus Wittich, Berkeley: University of California Press 1968, 422–39. See also Wolfgang Schluchter, *The Rise of Western Rationalism*, Berkeley: University of California Press 1981, 43–8.

10. Weber, *Economy and Society*, 422.

11. ibid., 426, 432, 438; Schluchter, *Western Rationalism*, 44, 168.

12. Max Weber, *The Protestant Ethic and the Spirit of Capitalism*, New York, Scribner 1958, 117.

13. Weber, *Economy and Society*, 1165, 560–1.

14. *A Catechism of Catholic Doctrine* Dublin: Gill 1951, 101.

15. Nicholas Abercrombie *et al.*, 'Superstition and Religion: The God of the Gaps' in *A Sociological Yearbook of Religion in Britain* Vol.3, London: SCM Press 1970, 98.

16. David Martin, *The Religious and the Secular,* London: Routledge and Kegan Paul 1969, 107.

17. Connolly, *Priests and People*, 148.

18. Patrick Logan, *Making the Cure*, Dublin: Villa Books 1972, 1.

19. Patrick Logan, *The Holy Wells of Ireland*, Bucks.: Colin Smythe 1980, 14.

20. See Weber, *Economy and Society*, 422.

21. Nic Ghiolla Phadraig, personal communication.

22. See Colm Tobin (ed.), *Seeing is Believing Moving Statues in Ireland*, Mountrath: Pilgrim Press 1985.

23. Research and Development Commission, 'Solemn Novena to Our Lady of Perpetual Succour', Dublin 1980.

24. Hugh Kelly, *A History of the Novena of Grace*, Dublin: Irish Messenger 1965, 15.

25. Research and Development Commission 'Report No.1: Religious Practice', Dublin 1975, 63.

26. *Catechism of Catholic Doctrine*, 67.

27. Peadar Kirby, *Is Irish Catholicism Dying?* Cork: Mercier Press, 1984, 31.

28. T. Inglis, 'Dimensions of Irish Students' Religiosity', *Economic and Social Review*, XI (1980), 244, 247.

29. Research and Development Commission, 'Report No.21, Religious Beliefs, Practice and Moral Attitudes: A Comparison of Two Irish Surveys 1974–1984' Maynooth: 1985, 35, 61.
30. M. Nic Ghiolla Phadraig, 'Alternative Models to Secularisation in Relation to Moral Reasoning', in *CISR Religion, Values and Daily Life*, Acts of the International Conference on the Sociology of Religion, Lausanne, 1981, 367–8.
31. Inglis in *Economic and Social Review* XI (1980).
32. Irish Episcopal Conference, *Conscience and Morality*, Dublin: Irish Messenger 1980, 22,16.
33. Bishop James Newman, quoted in the *Irish Times*, 30 September 1981.
34. Irish Episcopal Conference, 'Conscience and Morality', 16.
35. K. O'Doherty, 'Where Have all the Faithful Gone?', *The Furrow*, XX (1969), 588.
36. Nic Ghiolla Phadraig in *Social Studies* V (1976), 121.
37. Nic Ghiolla Phadraig, personal communication.
38. Nic Ghiolla Phadraig in *Social Studies* V (1976), 144.
39. M. MacGreil, 'Church Attendance and Religious Practice of Dublin Adults' in *Social Studies* III (1974), 181.
40. Inglis in *Economic and Social Review* XI/1980, 247.
41. See Michael Fogerty, Liam Ryan and Joseph Lee, *Irish Values and Attitudes*, Dublin: Dominican Publications 1984, especially 125–6.

Chapter 3, Church Organisation and Control, pp. 33–62.

1. Weber, *Economy and Society*, 603.
2. ibid, 1393.
3. *Irish Times*, 18 August 1983.
4. Quoted in L. Ryan, 'Church and Politics: The Last Twenty-Five Years', *The Furrow*, XXX (1979), 12.
5. Jean Blanchard, *The Church in Contemporary Ireland*, Dublin: Clonmore and Reynolds 1963, 17, 19.
6. Research and Development Commission, 'Report No.4: Attitudes to the Institutional Church', Dublin 1976, 67.
7. Blanchard, *The Church in Contemporary Ireland*, 20.
8. T. Inglis, 'Decline in Numbers of Priests and Religious in Ireland', *Doctrine and Life*, XXX (1979), 87.
9. Research and Development Commission, 'Irish Catholic Clergy and Religious, 1970–1981', Maynooth 1983, 4.
10. J. Abbot, 'Visitations by Priests in Irish Rural Parishes', *Irish Ecclesiastical Record*, XCVI (1961), 10.
11. Research and Development Commission, Report No.4, 25.
12. Abbot, in *Irish Ecclesiastical Record* XCVI (1961), 3.
13. ibid, 9.

14. L. Ryan, 'Faith Under Survey', *The Furrow*, XXXIV (1983), 5.
15. Inglis in *Economic and Social Review* XI (1980), 244, 247. Research and Development Commission, 'Students and Religion', 24.
16. Since 1975, the Episcopal Commission for Research and Development has carried out three major social surveys on young Catholics: 'Students and Religion 1976', 'A Study of Religion among Dublin Adolescents', and 'A Survey of Senior Students' Attitudes to Religion, Morality and Education.'
17. This fault is beginning to be rectified. See Tony Fahey, 'Female Asceticism in the Catholic Church: A Case Study of Nuns in Ireland in the Nineteenth Century', Ph.D. dissertation, University of Illinois, 1981.
18. Research and Development, 'Irish Catholic Clergy', xiii, xii.
19. Inglis, in *Doctrine and Life*, XXX (1979), 87.
20. Research and Development, 'Irish Catholic Clergy', 83.
21. Inglis, in *Doctrine and Life* XXX (1979), 98.
22. Research and Development Commission, Report No. 4, 30.
23. Evelyn Bolster, *The Knights of St Columbanus*, Dublin: Gill and Macmillan 1979, 32.
24. Desmond Clarke, *Church and State*, Cork: Cork University Press 1984, 202.
25. Quoted in Christina Murphy, *School Report*, Dublin: Ward River Press 1980, 155.
26. Quoted in John Whyte, *Church and State in Modern Ireland*, 1923–1970, 1st edn., Dublin: Gill and Macmillan 1971, 306.
27. *Solas* No. 6 (Easter, 1985), 4.
28. *Irish Times*, 20 November 1985.
29. Charles McCarthy, *The Distasteful Challenge*, Dublin: Institute of Public Administration 1968, 109.
30. *List of Post-Primary Schools 1982–1983*, Dublin: Government Publications 1983, 1–11.
31. Nic Ghiolla Phadraig, *Social Studies* V (1976), 144.
32. Whyte, *Church and State*, 18.
33. *Irish Times*, 9 March 1985.
34. E, Brian Titley, *Church, State and the Controlling of Schooling in Ireland 1900–1944*, Dublin: Gill and Macmillan 1983, 153.
35. Clarke, *Church and State*, 215.
36. Ryan in *Furrow*, XXX (1979), 15.
37. See Whyte, *Church and State*, 281.
38. Letter from the Irish Hierarchy to the Taoiseach, 5 April 1951, quoted in Whyte, *Church and State*, 426.

Chapter 4, Power and the Catholic Church in Irish Social, Political and Economic Life, pp. 63–94.

1. Nic Ghiolla Phadraig in *Social Studies*, V (1976), 120.
2. Research and Development, 'Students and Religion 1976', 39.
3. Nic Ghiolla Phadraig, in *Social Studies* V (1976), 148–149. MacGreil found that in the case of monthly Holy Communion, 'manual workers are almost 20% less frequent participants than the higher status occupations'. There was a similar trend in relation to education which showed 'a steady increase in frequency of participation in Mass and Communion as standard of education increases'. MacGreil, in *Social Studies*, III (1974), 185, 181.
4. Research and Development, 'Report No.4'. 4.
5. P. O'Healai, 'Moral Values in Irish Religious Tales' *Bealoideas*, XLII–XLIV (1974), 212.
6. E. Leyton, 'Conscious Models and Dispute Regulations in an Ulster Village', *Man*, I (1966) 535–6.
7. P. McNabb 'Social Structure', in *Limerick Rural Survey*, ed. Jeremiah Newman, Tipperary: Muintir na Tire 1964, 198.
8. Damian Hannan and Louise Katsiaouni, *Traditional Families?* Dublin: Economic and Social Research Institute 1977, 84. Hutchinson cites examples from U.S.A., Portugal, Brazil and Mexico. He argues that the chief function of mutual aid in Ireland, as in other similar societies, 'was not that of easing a man's personal burden of labour; it was that of providing a degree of security to the people...'. B. Hutchinson, 'On the Study of Non-Economic Factors in Irish Economic Development' *Economic and Social Review*, I (1970), 522. Gibbon rejects the notion that the mutual aid system has the function of providing security, or that it is part of the struggle to attain social prestige, and claims that it was part of the exploitation of small farmers by large farmers. P. Gibbon, 'Arensberg and Kimball Revisited', *Economy and Society*, II (1973) 487.
9. Nic Ghiolla Phadraig, in *Social Studies* V (1976), 135. Heeran found that 58% of her school-leaver respondents perceived their mother as extremely or very religious, compared with 34% who so described their fathers, see Rita Heeran, 'Attitudes of School Leavers to Missionary Religious Vocation', Dublin: Irish Missionary Union 1976, 34A.
10. E. Viney, 'Women in Rural Ireland', *Christus Rex*, XXII (1966), 334.
11. P. McNabb in *Limerick Rural Survey*, 199.
12. M. Gallagher, 'What Hope for Irish Faith?' *The Furrow*, XXIX (1978), 611–12.
13. Blanshard, *The Irish and Catholic Power*, 186.
14. See, for example, Whyte, *Church and State*, 44–7.
15. *The Irish Rosary* (March 1951), 70.
16. Brian Inglis, *West Briton*, London: Faber and Faber 1969, 107.
17. Whyte, *Church and State*, 368n, 313.
18. *Irish Times*, 22 August 1983.

19. Whyte took only 'those measures in regard to which I have evidence that, at any stage, one or more bishops were consulted or made representations.' He is thus able to conclude that the influence of the Catholic hierarchy on state policy 'has been fairly rarely exercised'. Whyte, *Church and State*, 363, 362.
20. ibid, 363–4.
21. ibid. 365. Basil Chubb. *Government and Politics of Ireland*, 2nd edn., London: Longmans 1982, 18.
22. Whyte, *Church and State*, 36, 42.
23. *Constitution of Ireland*, Dublin: Government Publications 1980, 2.
24. Quoted in Whyte, *Church and State*, 312, 313.
25. Ryan in *Furrow* XXX (1979), 12–13.
26. *Irish Times*, 13 February 1985; 30 November 1984.
27. Whyte, *Church and State*, 249, 368.
28. *Irish Independent*, 1 January 1985.
29. Nic Ghiolla Phadraig in *Social Studies* V (1976), 126–7.
30. *Irish Times*, 3 September, 16 August, 20 August, 1983. *Irish Independent*, 23 August 1983.
31. *Irish Independent*, 26 August 1983;
32. *Irish Times*, 17 August 1983; *Irish Independent*, 19 August 1983; *Irish Times*, 22 August 1983; *Irish Independent*, 28 August 1983; ibid. 2 September 1983; *Irish Times*, 31 August, 2 September 1983; *Irish Independent*, 3 September 1983.
33. *Irish Press*, 16 August 1983; *Irish Independent*, 1 September 1983;
34. *Irish Independent*, 1 September, 18 August 1983; *Irish Press*, 19 August 1983; *Irish Times*, 19 August 1983, 20 August 1983; *Irish Independent*, 24 August 1983.
35. *Irish Times*, 5 September 1983.
36. *Irish Times*, 12 June 1986.
37. ibid.
38. *Irish Times*, 20 June 1986.
39. *Irish Times*, 28 June 1986.
40. Bolster indicates that the Knights of St Columbanus were a major, but, as a secret organisation, also a covert, factor in much of the early social legislation of the Irish State, see Bolster, *The Knights*, 51.
41. J. Murphy, 'Censorship and the Moral Community', in *Communications and Community in Ireland*, ed. Brian Farrell, Cork: Mercier Press 1984, 62.
42. Chubb, *Government and Politics*, 32. For a more detailed account of the 'nightie' incident and the general impact of the Late Late Show, see M. Earls, 'The Late Late Show, Controversy and Context', in *Television and Irish Society*, ed. Martin McLoone and John MacMahon, Dublin: RTE 1984, 107–22.
43. *Irish Times*, 29 September 1984.

Chapter 5, The Growth in Power of the Institutional Church in Nineteenth-Century Ireland, pp. 97–129.

1. Submission from the Irish Privy Council (1719), quoted in William Burke, *The Irish Priests in Penal Times (1660–1760)*, Shannon: Irish University Press 1969, 200–1.
2. *Quoted in Jeremiah Newman, Maynooth and Georgian Ireland*, Galway: Kenny 1979, 33. See also John Healy, *Maynooth College: Its Centenary History*, Dublin: Browne and Nolan 1895, 87–125.
3. William Lecky, *A History of Ireland in the Eighteenth Century*, Vol.1, London: Longmans, Green and Co. 1916, 146, 151.
4. Patrick Corish, *The Catholic Community in the Seventeenth and Eighteenth Centuries*, Dublin: Helicon, 74.
5. Maureen Wall, *The Penal Laws 1691–1760*, Dundalk: Dundalgan Press 1976, 11–16.
6. Lecky, *History of Ireland*, 160.
7. Corish, *The Catholic Community*, 76.
8. N. Burke, 'A Hidden Church?: the structure of Catholic Dublin in mid-eighteenth century' in *Archivum Hibernicum* XXXII (1974), 85.
9. Sidney Smith, *A Fragment on the Irish Roman Catholic Church*, London: Longman 1845, 7.
10. Lecky, *A History of Ireland*, 148.
11. The hedge-school is a legend which still needs to be disentangled from romantic myth. Dowling gives an adequate description without analysing their numbers, their curricula, or their relation to the wider community, see Patrick Dowling, *The Hedge-Schools of Ireland* Dublin: Talbot 1935; see also Phillip O'Connell, *The Schools and Scholars of Breiffne*, Dublin: Browne and Nolan 1942, 52ff., 357ff., Donald Akenson, *The Irish Education Experiment*, London: Routledge and Kegan Paul 1970, 45–8.
12. Corish, *The Catholic Community*, 103.
13. Quoted in Wall, *The Penal Laws*, 9.
14. Lecky, *History of Ireland*, 233.
15. John Robbins, *The Lost Children: A Study of Charity Children in Ireland 1700–1900*, Dublin Institute of Public Administration 1980, 10–59.
16. Lecky, *History of Ireland*, 235.
17. Wall, *Penal Laws*, 9.
18. Quoted in T. Corcoran, *Education Systems in Ireland from the Middle Ages*, Dublin: University College 1928, 114.
19. ibid., 113.
20. Commissioners of the Board of Education, 14th Report (1812), 5.
21. As Akenson notes: 'Ireland underwent no industrial revolution, no significant urbanisation, no breakdown in the agrarian order and family structure, and did not experience any of the other forms of

social revolution that usually presage the creation of state systems of formal education.' *Education Experiment*, 3.

22. Seamus Breathnacht, *The Irish Police: From Earliest Times to the Present Day*, Dublin: Anvil Books 1974, 24.

23. Frederick Maitland, *Justice and Police*, London: Macmilan 1885, 105.

24. Breathnacht, *Irish Police*, 24.

25. R.B. McDowell, 'Ireland on the Eve of the Famine', in *The Great Famine*, ed. R. Dudley Edwards and T. Desmond Williams, Dublin: Browne and Nolan 1956, 28.

26. Galen Broker, *Rural Disorder and Police Reform in Ireland 1812–36*, London: Routledge and Kegan Paul 1970, 231.

27. Conor Brady, *Guardians of the Peace*, Dublin: Gill and Macmillan 1974, 3.

28. Breathnacht, *Irish Police*, 36–7.

29. Broeker, *Rural Disorder*, 228.

30. Robbins, *Lost Children*, 51.

31. John Douglas, *Observations on the necessity of a legal provision for the Irish poor*, Dublin: Wakeman 1828, 4.

32. ibid., 7–8.

33. McDowell in *The Great Famine*, 33.

34. Maurice Bruce, *The Coming of the Welfare State*, London: Batsford 1968, 97.

35. 18th Report of the Inspectors General on the General State of Prisons in Ireland (1839).

36. Mark Finnane, *Insanity and the Insane in Post-Famine Ireland*, London: Croom Helm 1981, 20.

37. *State of Ireland*, Report from Select Committee, Vol.8 (1825), 823.

38. *Emigration from the United Kingdom*, Report from Select Committee, Vol.5 (1827), 313.

39. See H.J. Johnson, *British Emigration Policy 1815–1830*, Oxford: Clarendon Press 1972, 71.

40. *Poor Law*. Report from Commissioners, Vol. 34 (1836) Appendix G, 'The State of the Irish Poor in Great Britain', iii, x, xxxvii, xxxix.

41. For an overall impression of the range and extent of these reports, see Arthur and Jean Maltby, *Ireland in the Nineteenth Century*, New York: Pergamon Press 1979.

42. Wall, *Penal Laws*, 58; Lecky, *History of Ireland*, 168.

43. Lecky, *History of Ireland*, 168.

44. See, for example, J. Colquhon, *Ireland: Popery and Priestcraft the Cause of Her Misery and Crime*, Glasgow: 1836.

45. Wall, *Penal Laws*, 66.

46. Quoted in Donal Kerr, *Peel, Priests and Politics*, Oxford: Clarendon Press 1982, 266.

47. Theobald Wolfe Tone, *An Argument on Behalf of the Catholics of*

Ireland, Dublin: The United Irishman 1792, 12.

48. See John Brady and Patrick Corish, *The Church under the Penal Code*, Vol. 4, *History of Irish Catholicism*, ed. Patrick Corish, Dublin: Gill and Macmillan 1971, 39–43.

49. Wall, *Penal Laws*, 66.

50. See P. Corish, 'Gallicanism at Maynooth: Archbishop Cullen and the Royal Visitation of 1853', in *Studies in Irish History*, ed. A. Cosgrove and D. McCartney, Dublin: University College 1979, 176–7. Keenan disagrees with Corish and argues that throughout the nineteenth century Ireland was uniformly Tridentine, and that there was only 'one image of the Church loyal to the Pope' see Desmond Keenan, *The Catholic Church in Nineteenth-Century Ireland, Dublin: Gill and Macmillan* 1983, 240.

51. For a description of the Relief Acts, see Dennis Gwynn, *The Struggle for Catholic Emancipation*, London: Longmans 1928, 8–93.

52. ibid., 150.

53. J. F. Broderick *The Holy See and the Irish Movement for the Repeal of the Union with England 1829–1847*, Rome: Gregorian University Press 1951, 21.

54. J. Murphy 'The Support of the Catholic Clergy in Ireland, 1750–1850', in *Historical Studies*, V (1965), 118.

55. Quoted in Kerr, *Peel, Priests*, 120. Kerr provides a detailed discussion of Church/State relations during this period, see especially 141–211.

56. ibid., 158–62, 202–8.

57. Desmond Bowen, *Paul Cardinal Cullen*, Dublin: Gill and Macmillan 1983, 254–5, 298.

58. Corish, *The Catholic Community*, 42, 49–51, 57, 67.

59. See John Brady, *Catholics and Catholicism in the Eighteenth Century Press*, Maynooth: Maynooth Univeristy 1965.

60. Larkin, in *American Historical Review*, LXXX (1975), 630.

61. Connolly, *Priests and People*, 33.

62. ibid., 38.

63. George O'Brien, *Economic History of Ireland from the Union to the Famine*, London: Longmans 1921, 17–19. (£1 = 20 shillings).

64. Kerr, *Peel, Priests*, 238–48.

65. Connolly, *Priests and People*, 48–51.

66. Murphy in *Historical Studies*, V (1965), 104–108.

67. Kerr, *Peel, Priests*, 36.

68. Connolly, *Priests and People*, 204.

69. Murphy in *Historical Studies*, V (1965), 107.

70. ibid. 105.

71. ibid. 114–17, 104.

72. Connolly, *Priests and People*, 53.

73. Murphy in *Historical Studies*, V (1965), 104.

74. Kerr, *Peel, Priests*, 19.
75. Quoted in Myles O'Reilly, *Progress of Catholicity in Ireland in the Nineteenth Century*, Dublin: Kelly 1865, 24.
76. ibid., 24.
77. ibid., 25.
78. Fahey, 'Female Asceticism', 86.
79. See Martin Brennan, *Schools of Kildare and Leighlin 1775–1835*, Dublin: Gill 1935, 62–3.
80. Corcoran, *Education Systems*, 89–90.
81. Akenson, *Education Experiment*, 52.
82. Dowling, *Hedge Schools*, 52.
83. Corcoran, *Education Systems*, 115, 125, 129.
84. ibid., 129.
85. Akenson, *Education Experiment*, 90.
86. Corcoran, *Education Systems*, 151–3.
87. ibid., 165.
88. Akenson, *Education Experiment*, 384–5.
89. Fahey, 'Female Asceticism', 93.
90. See Brendan Hensey, *The Health Services of Ireland*, Dublin: Institute of Public Administration 1959, 3–7.
91. Sarah Atkinson, *Mary Aikenhead, Her Life, Her Work and Her Friends*, Gill 1879, 238.
92. An Irish Sister of Charity, *The Life and Work of Mary Aikenhead*, London: Longmans 1924, 146, 158.
93. Select Committee on Medical Charities Vol.10 (1843), 198. See Edward Mapother, *The Dublin Hospitals*, Dublin: Fannin 1845.
94. Dublin Hospitals Commission Vol.35 (1887) xlii.
95. Fanny Taylor, *Irish Homes and Irish Hearts*, London: Longmans 1867, 25–7, 32, 54, 67–9.
96. Robbins, *Lost Children*, 294.
97. Quoted in Robbins, *Lost Children*, 305.

Chapter 6, The Irish Civilising Process, pp. 130–65.
1. Linda Spear, 'The Treatment of Sexual Sin in the Irish Latin Penitential Literature', Ph.D Dissertation, Univeristy of Toronto, 1979, 42, 36.
2. ibid., 425.
3. Norbert Elias, *The Civilizing Process*, I: *The History of Manners*, Oxford: Basil Blackwell 1978, xv.
4. ibid., 80.
5. The shift from physical punishment to a confinement of the body is documented by Foucault,, see Michel Foucault, *Discipline and Punish: The Birth of the Prison*, New York: Pantheon 1977, especially 136–41.
6. Elias, *History of Manners*, 101.

7. M. Turner, 'The French Connection with Maynooth College 1795–1855' in *Studies*, LXX (1981), 78–80.
8. Connolly, *Priests and People*, 185.
9. Ruth Clark, *Strangers and Sojourners at Port Royal*, Cambridge: Cambridge University Press 1932, 216.
10. Keenan, *Catholic Church*, 22.
11. Healy, *Maynooth College*, 274.
12. Bowen, *Cardinal Cullen*, 44–5.
13. Keenan, *Catholic Church*, 97.
14. Turner, *Studies* LXX (1981), 81–2.
15. Healy, *Maynooth College*, 283.
16. Quoted in E. Larkin, 'Church, State and Nation in Modern Ireland' in *American Historical Review*, LXXX (1972), 1255.
17. ibid., 1256.
18. Connolly, *Priests and People*, 45.
19. ibid., 47.
20. Turner, *Studies* LXX (1981), 81.
21. Connolly, *Priests and People*, 113.
22. Quoted in Connolly, *Priests and People*, 113.
23. L. McRedmond, 'The Church in Ireland', in *The Church Now*, ed. John Cumming and Paul Burns, Dublin: Gill and Macmillan 1980, 30.
24. Connolly, *Priests and People*, 2–3, 143, 162, 189–90, 192–3.
25. Phillipe Aries, *Centuries of Childhood*, New York: Vintage 1962, 100.
26. Elias, *History of Manners*, 180.
27. K. Nowlan, 'The Catholic Clergy and Irish Politics in the Eighteen Thirties and Forties', in *Historical Studies* IX (1974), 121.
28. Connolly, *Priests and People*, 225.
29. ibid., 239–52; see also Murphy in *Historical Studies* V (1965), 111.
30. T. Garvin, 'Defenders, Ribbonmen and Others: Underground Political Networks in Pre-Famine Ireland', in *Past and Present*, XCVI (1982), 143.
31. ibid., 151. see also Connolly, *Priests and People*, 238.
32. Bowen, *Cardinal Cullen*, 254–5.
33. Quoted in Connolly, *Priests and People*, 1.
34. ibid. 126.
35. Alphonsus Liguori, *Sermons for all the Sundays*, Dublin: Duffy 1842.
36. Turner, *Studies*, LXX (1981), 80.
37. Garvin, *Past and Present* in XCVI (1982), 148.
38. Quoted in Connolly, *Priests and People*, 132.
39. ibid., 54.
40. *Catholic Penny Magazine* (1834–35), 163–4.
41. D. Miller, 'Irish Catholicism and the Great Famine', in *Journal of Social History*, IX (1975), 86–7.

42. Larkin in *American Historical Reviews* LXXVII (1972), 636.
43. ibid., 644–5.
44. Keenan, *Catholic Church*, 148–52.
45. Connolly, *Priests and People*, 90.
46. Dublin Diocesan Archives, Archbishop Murray files.
47. Connolly, *Priests and People*, 121.
48. Alexander Irwin, *Roman Catholic Morality*, Dublin: Miliken 1836, 13.
49. Liguori, *Sermons*, 245.
50. Murphy, in *Historical Studies* V (1965), 103.
51. Benedict Vavly, *A Guide for Priests*, Dublin: Gill 1879, 78, 303, 307, 308.
52. ibid., 299.
53. ibid., 112.
54. Dublin Diocesan Archives, Murray Papers.
55. Quoted in Connolly, *Priests and People*, 83–4.
56. DDA, Murray Papers, 'Return for Ballymore Eustace', 1833.
57. See, for example, *Rules for the Regulation of the Christian Doctrine Confraternity of St. Patrick*, Waterford: Hanton 1839.
58. *First Report of the Catholic Book Society*, Dublin: Crean 1828, 5, 11–12.
59. T. Wall, 'The Catholic Book Society and the Irish Catholic Magazine', in *Irish Ecclesiastical Record*, CI (1964), 294–5.
60. Anon, *The Accomplished Youth: Containing a Familiar View of the True Principles of Morality and Politeness*, London: Crosby 1811; anon, *Moral Essays in Praise of Virtue*, Dublin: Jones, 1821; William Pinnock, *A Catechism of Morality*, London: Whittaker 1827.
61. Elias, *History of Manners*, 140.
62. Quoted in Bowen, *Cardinal Cullen*, 137–8.
63. Quoted in Norman Atkinson, *Irish Education*, Dublin: Figgis 1969, 69.
64. Quoted in J.M. Goldstrom. *The Social Content of Education 1808–1870*, Shannon: Irish University Press 1972, 53–4.
65. *The Schoolmistress or Instructive and Entertaining Conversations between a Teacher and her Scholars*, Dublin: Bentham and Gardiner 1824, 14–15.
66. ibid., 19.
67. *An Outline of the General Regulations and Methods of Teaching in the Male National Model Schools*, Dublin: John Foulds 1840, 6, 5.
68. Commissioners of National Education, *An Analysis of School Books*, Dublin (1853), 15.
69. Christian Brothers, *Christian Politeness*, Dublin: Powell 1857.
70. ibid., 21.
71. ibid., 9.
72. ibid., 23, 28.

73. Elias, *History of Manners*, 161–91, 162.
74. Henry Tuke, *On Chastity and Temperance*, Dublin: Graisberry and Campbell 1836, 7.
75. Elias, *History of Manners*, 182.

Chapter 7, The Transformation of Irish Society, pp. 166–86.
 1. Bowen, *Cardinal Cullen*, 169–75.
 2. Desmond Bowen, *The Protestant Crusade in Ireland 1800–1870*, Dublin: Gill and Macmillan 1978.
 3. W. D. Borrie, *The Growth and Control of World Population*, London: Weidenfeld and Nicolson 1970, 52; Thomas MacKeown, *The Modern Rise of Population*, London: Edward Arnold 1976, 1–2, 32.
 4. Ferdinand Braudel, *The Structures of Everyday Life*, I: *Civilization and Capitalism 15th–18th Century*, London: Collins 1981, 32.
 5. P.E. Razzell, 'Population Change in Eighteenth-Century England: A Re-Appraisal', in *Population and Industrialization*, ed. Michael Drake, London: Menthuen 1969, 131.
 6. K. H. Connell, *The Population of Ireland 1750–1845*, Oxford: Clarendon Press 1950, 25; Clarkson, 'Irish Population Revisited, 1687–1821' in *Population, Economy and Society*, ed. J. M. Goldstrom and L.A. Clarkson, Oxford: Clarendon Press 1981, 26.
 7. See McKeown, *World Population*, 18–43. Calvin Goldscheider, *Population, Modernization and Social Structure*, Boston: Little Brown 1971, 122–34.
 8. H. J. Habakkuk, *Population Growth and Economic Development since 1750*, Leicester: Leicester University Press 1971, 45; see also K. Gaskin, 'Age at First Marriage in Europe before 1850: A Summary of Family Reconstruction Data', in *Journal of Family History* III (1978), 29.
 9. M. Petersen, 'The Demographic Transformation in the Netherlands', in *American Sociological Review*, XV (1960), 346.
10. E. Shorter, 'Illegitimacy, Sexual Revolution and Social Change in Modern Europe', in *Journal of Interdisciplinary History* II (1971), 256.
11. E. Shorter, 'Female Emancipation, Birth Control, and Fertility in European History', in *American Historical Review* LXXVIII (1973), 628.
12. Borrie, *World Population*, 80–1; see also, Michael Anderson, *Approaches to the Study of the Western Family*, London: Macmillan 1980, 18.
13. Liam Cullen, *An Economic History of Ireland since 1660*, London: Batsford 1972, 100.
14. Connell, *Population of Ireland*, 56.
15. ibid., 90.
16. L. A. Clarkson, 'Marriage and Fertility in Nineteenth-Century

Ireland' in *Marriage and Society*, ed. R. B. Outhwaite, London: Europa 1982, 237.

17. L. Cullen, 'Population Growth and Diet 1660–1850' in *Irish Population, Ecnomy and Society*, 93–4.
18. C. O'Grada, 'Irish Population Trends 1700–1900', unpublished paper, University College Dublin 1981, 14.
19. Connell, *Population of Ireland*, 156.
20. M. Drake, 'Marriage and Population Growth in Ireland, 1750–1845', in *Economic History Review* 2nd series, XVI (1963), 311–12. O'Grada indicates that once the 1841 census is corrected for birth under-estimation it shows a comparatively high level of marital fertility i.e. 350 per 1,000 married women aged between 15 and 45 years. This was higher than the reported ratio in England and Wales in the 1850s (281:1000), and Prussia (314) and France (196) in the 1880s (O'Grada, *Population Trends*, 20–1; see also G. S. L. Tucker, 'Irish Fertility Ratios before the Famine', in *Economic and History Review*, 2nd series, XXIII (1970) 280.
21. L. Cullen, 'Irish History without the Potato' in *Past and Present* XL (1968) 79.
22. J. Mokyr, 'Irish History with the Potato' in *Irish Economic and Social History* VIII (1981), 27.
23. Cullen in *Irish Population*, 94.
24. There were widespread famines in 1727–30 and 1740–41. Drake suggests that the latter famine was equally devastating as the Great Famine. (M. Drake, 'The Irish Demographic Crisis of 1740–41', in *Historical Studies* VI (1968), 101–24.
25. Clarkson links the decline in famine and disease to improved medical technology and a lower level of urbanisation in Ireland. (Clarkson in *Irish Population*, 30–4).
26. Kennedy estimates that 801,000 emigrated between 1845–49. (Kennedy, *The Irish*, 42) Lee estimates that 800,000 died from hunger and between 1845–1851. (Joseph Lee, *The Modernisation of Irish Society*, Dublin: Gill and Macmillan 1973, 1.
27. Clarkson in *Irish Population*, 28.
28. ibid., 26; see also, J. Lee, 'On the Accuracy of the Pre-Famine Irish Censuses', in *Irish Population, Economy and Society*, 54.
29. F. J. Carney, 'Pre-Famine Irish Population: The Evidence from the Trinity College Estates', *Irish Economic and Social History* II (1975), 42.
30. For the pioneering discussion of the stem family in Ireland, see Conrad Arensberg and Solon Kimball, *Family and Community in Ireland*, Cambridge [Mass.]: Harvard University Press 1940. For a criticism of this study see P. Gibbon, 'Arensberg and Kimball Revisited', in *Economy and Society* II (1974), 479–98; see also, P.

Gibbon and C. Curtin, 'The Stem Family in Ireland', in *Comparative Studies in Society and History* XX (1978), 429–47; T. Varley, 'The Stem Family in Ireland Reconsidered', in *Comparative Studies in Society and History* XXV (1978), 381–92. In terms of the prevalence of the stem family system in Ireland from 1841, see D. Fitzpatrick, 'Irish Farming Families before the First World War', *Comparative Studies in Society and History* XXV (1978), 339-74. There is some debate within this research as to what extent the classical stem family, i.e. three-generational household, pertained to Ireland. Gibbon and Curtin conclude that the stem family was not the most common form of family in Ireland, even at the time that Arensberg and Kimball did their research. However it was more common than elsewhere, and there was a very large number of extended families, together with a relative scarcity of nuclear and simple families (p. 439). But if the inheriting son postponed marriage not only until the father died but also until after he died, and if one or two brothers and sisters stayed on the farm unmarried, then there would be an extended family constituted basically within stem-family practices.

31. Connell, *Population*, 27–8.
32. Kennedy, *Irish*, 42–3, 212.
33. Walsh notes that during the 120 years following 1841 'Ireland had the highest emigration rate in Europe, and was the only European country in which emigration exceeded natural increase, leading to a persistent decline in population'. B. Walsh, 'A Perspective on Irish Population Trends', in *Eire* IV (1969), 8.
34. Kennedy, *Irish*, 66–109.
35. Raymond Crotty, *Irish Agricultural Production*, Cork: Mercier Press 1966, 41.
36. M. Drake, 'Marriage and Population Growth in Ireland, 1750–1845' in *Economic and History Review*, 2nd series XVI (1963), 311.
37. J. Lee, 'Marriage and Population Growth in Pre-Famine Ireland' in *Economic and History Review*, 2nd series XXI (1968), 285,291.
38. Kennedy, *Irish*, 140–3.
39. ibid., 146, 148.
40. ibid., 152 (emphasis in original).
41. ibid., 159.
42. ibid., 160.
43. ibid., 154.
44. ibid., 147.
45. Murphy in *Historical Studies* V (1965), 108–9.
46. K. H. Connell, *Irish Peasant Society*, Oxford: Clarendon Press 1968, 126, 121.
47. McNabb in *Limerick Rural Survey*, 222–3.
48. Richard Stivers, *The Hair of the Dog*, London: Pennsylvania State

University Press 1976, 75–100. Edward Shorter, *The Making of the Modern Family*, New York: Basic Books 1975, 209.

49. Stivers, *Hair of Dog*, 73–4.
50. A social history of the Irish pub has yet to be written, which is strange for a society traditionally associated with pub life. Just when, where and how pubs proliferated in Ireland deserves more attention than that brief period of temperance in the 1830s and 1840s which seems to have captured the imagination of some Irish historians.
51. Stivers, *Hair of Dog*, 86.
52. For a discussion of the importance of the gift relationship in attaining social prestige, see Marcell Mauss, *The Gift*, Glencoe: The Free Press 1952, especially 10–12.
53. Stivers, *Hair of Dog*, 87.
54. M. Peillon, 'Irish Festivities in Comparative Perspective', in *Maynooth Review* VI (1982), 39–59.
55. McNabb in *Limerick Rural Survey*, 233.
56. Stivers, *Hair of Dog*, 69, 70–1, 74.
57. For an account of the practices involved in making an Irish match, see Arensberg and Kimball, *Family and Community*, 109.
58. Kennedy, *Irish*, 175–6.
59. ibid., 193.

Chapter 8, The Irish Mother, pp. 187–214.

1. 'The Trimming of the Rosary', quoted in Patrick Griffith, *Christian Mothers: Saviours of Society*, Dublin: Browne and Nolan 1926, 62.
2. E. Hynes in *Societas* VIII (1978), 149.
3. Crotty, *Irish Agricultural Production*, 37–8.
4. J. Lee, 'Women and the Church since the Famine', in *Women in Irish Society*, ed. M. McCurtain and D. O'Corrain, Dublin: Arlen House 1978, 37.
5. Referred to in J. M. Goldstrom, 'Irish Agriculture and the Great Famine', in *Irish Population, Economy and Society*, 162.
6. Connell, *Population of Ireland*, 47–85, especially 55, 82, 83.
7. Crotty, *Agricultural Production*, 29–30.
8. S. Clark, 'The importance of agrarian classes: agrarian class structure and collective action in nineteenth-century Ireland', *British Journal of Sociology*, XXIX (1978), 25–30.
9. Connolly, *Priests and People*, 17, 23.
10. E. Larkin, 'Church, State and Nation in Modern Ireland', *American Historical Review*, LXXX (1975), 1245–7.
11. Clarke in *British Journal of Sociology*, XXIX (1978), 29,30.
12. Larkin in *American Historical Review*, LXXX (1975), 1248.
13. Quoted in M. Moynihan, ed., *Speeches and Statements by Eamon de Valera*, Dublin: Gill and Macmillan, 466.

14. *Census of Population of Ireland, 1841.* General Report, xiv; *Census of Population, 1891.* General Report, 9.
15. Lee in *Women in Irish Society*, 37–8.
16. *Report of Poor Law Commissioners*, 1836 (Vol. 34) Appendix G, 'The State of the Irish Poor in Great Britain', xiii.
17. G. Rattray Taylor, *Sex in History*, New York: Harper and Row 1970, 81.
18. Alexander Humphreys, *New Dubliners*, New York: Fordham. University Press 1966, 139. For similar descriptions of Irish love and marriage see Donald Connery, *The Irish*, New York: Simon and Schiester 1968, 192–213. Richard O'Connor, *The Irish*, New York: Putman 1971, 141–70. Alan Bestic, *The Importance of Being Irish*, New York: William Morrow 1969, 107–19.
19. J. Michelet, *Priest, Women and Families*, London: Longmans 1846, esp. 114–19, 148–9.
20. R. Stivers, 'The Irish-American Experience with Alcohol', Paper presented at MidWest Sociological Association Meeting, Chicago 1984, 11.
21. *Catholic Penny Magazine* (1834), 13. This was very similar to the advice being given by contemporary Puritan moralists. See, for example, William Pinnock, *A Catechism of Christian Morality*, London: Whittaker 1827, 57; Henry Tuke, *Temperance and Chastity*, Dublin: Graisberry and Campbell 1815, 7. Tuke's advice was typical in that temperance was put forward, along with economy, industry and honesty, as the virtue to be attained by boys, while chastity was seen as the specific task of girls.
22. Quoted in Dominick Murphy, *Sketches of Irish Nunneries*, Dublin: Duff 1865, 64.
23. *Agricultural Class Book*, Dublin: Commissioners of National Education 1854.
24. *The Schoolmistress*, 17.
25. *Reading Book for the Use of Female Schools*, Dublin: National Commissioners of Education 1845.
26. *Report of Commissioners of National Education in Ireland* (1853), 7.
27. Fahey, 'Female Asceticism', 90–2.
28. Katherine Tynan, *Twenty-five Years*, London: Smith Elder 1913, 56.
29. Akenson, *Education Experiment*, 140, 321, 346.
30. Quoted in Fahey, 'Female Asceticism', 94.
31. Hasia Diner, *Irish Immigrant Women in the Nineteenth Century*, Baltimore: John Hopkins University Press 1983, 67.
32. Connell, *Peasant Society*, 113–61.
33. J. Murphy, 'Priests and People in Modern Irish History', *Christus Rex* XXIII (1969), 258.
34. Taylor, *History of Sex*, 107.

35. Griffith, *Irish Mother*, 58.
36. Lockington, *Soul of Ireland*, London: Harding and More 1919, 66.
37. Quoted in Humphreys, *New Dubliners*, 139.
38. N. Walsh, *Woman*, Dublin: Gill 1903, 23.
39. Pope Pius XII, *Woman's Place in the World*, Dublin: Catholic Truth Society of Ireland, 8.
40. Griffith, *Christian Mothers*, 55–6.
41. Hannan and Katsiaouni, *Traditional Families?*, 228.
42. Nancy Scheper-Hughes, *Saints, Scholars and Schizophrenics*, Berkeley: University of California Press 1979, 179–80.
43. McNabb in *Limerick Rural Survey*, 228.
44. Scheper-Hughes, *Saints*, 180–2.
45. Connell, *Peasant Society*, 121.
46. Scheper-Hughes, *Saints*, 184.
47. Hutchinson in *Economic and Social Review*, I (1970), 525.
48. Scheper-Hughes, *Saints*, 172, 117, 134, 137, 157.
49. Stivers 'Experience with Alcohol', 11.

Chapter 9, The Influence of the Catholic Church on Modern Irish Society, pp. 215–27.

1. Humphreys, *New Dubliners*, 20.
2. R. D. C. Black, *Economic Thought and the Irish Question 1817–1870*, Cambridge: Cambridge University Press 1960, 157.
3. J. Lee, 'Capital in the Irish Economy', in *The Formation of the Irish Economy*, ed., L. M. Cullen, Cork: Mercier Press 1968, 62; Lee, *Irish Society*, 16.
4. Larkin in *American Historical Review*, LXXII (1967), 874.
5. L. Kennedy, 'The Roman Catholic Church and Economic Growth in Nineteenth Century Ireland' in *Economic and Social Review*, X (1978), 52.
6. ibid., 55.
7. Hutchinson, in *Economic and Social Review*, I (1970), 528.

Index